A Mass Murder

Peter Hyson

A Mass Murder by Peter Hyson

© Peter Hyson 2024 Published by The Cotswolds Press 2024

The right of Peter Hyson to be identified as the author of this work has been asserted by him in accordance with the Copyright, Designs and Patents Act 1988

Cover design by Emma O'Brien, Illustrator & Maker of Monsters www.emmajaneobrien.com

All rights reserved. No part of this book may be reproduced, stored in a retrieval system, or transmitted in any form or by any means, electronic, mechanical, photocopying, recording or otherwise, without the prior written permission of the author.

This is a work of fiction. Any similarity to any events or persons living or dead is unintentional and purely coincidental.

ISBN 978-1-7393489-3-9 (e-book)
ISBN 978-1-7393489-4-6 (paperback)

Dedication

No novel ever emerges in isolation. So many people contribute, professionally, emotionally, intellectually. And to each I'm profoundly grateful.

But this book is dedicated not to people but to places! The villages I've been to who have inspired the characters named after them and to who've provided me with inspiration, challenge – and sometimes even coffee!

Thank you!

Preface

Having set myself the challenge of writing a series of stories where all the characters mirror actual British place names, the challenge grows bigger with each new title! Not only does my list of options shrink, followers of the series (thank you, you know who you are!) would soon catch on if each story only introduced one new character (place)! Although being a familiar figure is no guarantee of safety...

In *A Mass Murder*, amateur sleuth Catherine de Barnes returns to her homely but worryingly homicidal Cotswold village of Much Slaughter after a contract that may not have gone quite to plan. But then neither does her return. She's barely unpacked her luggage before being sucked into investigating the murder of locum vicar, Reverend Mark Cross, and the disappearance of a missing church artefact, which might be a valuable heirloom worth killing for – or a worthless trinket. All of which rekindles her precarious connection with Chief Inspector Glen Parva, while she attempts to salvage her relationship with Dr Linton Heath and make up with close friend Cherry.

Spend time enjoying coffee and cake in Skye Green's boutique Crimson Courgette Coffee Emporium and languish in the chilly vestries of not one but two churches, Much Slaughter's St Cyril the Obtuse and its near neighbour St Ignatius of the Vault. Meet an eccentric local antiques dealer, a flighty TV runner, a major, and a church warden with a secret past. And much, much more...

No Cotswold Capers tale would be complete without the tails of Catherine's Golden Retriever Dagenham and his bestie, the shaggy Old English Sheepdog, Barking.

For more about the characters, their place names and to sign up for the quarterly newsletter *Continuing Capers* see: www.peterhyson.com. And watch out for *Who Killed the Dame*, the next in the captivating series when the village drama society stages way more drama than it anticipated.

Chapter 1

Halfway up the steep incline to the vicarage and despite my desperation to be reunited with my beautiful Golden Retriever, I have to cling onto the metal handrail, my breath coming in wheezy gulps. That's par for the course. What isn't, are my shaking legs, making me feel I'm back on board the rolling ship which has been home for the last three months. At least I'm only sporting a large backpack rather than my full retinue of cases which will be couriered over tomorrow.

They say the mind plays strange tricks, but this time it's the heart because I fear the welcome I'm about to get from my friend Cherry. She has several public roles in Much Slaughter, and I very much hope today she'll be in vicar's partner mode.

'A two-word text and fifteen minutes' warning? Really? Is that all I mean to you?'

In the doorway, Cherry Willingham's scowling face is a far cry from the warm one I'd left three months earlier. Even her mass of unkempt frizzy chestnut hair seems to bristle with the electricity of anger. It seems she's in the mindset of our local coach and ex-rugby player which, believe me, is the one you'd least want to encounter. Even being treated as a member of her nursery school would be preferable.

Can't say I blame her, though. Having left the village on such a high after I'd tracked down a local cop-killer, and with a twelve-month cruise ship contract in my pocket to teach chocolate-making, here I am back on her doorstep, only weeks later with, as she rightly points out, only the briefest of warnings. I mean, there were very good reasons for my behaviour, but even so, it's not a great way to treat a friend.

'Yes, I'm sorry, Cherry.'

'Catherine, you don't neglect the people you claim to be your friends. Even if you have only been here for a year. You keep in touch. You share things. I thought we, I thought I, meant more to you.'

My head droops in shame. 'I know, you're right. It's just, well, the past few weeks got worse and worse and I felt so ashamed, until all I wanted was to creep back into Wisteria Cottage and lock myself away with my lovely dog.'

On cue, my lovely Dagenham whines from deep within the house. 'You and Wickham are the only ones who know I'm back. Oh, and Linton has some idea.'

Cherry shakes her head and flings the door back, marching across the hall and doing the same thing with the kitchen door. Dag bounds out, his tail wagging like an aeroplane propeller, his tongue lolling in excitement. But halfway across the hall he stops, skidding slightly on the polished floor, and gives me a withering doggy-glare as he's joined by his best mate, the massive Old English Sheepdog and self-appointed vicarage guardian, Barking. They both slump to the floor and Daggers stares at me for a moment before giving Barking a long lick.

Hmm. My return might not be as straightforward as I'd assumed. My heart lurches and I suddenly feel quite nauseous as I reach out to steady myself on the doorpost.

'How's Scott getting on?' I ask Cherry. Scott is our vicar and Cherry's partner, although they've embraced the trendy 'living together apart'.

'He's on retreat, Cat. How do you think he's getting on? It's not exactly gourmet banquets and late-night dancing. Unlike some.'

Ouch.

'Meanwhile, I get to field all his late-night visitors and early morning phone calls. And I'm still trying to tidy up his mess. So, no, keeping this place occupied while he's away, it's not going well.' She shoos a still-reluctant Dagenham outside and closes the door behind us.

Two minutes later, Dag and I are walking down the drive, with our tails between our legs.

My cottage has been described as 'the perfect thatched idyll for the perfect rural dream' (the real estate blurb) or 'a complete cliché' (my snarky boss in London when I'd told her I was upping sticks and exiting job, marriage, and the capital for the Cotswolds village of Much Slaughter). And starting my own business – she'd burst out laughing at the idea of me even getting round to writing a business plan, never mind getting a business off the ground. But she'd been wrong about the business and the business plan: well, there was plenty of time over the next couple of weeks to get back to that since there was absolutely nothing else in the diary.

That had been a little more than twelve months ago. Oh, and two murder investigations later – but that's a different saga. Then the last three months working on Caribbean cruise ships – but the less said about that the better. Chapter closed.

Now all I want to focus on is coffee and cake with my clutch of wonderful friends, while I re-establish my fledgling chocolate business.

One more corner to round before I can start to nest in my own space and not in a six by four doll's house cabin, often bent double.

Fate, naturally, has different plans...

My rural idyll is ablaze with floodlights and the road is jammed with trucks and clusters of very busy people in an array of scruffy Victorian country gear, their breath clouding in the chilly March evening. To say nothing of a giant spaghetti of heavy black cables covering the pavement in front of my cottage and much of the road. Plus a herd of loudly bleating sheep and a van of barking dogs that have Dagenham growling like a bear.

My heart erupts in kettledrum thumps and nausea. Why on earth hadn't anyone warned me about the film crew? *Possibly because you didn't tell them you were coming back?* Okay, fair point, but this is the last thing I need after a fraught four-hour train and taxi journey from Southampton Docks. And a far from auspicious encounter with Cherry. I really can't face clambering over all those cables only to get into rooms ablaze with stray light from the lamps outside.

Thankfully, there's a light in my neighbour's cottage, and in the blink of an eye I'm inside, where the wonderful Wickham Skeith, bless him, has already set out a tray with a huge mug of hot chocolate, half a dozen dark chocolate biscuits and an uncut chocolate sponge cake covered in creamy chocolate icing. He knows me all too well.

He also knows the art of diplomatic silence, perhaps through decades of running his bookselling business, although he'd be the first to insist it was a shop not a library. Anyway, he's perfectly content watching me decimate the goodies and add a mountain of calories to my daily intake.

A few minutes later, I release a contented sigh. This is indeed what I've come back for. Healing has begun and I turn to my lovely friend. 'Wickham, do you think it would look too out of place if I put a gated wall around my cottage?'

'Why not go the whole hog and add a moat and drawbridge?' His rheumy blue eyes twinkle underneath his thick grey curls.

'Very funny. All I wanted was a quiet return, to lock myself in Wisteria Cottage and never come out, at least for a while. And what do I find? Half of Hollywood camped on my doorstep with enough light to be seen from space.'

'Hmm, yes. Understandable. They've been here a couple of weeks, apparently filming some series to do with sheep and dogs.' Dag raises a sleepy eyelid at the mention of sheep and dogs, decides it's not worth the effort and resumes snoring in front of the fire. 'My fault, I'm afraid.

I told them you'd be away for far longer than they'd be here so they set their equipment up on that assumption, and to save the rest of us being unduly disturbed. Anyway, they'll be finished in a couple of days. I've made up my spare room so you can stay here until they're gone. And you're welcome to host the gang here, if you don't want to be seen in the village for a while, to explain why you flunked it.'

'I didn't flunk it!'

He turns, the biggest grin on his face. 'That's more like the Catherine de Barnes we know and love!'

I giggle. *You fell for that one!* 'Yes, alright. You've made your point, cheeky thing.'

Wickham pats my arm. 'Their loss, our gain, Catney. I for one am very glad they tore up the contract.'

'That's what was so lucky. Turns out, they shouldn't have given me a twelve-month contract until I'd proved myself. Not that I'm complaining, it allowed me to gain some very useful business contacts. To say nothing of getting back to where my heart truly is.'

Wickham's thick eyebrows wiggle and I hasten to reassure him. 'The place, not the romance.'

His eyebrows lift even higher, a smile now playing around his mouth. I rush on.

'And just so we're absolutely clear, I have absolutely no idea how Linton will react to my actual physical presence in the village.'

'But you told him you were coming back, right?'

I squirm in his armchair. 'Um, yes. That is, I told him I was coming back. I just didn't tell him exactly when.' The prospect of spending every day in the village with Dr Linton Heath's radioactive anger beaming out from his Bedside Manor home was truly awful.

If Wickham's eyebrows rise any further, I swear they'll be hovering above his head, but thankfully I'm spared any further explanation by a loud hammering on the front door. Wickham leaps up and seconds later ushers in my friend Skye Green. My broad smile fades somewhat as I remember she wasn't one of the people I'd told. But unlike Cherry, her welcome-home smile is as wide as mine and we flop into each other's arms. I'm enveloped in her mass of startlingly purple hair. Skye has enough hair dye colours to equip an entire theatre dressing room, all part of her carefully curated hippy bohemian image.

'I heard you were back, Cat.'

I'm about to ask how on earth she knew, but of course the village grapevine makes the internet look decidedly sluggish. Although, given that the taxi dropped me outside the vicarage and the walk from there to Wickham's passes only a handful of cottages, all of which would have had their heavy curtains drawn to conserve heat, it's still pretty impressive.

I'm spared the embarrassment of what to say next by another knock on the door, then Wickham ushers in an uncharacteristically sheepish Cherry. She marches straight up to me and I'm wrapped in my second huge hug, although this time I don't need sunglasses, as I'm submerged into chestnut hair instead of purple. A muttered 'sorry' emerges from the tresses.

'Me too. I feel like such a failure and I've no idea how I'm going to show my face in the village.'

I pull back, only for Wickham to put a hand on my shoulder. 'Catney, all you need is an excuse to get involved again. Perhaps another murder?' He laughs. I don't. 'Besides,' he squeezes my shoulders softly, 'this is Much Slaughter, we support our own.'

There's a lump in my throat the size of a boulder as the other two nod agreement. 'I know.' I say. 'I'm just so embarrassed. I mean, you were all so wonderful and supportive when I left. So generous.' I'm determined not to cry, but I can't help gulp. 'How will I ever face Linton?'

'Ah yes, the good doctor. Now there's an interesting point.'

The boulder moves to my stomach and I feel sick. 'Don't tell me. He's got a girlfriend.' I can't tell you how many nightmares have featured versions of that scenario.

'No, no, nothing like that. It's just...' Wickham smiles, gently. 'Quite the opposite, in fact. There just seems to be, less of him.'

'Oh for goodness' sake. Men!' Skye plants her hands on her hips and shakes her head so her hair flails like trees in the wind. 'What Wickham's trying to say is that our beloved doctor is mooching around like a love-sick puppy and the sooner you get over there and mend fences the better.'

My shoulders droop. 'I can't face him. What will he think of me? Especially since we'd agreed to keep everything low key and use the year I'd be away to see how things go. He'll think I can't commit to anything, that I just ran away.'

Skye suddenly leaps up. 'I need the loo,' She bolts out of the room, giving Cherry what looks like a furtive stare as she hurries past the startled Wickham who's *en route* to the kitchen. Although, in a lifetime first, I don't think I can face any more chocolate.

Cherry slides across on the sofa and puts her hand on my arm, gently. 'You okay, hon?'

I nod as we both stare into Wickham's log fire. She's clearly still upset with me but I appreciate her making the effort and I give her arm a squeeze in return. 'At least Wickham's letting me stay here until I can get back into my cottage properly. And he's said you're all welcome, at any time.' Cherry nods.

Moments later, Skye returns, giving Cherry a knowing wink, before plonking herself down on one of the dining chairs as Wickham comes in with the tray.

Okay, it would be rude not to. 'Just a smidgen please, Wickham.'

He smiles and delivers a slice of cake the size of California, before being the perfect host to everyone else. Then, as if on cue, they turn to me. I suppose it was inevitable: the only question was who'd be the first to broach it.

'Would you like to tell us what happened? You don't have to, but it might help.' It's Wickham.

I wince, then smile. 'In a nutshell, it turns out I'm not so good when I'm surrounded by a couple of thousand pampered passengers. Most of whom seemed to think I was at their beck and call 24/7. Passengers who didn't think me saying, "No, Madam, I have absolutely no idea where Canasta for not-quite-beginners is being held today," cut it. Not to mention, my cabin was so deep in the bowels of the boat, I'm surprised we weren't scraping the seabed. And a cabin-mate whose snores could damage the sonar monitoring of several countries.' I shrug to emphasise the story I've crafted.

Wickham and Skye both chortle, then drain their mugs, then my neighbour makes eye contact and stares quizzically at me while slowly raising one questioning eyebrow.

'Okay, okay. Most of them weren't *that* bad. They were quite nice, actually. Especially three American ladies in their late forties who came to every one of my workshops simply because they wanted to keep up their choc stocks! Apparently, they were on a Girls' *Long Weekend* which, when I asked how long that was, they said, giggling, 'So far, three months and counting!' They were huge fun. And I did come away with some great contacts...'

Wickham's eyebrows rise like Tower Bridge.

'It was business, nothing else. There was barely time to pursue sleep, never mind love. Not that I wanted to.' I gulp and turn away, blushing. I busy myself with tickling Dag's ears. He's unimpressed at having his sleep disturbed but still manages to drift off again, not something I've managed to do while having my ears tickled by my dishy doc... enough of that... 'So, what's been happening in Much Slaughter while I've been away?'

But before anyone can answer, there's another knock on the front door and Skye leaps up like a cat on a hot tin roof, returning moments later to usher in... the very hesitant but still gorgeous medical hunk otherwise known as Dr Linton Heath. Now also likely to be known for the rest of eternity as my 'ex'.

My friends jump up in welcome, but my own legs refuse to operate, and Linton looks every bit as wobbly. Skye jerks her head and Cherry and Wickham follow her out, like rats deserting a sinking ship. Perhaps not an appropriate metaphor.

In the ensuing silence, Linton and I take a deep breath.

'Linton, I can...'

'Cat, I can't...'

'You first.' I smile weakly, relieved to duck the initiative.

Chapter 2

My heavy eyelids struggle open, my body aching, protesting it's far too early. The bedside clock backs this up, brightly projecting 05.15 onto the ceiling of an otherwise pitch blackness and I groan. Unfortunately, my mind is already springing into action, still wedded to Caribbean rather than UK time. Although as it does a smile slowly spreads over my face and I carefully turn to gaze at the bare shoulders lying next to me, rising and falling in time with the good doctor's shallow breathing.

I slide a little closer, throwing my arm around his torso, feeling my warm flesh against Linton's. My gentle sigh ruffles the hairs on the nape of his neck. Yes, I had to admit it, last night's conversation ended far better than I'd dared to hope.

We talked into small hours, and then retired exhausted to Wickham's spare room, even though Dr Heath's official residence at Bedside Manor is only a few hundred yards away. But even that seemed too far, once I'd apologised for not telling him exactly when I'd be back because I wasn't sure how he'd take it and he'd roundly told me off for doubting his feelings. End result – we'd agreed to move forward and 'take things slowly'. As it turned out soon after, maybe not that slowly… Maybe the fact I'd forgotten to pack my pjs helped.

Linton stirs, turns over, opens one sleepy eye and looks rather startled, so I kiss him gently on his soft lips and we both slide back into oblivion, my arms hooked round him, his snoring mingling with Dagenham's, the two special males in my suddenly improving life.

Can there be anything better than slowly waking (a couple of hours later) to the aroma of fresh coffee and snuggled in the arms of a lovely man with Daggers curled up at the foot of the bed? Especially after three months 'solitary' in a staff bunk in a cabin hardly large enough to swing a mouse, never mind the proverbial cat. I could happily nestle here for the rest of my life, cocooned from explaining my odyssey to anyone else, free from the pressures of resurrecting my chocolate business and free from, let's be honest, murders and their accompanying grumpy police officers – and I don't think Chief Inspector Glen Parva would disagree with that last one.

Thank goodness all of that was literally last year and this new one stretches ahead, filled with the joys of spring and settling back, next door, into Wisteria Cottage, exploring the quiet country life and reuniting with old friends. And, as Linton stirs in my arms, exploring life with a new relationship. I resolve to take life at its own pace and see what happens. *And we all know how long your resolve lasts, don't we, Cat*?

The bedside clock now beams a much more respectable 07.45 onto the ceiling and my contented sigh causes Linton to stir. He slowly stretches his muscles before leaning over and planting the most delicious kiss full on my lips. It's delicious it almost makes me forget breakfast. Almost. Until my rumbling stomach gives the game away and he grins before padding off to shower.

Meanwhile, I give thanks for an understanding man who's prepared to give me a second chance. I'd been pushing my luck when I persuaded him I needed to work on the cruise ships just as we'd begun to get serious. He'd made it clear that committing was a big step for him. So we'd both agreed, a few hours earlier, that it wasn't going to be easy and that it could fall apart. Neither of us had a great track record, and communication during our three months apart wasn't exactly overflowing, being a weekly email (his more of a village newsletter and mine more of a letter to an agony aunt, bewailing life's tribulations) and a couple of video calls, one of which ended in a blazing row about something which we can't now recall.

After that, we'd both decided to 'give it a rest for a while', although as soon as the call ended I'd no idea whether the agreement was to pause emails and calls, or to not see each other again as long as we both should live.

The result was, I didn't know how to make the next move. And, as I'd learnt last night, neither did he, both of us assuming that was the end. Apparently, after the row, Linton had been told off by Wickham for behaving like a bear with a sore head, while I'd been told off by the chief petty officer (CPO) for reporting on duty with eyes so red they might have been the ship's portside warning lamp. (See, I did learn some jargon.) Luckily, the CPO didn't see my tear-drenched pillow hung out to dry, which, at the time, was exactly what I wished would happen to my landlocked lover.

Since all that's a thing of the past, I take a few moments to lie back, my hands behind my head, my tangled mass of blond hair across the bare flesh of my chest and slowly and nosily gaze around Wickham's pretty, if rather dated, spare room. Which I hadn't been able to do a few hours earlier, due to the, erm, darkness of night. *Yes, Cat, that was definitely the reason*.

I'm currently luxuriating in a soft, deep mattress on a huge, dark, oak framed bed which feels as it ought to be a four-poster, complete with hanging damask trappings. In the far corner, on each side of the room, I pick out heavy oak chairs with flowery cotton upholstery. And there's a deep pile cream and rose carpet that just invites padding around on, barefoot. Not to my taste, but I have to admit, at this moment in time, it's wonderfully comforting.

Beyond the heavy damask curtains, I imagine the villagers of Much Slaughter beginning to stir on their daily rounds. And it strikes me just how much I'm now looking forward to seeing the surprise on their faces as they realise, *I'm back.* As if to celebrate, St Cyril's church clock strikes eight and there's a clatter of milk bottles being delivered on the doorstep.

'Still embracing the cruiser's life of luxury, are we? Lying in bed all day?' Linton arrives back from the bathroom down the corridor, standing in the doorway with a very small fluffy white towel wrapped round his waist and a very wide smirk across his face. He stares at my reclining figure for several seconds before realising my state of undress and hastily closes the door. Which gives me ample time to return the compliment and inspect and admire his fit and refreshed body. Judging by the glistening muscles, he's even managed to find some lotion. Which is not something I'd have expected to find at Wickham's, which just goes to show you should never judge, even a tweeded bibliophile.

Sadly, the same freshness doesn't extend to Linton's clothes, which are scattered across the floor, and it's now dawning on him too that he'll have to face the Walk of Shame back to Bedside Manor, wearing the same clothes as the previous evening. It may only be a couple of hundred yards but, trust me, in a village like Much Slaughter, word will spread like wildfire.

He winces, then turns to me, his dark eyes twinkling. 'It was worth it.'

It absolutely was.

He's also right, I can't lie in bed all day, just as I couldn't on the ship, so I leap out of bed, and I'm immediately gathered into an encompassing bear hug and lingering kiss.

'Breakfast in ten.' Wickham's voice rattles through the (thankfully now closed) bedroom door causing us to leap guiltily apart and then re-embrace in a fit of giggles we try to stifle.

Unlike Linton, I have the blessing of an overnight bag tiding me over until the courier delivers my luggage so I can at least climb into clean underwear, cotton shirt, thick jumper and a not-too-crumpled pair of jeans. My blond curly hair is a different matter, resembling a tangled jungle and resists all efforts to drag a brush through it. Ah, well, that'll just have to wait until

I'm back in my cottage. At least with hair as wavy as mine, no-one will think twice about why it looks so ruffled.

A rapid shower and some light makeup later, I slip into a wicker chair at Wickham's neatly laid breakfast table, to be greeted by another of Linton's full-on kisses that's only slightly spoilt by the aftertaste of tomato ketchup from the huge bacon sandwich he's already half-devoured.

I settle myself contentedly at the table, admiring the green and white gingham cloth, which has been ironed immaculately, and laid with three place settings and enough cutlery, plates, jams and marmalades to service a cruise liner breakfast... not a memory I want to resurrect.

Instead I focus on the fact that after some frantic texting resulting in an avalanche of happy emojis, I'll soon be reuniting with the best friends in the world, in one of the nicest villages in the world, while relaxing in one of the best coffee shops in the world. Wickham has been a comms hub for weekly village updates – and welcome they were too – but they never got beyond, 'Skye held a coffee morning and twenty people attended' or 'Scott's been packing his trunk for his thirty-day retreat' or 'there was a queue of six people outside the vet's this morning'. All fact and no feeling. As if Charles Darwin had written *Pride and Prejudice*. Even the occasional texts from friends themselves left more gaps than they filled. So I can hardly wait for a proper face-to-face natter.

Mein host has already deposited two large cafetières on the table (he knows where my priorities lie) and I'm breathing in the rich aroma of freshly ground beans and eagerly anticipating my first mouthful of steaming coffee in Wickham's largest mug (or soup-bowl, as he cheekily refers to it) when the door bursts open and Skye explodes in.

This morning, she looks even more dishevelled than me, her matted purple hair drooping over her shoulders onto a white cotton shirt that looks as if it's never crossed the path of an iron. Her long flowery skirt flaps around her ankles and her bright red lace-up boots.

'Sorry, couldn't wait any longer. Spill the beans, Ms de Barnes. How did it go?' Her eyes latch onto mine like lasers.

I shake my head and try to look cross. After all, things with Linton could have gone either way and from our online meetings and carefully composed messages, my expectations were lower than the limbo poles we used to amuse the cruise passengers. The odds had been high that this morning I'd be drowning my sorrows in Wickham's strong brew.

'How did it go? You mean, after you meddled in my private life without so much as a by-your-leave? How do you think it went?' Which was as far as I could go, before I had to give up the pretence. A huge smile spreads across my face. 'Despite your interfering text – not too bad, actually. I thought he'd...'

'And where's the hunk now?'

Linton clears this throat with a discrete cough from his seat hidden behind the door, then jumps up and mutters, 'I'm sure I need to – erm – make some house calls...'

'Seems you've made one already.' Skye wiggles her eyebrows and grins. No, not a grin, something much more lascivious.

I wag my finger at her and smile widely. 'I'll have you know, young lady, we were as chaste as teenagers.'

She cocks her head on one side, staring at me like a predatory animal, then plonks herself down at the table. 'Don't know what you were like as a teenager, but no-one would've called me chaste!'

Further explanation is spared by the phone in the hallway ringing, the echoes making us start in surprise. Wickham hurries into the room, deposits more bacon sandwiches and several toast racks, then leaves again to answer his phone.

A minute or so later he reappears and it's obviously not good news. 'Sorry, all, I need to dash. Linton, you should probably join me. Seems there's been an incident at the church, and they need a doctor *and* a church warden.'

The mind boggles at why they'd need both, especially since there's at least thirty minutes before the midweek service begins, which, in Much Slaughter, means at least twenty-nine minutes before anyone arrives at the church. That's intriguing enough to ensure I'll be tagging along.

Skye waves us out. 'I'll clear up here. Then I need to open up my coffee shop. Let me know...'

Chapter 3

From Wickham's cottage to the Church of St Cyril the Obtuse would normally take about five minutes. We manage it in two, approaching the top of the steep rise puffing like steam engines, my heart racing with an unhealthy mix of exertion, caffeine and apprehension. Linton is already one hundred yards ahead. I'm busy admiring his fit rear when he nears the church and I realise just how inappropriate that is, and blush even more.

Silhouetted against the open church door is a stocky figure in an expensive-looking Argyle v-necked jumper over a crisp white polo shirt and baggy trousers, his white trainers mud-splattered. The doctor barely slows and disappears inside, while the figure, who I recognise as the local antique dealer, pivots and hurries after him.

I reach the door some distance ahead of my sexagenarian neighbour and grind to a halt. The church is empty, and I stare around for a few seconds, waiting for my eyes to adjust to the gloom, as if I'm expecting something to appear, since this is a church, some divine apparition perhaps.

Voices swell from the front, from the vestry, and Wickham reaches my side, then pushes past to place himself between me and any untold danger. I suppress a giggle at a frail 69-year-old protecting me but remind myself he's just being a gentleman and trot after him, executing a quick overtaking manoeuvre as we reach the vestry door.

Whatever I thought I was preparing myself for most definitely isn't what I find, and I stop abruptly, horrified.

An elderly vicar in a black clerical cassock lies face down in a pool of blood. His arms are splayed out wide at ninety degrees to his torso, as still and grey as the medieval stone sarcophagus next to him. One of our large brass candlesticks lies on the stone floor just beyond his left hand.

My blood runs cold, not just at the terrible sight, but because this is now the third suspicious death, and I've only been in the village about fifteen months. The deaths have, however, taught me a few things, in addition to an eminent local Chief Inspector's dislike of 'interfering busybodies', and in particular, the importance of taking in the details of the scene before me.

Linton looks up as we enter, two of the fingers of his right hand on the reverend's neck, and he shakes his head. The antiques dealer lets out a high-pitched wail and clasps the cravat round his throat as if he's being strangled.

Wickham hurries across and guides him into a carved wooden chair by the desk on the far wall. He extracts a white handkerchief and offers it to the poor man. 'Take your time, Dale. Have you called the police?'

Dale just stares ahead, out through the ornate wooden screen into the sanctuary beyond, his ashen face in sharp contrast to the deep yellow Pringle golf sweater he's wearing. It's obvious we'll get nothing out of him at the moment so I turn to Wickham. 'Do you have any idea who *he* is,' gesturing at the body, 'and what he's doing here?'

For a moment, my neighbour looks taken aback. 'He's our locum vicar, covering while Scott's on retreat. He was meant to be taking today's communion service.'

Of course. Just one of the things to have changed since I've been away. Chastened, I let my gaze wander slowly around the room.

I'd only been in here a few times – most of the villagers refer to it as the Holy of Holies and refuse to come in, leaving it for clergy to robe in, wardens to fill in service registers and treasurers to count collections. *Ah, good point.* I turn to the huge safe in the far corner but it's closed and so presumably locked. (Even I know better than to wander across a crime scene to check.)

The desk has a few books and churchy pamphlets on it, along with the official church black ink bottle and several pens and pencils, but it's all neat and, to my familiar eye, in order. A long black clerical cassock hangs on the outside door with a crisp white surplice and beside it, on the chest of drawers, a purple stole has been laid out. Of course, it's Thursday and presumably he'd been getting ready for the midweek communion service. Oh good grief, people will be arriving any minute...

Wickham clears his throat, making the three of us jump like kangaroos. 'I ought to do a preliminary check to see if anything's missing. But, to be honest, I'm worried about disturbing the evidence before the police get here.' He glances at a gold pocket watch. 'Which should be any minute.'

As if he has the gift of prophecy, the heavy church door clangs open followed moments later by the vestry door. Except it's not our returning vicar who marches into the vestry.

The new entrant turns out to be my arch-nemesis, Chief Inspector Glen Parva. I'm gratified to see he looks absolutely gobsmacked, and not just at the victim. He stands frozen, staring from me to the body and back again as if refusing to believe his eyes. Seconds pass. Linton continues his careful check of the body while casting furtive glances in my direction, Dale snuffles and snorts while Wickham grasps the poor man's hands and mutters something or other I can't hear.

'Just as I thought my life was getting back to some semblance of normality,' the officer mutters to the corpse, although I've no doubt it's aimed at me rather than the unfortunate reverend. And, in fairness, as far as he knew, his favourite amateur sleuth (my words) was several thousand miles away aboard a cruise ship and out of his hair (and investigations) for another nine months. He is, however, a man of procedure, and I watch him take over. 'Right, tell me what we've got, Doc. I presume life is extinct?'

Linton nods.

'Who found the body?'

Dale lets out another plaintive wail. 'It's my fault. If only I hadn't...' and buries his head in his hands, sobbing.

The chief inspector shakes his head. 'Anyone?'

Wickham steps forward. He looks particularly grey, his wrinkled face deep with concern, and gestures to the other man. 'This is Dale Hill, Chief Inspector, he owns an antiques business over in Cirencester. And, before you ask, he's no relation to our own Mary Hill. He rang ...' he glances at his wristwatch, 'around twenty-three minutes ago.

Didn't make a lot of sense, other than I needed to get down here as soon as possible.'

'I see. And why you, if I might be so bold, Mr Skeith?'

I step closer. 'He's one of our church wardens, Inspector. He's the named contact on the notice board.'

'Ah yes, Ms de Barnes. Honouring us with your returning presence, I see. And another murder. Which is quite some coincidence. I suppose you just happened to be walking past the church when there happened to be the, let's see–' He lifts his right hand and counts on his fingers, 'third murder?'

'Actually, Inspector, I only got back late yesterday, and since my house was surrounded by TV types, I took refuge with my lovely neighbour. I was there with him when Dale called and I thought–'

'You'd poke your nose in – again.' Thankfully, he smiles. Just about. 'And how about you, Doc, how'd you get involved?'

Linton moves across from the body, stretching his legs. 'I just happened to be at Wickham's when Mr Hill phoned him.' And blushes.

Glen immediately demonstrates his excellent detective credentials by putting two and two together (or at least one and one together) and smirks.

Linton hops from foot to foot with embarrassment. 'Mr Hill, Dale, was waiting at the door when I arrived a couple of minutes after his call, and this is exactly what I found.' He waves his arm over the scene. 'These two were a few seconds behind. And, no, we haven't touched anything. Other than my cursory inspection of the body. Oh - and Dale needing to sit down in shock. As you can see.'

Glen rolls his grey eyes and glances down. 'Any idea who he is? I mean, clearly a vicar, but...?'

'According to Wickham, he's our locum vicar while Scott's on retreat. His name's Mark Cross.'

Glen's eyebrows rise, I'm guessing, at the appropriateness at the vicar's surname for his role but unusually he says nothing.

'He's the vicar of St Ignatius of the Vault, a couple of villages away, across the hills.' Wickham shakes his head, looking sad. 'Today's service would have only been his third or fourth here.'

Glen stares at the recumbent incumbent for a few seconds, before turning back to us. 'And has anyone informed Reverend Willoughby yet? We'll need him back here, pronto. Someone needs to work out what's missing.'

'Missing, Inspector? I don't understand.' I turn towards him, feeling oddly defensive, as Wickham whips out his mobile phone and starts dialling.

The police officer stares down his nose at me for a few seconds, then sighs. 'Trust me, this'll be a theft gone wrong. It has all the hallmarks. Some local petty villain. My hunch is the reverend disturbed them.'

I can hardly believe my ears. How can a professional officer jump to a conclusion so quickly? 'But what could they have been after? This is a church vestry, not Fort Knox. And,' I point triumphantly, 'the safe looks locked.'

Glen gives it the briefest glance before turning to the body. 'I think you'll find *that's* the object of their villainy.' He points to where the candelabra lies in the pool of congealing blood.

'What, that old thing?' I realise I sound like a rich old aunt dismissing an invaluable family heirloom, but I can't help myself. 'I'd be surprised if that fetched even a couple of hundred pounds. For the pair.'

The police officer's eyes light up. 'Aha. So, Miss Clever Clogs, if there's a pair, where's the other one, hey? Answer me that.'

Okay, he has a point. But then Wickham returns to announce, 'the Reverend Willoughby will be with us shortly.' There's such a quaver in his voice, I look up. I've never heard him like this before. He looks shrunken, somehow, like a balloon that's lost air.

We all jump at the crash of a heavy oak door opening, the metal handle thumping an echo throughout the church. Moments later, a huge mustachioed face peers around the vestry door.

Glen scowls and mutters, 'What does that ruddy constable think he's doing? I told him absolutely no-one comes in.'

Oh dear, none of this is helping his famously fragile temper.

The newcomer puts on a broad smile and grasps the inspector by the arm. 'Don't blame him, Officer. I'm afraid I can be rather overwhelming to the lower ranks. Wing Commander Boothby Graffoe, RAF, retired. And church warden here, along with Wickham. Heard we'd had a spot of bother so thought I ought to show my face. Oh...' He swallows heavily as he catches sight of the body. 'Right, well, that seems to answer my question. What can I do, Officer?'

'Stop contaminating my crime scene. It's getting like Piccadilly Circus in here.' A vein starts pulsing in the inspector's neck.

I can feel the tension rising so I hurry across to the Wing Commander. 'Boothby, perhaps you could dismiss the congregation?'

'Spot of crowd control, eh. Absolutely. Leave it to me. While you make sure everything's tickety-boo here, Ms de Barnes.'

Glen tenses like a coiled spring at being side-lined while Boothby, completely oblivious, salutes the policeman, swivels on his heels, and marches off through the church.

Seconds later his voice booms back, 'You, Constable Chappie, you can stand down. No-one gets past my defences, what!'

Wickham and I stifle grins.

Glen shakes his head, then turns to Dale, who, I'm pleased to see, looks slightly less pale. 'Why are you here, anyway? Bit off the beaten track for a midweek service when there's a perfectly good church in Cirencester.'

'Oh no, Chief Inspector, I'm not here for the service.' Dale swallows hard before glancing across at the body and turning pale again. 'The reverend wanted to see me before the service.' He winces as Glen checks his dark glasses are clear of his face, flicks open his official police-issue notebook, his pencil poised like a snake ready to strike at some juicy morsel.

Dale takes out a huge spotted handkerchief and wipes his forehead, then twists the cloth around his fingers, his eyes straying towards the body, then flicking around the vestry.

'Well?' said Glen. He isn't the most patient of men at the best of times, and now he's getting close to exploding.

'Dale.' I crouch down in front of the poor man, after sending a warning glance at the impatient inspector. 'Why exactly were you here to see Reverend Cross? If it's not too personal a question to ask?'

'No, nothing like that.' The man suddenly looks very relieved. 'It was a professional matter. I needed to give him the results of a valuation and he wanted it to be discrete. But, oh God, if only I'd been on time…'

Glen raises an eyebrow and takes a deep breath, so before he can wade in, I cut him off. 'Dale, no-one's blaming you.' I can sense Glen stiffen. 'Are you saying you were late?'

The man nods, silently, staring mournfully at a spot of damp on the wall. 'It was a customer, you see. I'd only unlocked my shop door to pick up the file. But the person slipped in and, well, I couldn't exactly throw them out, could I? And I wasn't more than five minutes late. Honestly I wasn't. Ten, at the most. But if I hadn't…'

'It wouldn't have made any difference,' Linton mutters. 'He was already dead.' I squeeze his arm as Glen snorts, and I realise then that the poor man's going to be the prime suspect, but to my mind, you never get anything out of anyone if they're a gibbering wreck.

But anything Dale might have been tempted to say is halted as a young female constable taps on the door, crosses the room and whispers to Glen. Sadly, unlike in the films, it's impossible to hear what she's saying. Glen looks decidedly smug, and nods. I'm clearly not on his need-to-know list.

Then he clears his throat, and looks around the vestry from Wickham to Dale, then me. Only Linton seems to avoid the police-glare. 'In my long professional experience…' He's staring pointedly at me but I'm not going to be intimidated so I stare straight back. '…there are only two real reasons for a murder. Love, or money. And given that the reverend here is a man of the cloth, I reckon this won't be some torrid love affair.'

'Really? I mean, I'm no expert, but given that vicar-ing is hardly the quickest way to get rich, it's much more likely to be–'

'So we'll be pursuing two particular lines of enquiry.' Glen's clearly on a roll now. 'Because I'll bet we'll soon discover that this vicar has a shady past.' He glances at the body, then leans down and removes a piece of mud from the sole of the victim's shoe revealing the manufacturer. 'Just as I thought. Church's, a highly appropriate shoe manufacturer for a man of the cloth, and somewhat beyond his price range, I'd have thought. So maybe gambling, or blackmail?' He nods at his own cleverness.

'But Glen…' *No, Cat, don't get involved, leave it to the professionals.* 'Inspector, surely you don't kill someone you're blackmailing? That's literally killing the goose that lays the golden egg.'

'Greed.' Glen spits the word out. 'Or maybe theft.'

He pauses as a uniformed police officer peeps timidly around the vestry door and is summoned to Glen's side, where he whispers in his ear, taking exaggerated care to check we can't overhear. Glen nods, before dismissing him as imperiously as a Roman emperor. 'Seems we've found a witness.' He pauses to stare at each of us. 'Someone in one of the houses saw a posh old sports car race around The Green and scorch off in a cloud of smoke. They won't get far. We'll set up roadblocks.'

The heavy church door clangs again and we all swing round for the latest intruder as Glen's anger looks fit to burst at the interruption.

Chapter 4

This time, it's our home cleric, the Reverend Scott Willoughby, who bursts into the vestry, sweating profusely despite the cool morning, and looking decidedly angry. He catches sight of the pool of blood and the body and freezes.

'I'm sorry Scott.' Wickham looks anything but sorry. 'I know we're not supposed to interrupt your retreat. But under the circumstances ...'

His coolness seems to galvanise Scott, who glances round and shakes his head, his unkempt black hair swirling in the light. 'Right, well, I see that everything's in your capable hands.'

I'm about to thank him until I realise he's actually speaking to the chief inspector. Fair enough, I suppose.

Scott nods grimly at the doctor. 'We must stop meeting over dead bodies, Linton.'

Linton lets out a weary sigh and gazes at the chief inspector. 'The wound on the back of his head suggests he was hit from behind. It was probably enough to kill him outright. That's about as much as I can tell you. The rest is up to forensics and the post-mortem.'

He crosses to stand next to me and mutters, 'You okay, sweetheart?' I nod rather uncertainly and snatch his hand, luxuriating in the warmth and strength of his grip. We stay like that for several seconds until Glen rather pointedly clears his throat.

'Sorry to break up the happy scene but I do have a suspicious death to investigate.'

I can feel myself blush, and I drop Linton's hand as if it was red-hot. 'Yes. Absolutely.' I don my sleuth's hat and turn to Scott. 'Who had keys to the safe?'

'There are no keys, Cat, it's a combination safe.' Scott shakes his head as if I should somehow know. But who takes note of such minor details? *Erm, possibly a detective?*

Glen frowns and I can tell he's thinking that this is why amateurs shouldn't get involved. Although, as he now checks the safe himself, it probably hadn't occurred to him either.

'Maybe you'd like to open it, Vicar?' Glen can't keep the irritation out of his voice. It's a far cry from the last time we'd all been together at my farewell party. Three months and a lifetime ago, for all of us.

The heavy safe door swings back with a loud clang and we all instinctively lean forward as several ledgers spill out onto the stone vestry floor. The rest of the contents seem to be registers, dusters, and cloth bags for storing the cash from collections. And goodness knows what else.

'So, what's missing?' The Inspector still sounds irritated and I half wonder if he'd somehow expected to find the murderer in there, folded up like a conjurer's assistant.

Scott brushes the fallen ledgers aside with his foot and bends low to peer inside. He's about to reach in but pauses and looks questioningly at Glen.

The policeman gives a curt nod and the vicar rummages around for a few seconds, the pile at his feet growing as items are none too carefully extracted. I don't think Scott's mood is much better than Glen's.

'Well, Inspector, as far as I can tell, the only items missing are a brass chalice and paten, but they're only plated, so not worth anything. We just use them for home communions. Even the other candelabra's still there.' He reaches inside and extracts a second candelabra, a carbon copy of the one on the floor, apart from the bloodstains, that is. He places it on the vestry table and we all stare at it.

I shudder, as I can't stop imagining it being swung towards our guest cleric. Then something occurs to me.

'Inspector, if the reverend had already unlocked the safe where both the candelabras are usually kept ready for the service – and presumably he'd have known the combination,' Scott and Wickham both nod, 'then why just take the chalice and patten? Why not take the candelabras: melted down they might be worth a few pounds, certainly more than the two missing items. But even then, surely they're hardly worth killing for?'

'Just goes to prove what I said earlier.' Glen snaps his notebook shut, then stares at each of us in turn before tucking his notebook away in an inside pocket. 'Mark my words, it'll be some local petty crook who thought there'd be something of value in the safe and was probably disturbed by the vicar when he'd got hold of the candle thing, and hit out in the heat of the moment.'

'That's all very well, Inspector, but who opened the safe?' I can't help being snappy. His casual approach irritates me, much as it did in our previous murder encounters. And look where he'd have ended up without my help. Being sued for wrongful arrest, quite probably.

Parva pauses for a moment, which I suppose is something. Then his face brightens and he speaks slowly, as if annunciating to a small child. 'Well, obviously the rent-a-rev opened it, went off to do something else and when he came back he disturbed the thief. An opportunist, like I said.'

He turns to Scott with a self-congratulatory nod. 'And you, Vicar, you might as well toddle off back to your month's holiday.'

I see Scott stiffen. But just as I think he's about to explode, he shrugs and mouths, 'Let it go,' at me and marches out, leaving me staring after him. This retreat thing certainly seems to have calmed him down, even after just a few days.

Wickham mutters, 'And just who's going to take our services now?' But Scott's already out the door, with Glen only a few paces behind.

This is outrageous. I grab the police officer's arm. Not a good move as he immediately swings round, his eyes narrowing and a vein throbbing in his neck. But I'm really not letting this go. He's got it so wrong.

'From what I've read, Inspector...' I see no need to enlighten him that it's from crime novels rather than textbooks, 'Isn't it at least as likely to be an affair of the heart? What if it's all about *love*.' Okay, maybe I slightly overemphasise the word, but come on, how many Agatha Christie motives hinge on romantic entanglements of one kind or another? 'Or maybe mistaken identity?' I'm not going to let go now.

'Oh yes.' The sarcasm drips off Glen's voice like oil off a spit-roast. 'There are so many other people you might mistake for a five foot six, bald, seventy-year-old clergyman in a black cassock.'

'Maybe they thought he was Scott?'

'That'll be the six foot one, fifty-year-old with a mop of black hair?'

'He's only forty–'

Glen's glare would melt one of our stone gargoyles.

We pause for a moment at the noise of a loudly revving car engine. Revving turns out to be doubly accurate as the reverend Scott lets out the clutch and rumbles down his driveway, presumably all to glad to be returning to his retreat.

'Inspector, there is one more thing you might like to be aware of.' Linton's voice cuts through the icy atmosphere and Parva quickly changes his glare to one of benign enquiry fixed on Linton.

The doctor plants his hands on his hips and gazes at the body, swivelling his head from side to side. Sherlock Holmes would approve, I think. 'The more I look at him, the more I think his body's been staged.'

'You mean moved?' Parva renews his glare, first to Wickham and then to Dale, before landing and locking in my direction.

'No, Inspector, not moved, rearranged. I don't think a blow from behind would have left him with his arms splayed out like that. It's as if he's been staged to look like a cross.'

'A crucifixion? That's hardly likely to be some chancer, then, is it?' The words tumble out of my mouth before I've a chance to stop them and my gut rumbles.

I'm saved from further police malevolence as the inspector's phone rings. He glances at the screen, grunts and marches into the main church, firmly banging the door behind him.

I scurry across and thrust my head and shoulders through the arch in the wooden screen between vestry and the sanctuary putting myself in imminent danger of a very undignified fall. The things I do in the course of my work. But he's too far away and all I can detect is a dull monotone. Then he half turns, causing me to withdraw, rapidly, snagging several strands of hair, and so letting out a squeak that echoes throughout the church, as if the church mouse had been cornered by the cat.

Wickham, meanwhile, has moved across to Dale and produced a glass of water from the desk. Judging by the air bubbles, I shudder to think how long it's been there, but it does restore a little more colour to the poor man, although he's still looking quite shaken.

As Dale drains the glass, my neighbour puts an arm around his shoulder to lift him. 'We should take him back to my house, Cat.'

Linton moves across to examine his eyes. 'I could give you a sedative.'

But Dale shakes his head and Wickham grins, 'Maybe a stiff whisky, instead!' This seems to meet with much more approval.

'Probably a good moment for me to move back into my cottage, then.' After the last few hours, all I want to do is curl up by the fire, preferably in the arms of my favourite doctor.

Linton may be thinking along similar lines as he smiles warmly at me. 'I've transferred my home visits to this afternoon so I have an hour or so. Maybe you'd like a hand?'

I blush. I most certainly would.

'To move your things back.' He gives a cheeky grin and lopes off to open the door and call, 'Inspector, if it's alright with you, we're going to take Dale back to Wickham's to recover. And I'll take Catherine with me – it'll keep her out of mischief for a while!'

Even I can hear the relief in Glen's agreement, although I'm sincerely hoping it'll be a case of out of one set of mischief, into another.

The first thing I notice as I push open the wooden door of Wisteria Cottage is how fresh it smells. I'd been preparing myself for the mustiness of three months unoccupied. Instead it smells of, well, spring. But of course, I'd underestimated my wonderful neighbour. Even with just two days' notice, the place is spick and span with vases of bright yellow daffodils in the hall so I just stand and breathe in the smells of my wonderful home. What had made me think I could leave it for a whole year?

My rumination is brought to a bone-juddering halt when Linton canons into me as he hauls a heavy suitcase over the threshold. 'Just met the courier. Would have been lighter to have carried you over,' he grins, then quickly disappears up the stairs using my luggage to avoid my flick at his ear.

'I'll put the kettle on,' I call after him. 'Not that you deserve it after your last comment.'

'No', he calls back down. 'I deserve several glasses of your best red wine after lugging several tons of your belongings over what feels like half the village.'

'For goodness' sake, it's barely twenty yards from next door, you wimp.' I have a huge smile as I slowly gaze round my kitchen, allowing myself to refamiliarise myself and appreciate all the homeliness. And luxuriate in all the space.

In my cabin I'd had to do a major reshuffle every time I wanted to brew a cup of tea. Here I can lay out the cups side by side next to the electric kettle and still have room for plates. Which reminds me... Yes, of course, Wickham's thought to get in milk. And one of those special home-baked fruit cakes from our village store, Rackem & Stackem. That man is an angel in tweeds. Running my finger over the cool kitchen surfaces brings an actual tear to my eyes and I don't consider myself a house-proud girl.

By the time Linton staggers downstairs, theatrically massaging his body as if he's just climbed Mount Everest with a grand piano on his back, the tea is brewing, the cake is sliced and plated and I'm leaning on the kitchen sink staring into my garden, taking in its clumps of yellow and orange daffodils and delicate white snowdrops. Bliss. Especially when I feel Linton's arms encircle me and his face nuzzles into my hair.

'Tea, doctor.'

He sighs but saunters across to drop into an armchair, a mock pout on his face. I deliver our tea and cake to the side table and settle on his knee to lean forward and wipe the pout away. He smells warm and homey, with only a slight undertone of... Well, in fairness, he's still not been home to change yesterday's clothes, to which there's now been added the aroma from portering my couriered belongings.

Goodness knows how long we snuggle there, periodically emerging for sips of tea and bites of cake. But, apart from last night, it's the nicest time I've spent in weeks. In fact, since that romantic pre-cruise dance evening months ago when, for the first time, I'd actually dared believe we might make a go of this. Then, the cloud on the horizon had been the job on the cruise liner. With that behind me, however ignoble the quitting, the horizon looks clear, sunny and warm, the only cloud being an unsolved murder. But then of course, that's Glen Parva's concern, not mine.

I snuggle back down and, I guess, doze, because the buzz of my phone awakens me to a text message. It's the wonderful Skye Green, demanding 'all the gory details' from my 'life on the ocean wave'. Her message is followed almost immediately by one from Cherry, demanding to know exactly what one should 'do with a drunken sailor'? Really, the minds of my friends...

My phone buzzes again.

Minutes later, after my phone's been buzzing like a hive of marauding bees, and with Linton now snoring unencumbered in the armchair, I've sent out a bunch of invites for coffee tomorrow morning in our 'fav' village café and been assured by my former gang that none of them would miss it for the world or let wild horses drag them away, or any other cliché they could muster. And the icing on the cake (literally) is Skye ordering a bumper batch of my chocolate-based goodies, destined to keep me elbow-deep in flour, butter, jam and eggs for half the night. I love it!

Chapter 5

As I push through the door of the Crimson Courgette Coffee Emporium, my arms laden with the ordered goodies, the first thing to strike me is that it hasn't change one iota since I left. Although I suppose that's hardly surprising, given the refurb Skye did when she took over a few months previously. The quirky record sleeves still cover the walls, interspersed with felt-tipped customer comments, a kind of legalised graffiti. Bunting hangs looped across the ceiling and the scattering of table lamps are adorned with an assortment of colourful paper and material shades. It feels homey long before I've reached my favourite alcove, which I'm thrilled to see Skye has commandeered with a Reserved sign amidst the Friday morning buzz of customers. Actually, that has changed: I don't remember it being *quite* so crowded before. Unless it's a coach trip, and glancing at the patrons who seem to be mainly older women in sensible shoes I suspect they're here for Royal Highgrove Gardens Tour.

Skye's excellent service continues as a huge mug of steaming chocolate and a large scone are delivered to me, to the obvious annoyance of several adjoining tables still waiting for their orders. Now this I have most definitely missed! I look around the room and announce, 'Best hot chocolate this side of Italy!' Skye's five foot four, willowy frame swells with pride.

'I'll join you in a minute, Cat. I've booked Auntie Rose specially.'

Skye's Aunt Rose was the previous owner of this place when it was Ye Olde Tea Shoppe, and she's been using her freedom since Skye took over to rack up the travel miles, so goodness knows where she's been hoicked back from.

Right on cue, Rose pokes her pepper-haired head around the kitchen door, gives me a huge grin and an equally big wave and disappears back just as the shop bell announces the arrival of Scott's partner Cherry, arm-in-arm with Boothby. The RAF officer (retired) halts on the threshold, and slowly scans the room, not, I realise, looking for me but for appreciation of how lucky he is to have a young lady on his arm. I shake my head at his display, but he's such a lovely man it's hard to begrudge him his ways, even if he is several generations behind the times. Providing he's inoffensive, of course.

While he's drinking in the looks, Cherry's also casting round the room, nodding at various familiar faces and smiling at the unknown ones. I grin. She's much more into the role of vicar's wife – or partner – than she'd like to admit. It suits her.

Boothby picks his way with surprising gracefulness through the tightly-packed tables and throws himself into the armchair opposite mine. Cherry peels away to lean into a table in the other corner, where she exchanges a few words with two serious-looking older men. They nod as she turns away, her habitual long skirt swishing around her equally habitual red Doc Marten boots. As she settles into my neighbouring chair, her mop of frizzy chestnut hair completely covers her face, so she sounds like a disembodied voice coming out of a hedgerow. 'Come on, girl, spill the beans about life on the ocean wave.'

I take a deep breath. Where on earth to start? As it happens, I'm spared the decision because a dark shadow looms over the table and I sense my friends tense. My heart thumps and my blood runs cold at the sight of our vet, Martin Dales. And at almost six feet tall, there's quite a lot of him, especially when he looks angry. Which is most of the time.

He swallows hard, his Adam's apple bobbing up and down. 'So, it's true, you're back?' He addresses the mug in front of me. 'Is it true you found the body?'

I nod slowly. 'I'm afraid so, Martin. And, before you ask, no, I don't think you were involved.' *Makes a change, Cat, after last time.*

He winces and turns to leave, adding, rather grudgingly, 'It's good to have you back, Catherine.' Which, considering a few months ago I'd nearly had him arrested for murder, I suppose might be considered quite magnanimous.

Martin walks away. At the door, he meets the arriving Wickham, and they conduct an elaborate dance, both grinning like the Cheshire Cat before briefly embracing like good pals. No reason why they shouldn't be, of course, I'd just never noticed. I wonder if I'm coming back with opened eyes, more attuned to things I'd missed when I was the newcomer and concerned with settling in.

Wickham crosses to our table almost as speedily as our vet did, but he at least does slide into a chair, even if he does then wriggle like a cat on a hot tin roof. 'Can't stop, Catherine, my bookshop resembles WH Smith's on Paddington Station today.'

'I'm just pleased you could pop in at all, neighbour of mine.'

'Actually, I've a favour to ask. Didn't want to mention it last night as it's business. Thought you'd want to settle back in first.'

I listen with interest. I still have some savings from my employment and marriage in London, but they're shrinking rather fast. Time to breathe new life into my chocolate-making business.

'It's like this, Catherine. I don't know how this might fit with your business plan, but I've got a significant birthday coming up next year and there's a big family event nearby. I wondered if you'd do me the honour of making a chocolate centrepiece.'

'Wickham, I'd be delighted!'

'It's my three score years and ten, as the Bard put it. So, I thought I should probably make an effort.'

Naturally that elicits a round of applause – even though he's made no secret of it for at least the while time I've been in Much Slaughter - and numerous assurances that he doesn't look a year over fifty.

'Of course I will, Wickham, I'd be delighted. *And* it fits perfectly with my business plan.' *Catherine de Barnes, you know perfectly well there's no such thing*. 'Closer to the time just let me know what you've got in mind and I'm sure we'll come up with something special. Phew, for a moment, I thought you were wanting something for next week!'

'Ah, well, that brings me onto the other, more pressing matter. Easter eggs.'

My ears prick up. It won't surprise you to know that Easter's one of my favourite times of the year because of its chocolate-potential: all those different types and sizes and fillings. Even if it does then need to be followed by several weeks of extra-brisk walks and trips to the gym. *Come off it, Cat, when have you ever even been inside a gym*? Okay, you got me there, but wasn't there some research saying imagining exercise was almost as effective as actually doing it?

Wickham's now in full flow. 'I've been thinking about Easter eggs picking up on famous book characters. I'd like you to make them, Cat, and we'll sell them in *Bound to Please* and here in the coffee shop. We can share the proceeds. I don't need an answer now, the end of the day's fine. We're already into Lent, you know.' He tosses a handful of paper onto the table and as quickly as he arrived, he's gone, leaving behind the faintest whiff of very expensive cologne.

We're just examining the fourth design when another shadow falls over our table and I look up to discover Chief Inspector Glen Parva, hovering with uncharacteristic uncertainty and shadowed by the ever-inquisitive Skye.

'Um, Ms de Barnes.' Oh dear, this formality doesn't bode well. 'I was wondering if...' His voice peters out and he looks around the room in some desperation.

'Glen, what is it? I say. How can I help?' Just because he wants to resort to old-fashioned formality, doesn't mean I have to. I thought we'd long passed that point.

He takes a deep breath, then mutters something indecipherable, as if he can't get the words out quickly enough.

'What? Slow down, Glen.'

'I wonder if you'd help me interview Dale Hill.'

I recognise the words but they make no sense. 'You want me to…?'

'Exactly.'

I never thought I'd see an embarrassed inspector, hopping from foot to foot, his face bright pink.

'The thing is, he's such a delicate flower, I thought he might respond better to a familiar female face.'

I suppose as olive branches go, it's not bad. Plus it'll be a great opportunity. Not to interfere, of course, but to, erm, keep abreast of how the case is progressing. Or not.

Glen could be reading my mind. 'I know I'm not going to stop you poking your nose in, so I might as well make sure your nose is poking in the right direction!'

Skye looks in danger of hysterics, she's laughing so much, She nods her head in the direction of the door. 'Go on, Cat, the inspector means now. I'll finish up here and we can start planning your business expansion this evening.'

Which is why, within the hour, and courtesy of Glen's very comfortable elderly Rover, we're marching down Cirencester's beautiful Sheep Street. Conversation on the journey had been limited to him informing me, 'We've done our research and it seems that the vicar was indeed pure as snow, with no hint of slush', while I wondered how to tackle the antiques dealer.

I needn't have worried. As we approach Treasures of Corinium, Glen crashes the shop door open. Dale Hill's face twitches as the police officer marches straight up to the desk.

'There's a back office, I presume?' He's so sure he's right he even leads the way. And, sure enough, moments later we're in a well-appointed and very comfortable looking room dominated by a large, leather-topped mahogany desk and an admiral's chair, along with a bookcase crammed with old leather-bound volumes and topped with various specimens of, if my limited knowledge serves me correctly, Spode China. Tasteful.

Glen takes the admiral's chair as Dale comes in bearing two folding chairs that seem to owe more to a church hall than to antiquity. Today, he's wearing a bright scarlet jumper, no doubt from the same expensive source, with the same baggy trousers. This time, black and white check socks are visible between his trouser turn ups and brown brogues.

Before either of us has chance to sit down, the officer flicks open his notebook. 'Now, Mr Hill, the name of the customer who was responsible for the fatal delay?'

Dale looks as if he's about to collapse rather than sit down and I grab his arm to help him into the chair. 'Dale, the Inspector isn't saying it's your fault, he's just hoping you might remember what happened. It must be really hard having to go over it again and I'm sorry, but it will really help us if you can.'

Dale gulps but nods. 'The trouble is, I do keep going over it. Every time I shut my eyes.'

I put my hand on his arm again. He's shaking really badly. 'Let's start with when you arrived at the path up to St Cyril's. Was anyone else around?'

He shakes his head. "It was still quite early, really. Let me think. The service starts at 10 and the vicar wanted to meet well before then. About ten past nine, I think.' Then he jolts. 'Actually, now you come to ask, yes. I did see something but most churchyards seem to attract courting couples so I deliberately didn't look any closer. They can get quite stroppy, you know. And I was late.'

Glen drums his fingertips on the leather. 'Who was it?'

'Oh, I've no idea, Inspector. I mean, I do spend quite a bit of time in Much Slaughter, the people there have such lovely, interesting items.' He catches the inspector's eye and hurries on. 'But I don't *know* that many people. And I certainly didn't recognise the person.'

Glen growls so I cut in as quickly as I can, 'Really helpful, Dale. Do you remember what they were wearing?'

He pauses for a few moments. 'Not really. As I say, I was in rather a hurry. I think something dark, maybe a black jacket? And maybe a dark cap or something?'

"Tall? Small? Skin colour?' Glen seems to have studied at the staccato school of interrogation. 'Maybe you could call into the police station and we'll try a photofit.'

The antiques dealer shakes his head as Glen looks up from his note taking. 'It wouldn't surprise me if it was one of those telly people, half of them look like they'd do you in as soon as look at you. From what I saw, they were all dressed in scruffy clothes.' I jump in.

'Inspector, that's probably because, they're filming something set on a Victorian farm. But anyway, that doesn't feel right to me, not in my gut.'

The police officer winces. Admittedly, it's not the most scientific way to conduct a case investigation, but as I've learnt in my previous murders (so to speak), my gut gives a good steer and I'm learning to trust it more and more.

Glen noisily flicks a few pages back in his notebook and stares at Dale for a few moments before putting on his best official police voice and asks, slowly and deliberately, 'Why exactly would Reverend Cross want the candelabras valued?'

'Oh, no, Inspector, it wasn't about valuing the candelabras. It was about the pyx back in St Ignatius.'

I have no idea what one of those is, but now I'm intrigued. 'Then why did he want to meet in St Cyril's? Surely it would have made more sense to have met there?'

Dale nods. '*I* thought it was odd, especially since the pyx was in the safe at St Iggy's. But Reverend Cross was insistent it had to be at St Cyril's. And it had to be before the service because he was busy for the rest of the day.'

Glen is finally looking interested, his pen scurrying over his notes.

'And that's when I found him.' He shudders.

Glen makes some more notes then jumps up and marches into the shop. 'Thank you, Mr Hill, it's a helpful new line. Now all I need is the name of that customer.'

Dale nods, picks up a huge ledger from his desk and passes it to the Inspector. Glen glances at it, nods and sets off down the corridor, ledger in hand.

Since he's my chauffeur, I have no option but set off in hot pursuit, like a police officer pursuing a miscreant.

As if on cue, my phone rings – the opening bars from The Beatles' *Savoy Truffle* which invariably makes my stomach rumble and my mouth water. 'Hello, Skye. Is everything okay?'

'It is with me, but you sound rather strange?'

'That'll be because I'm running after Glen.'

A loud giggle causes me to pull the phone away from my ear. I can still hear her laughter.

'Literally, not romantically. We're in his car...'

I'm getting some very strange looks from passers-by as I wheeze like an old boiler while shouting into a phone held at arm's length. Clearly this is unusual for Cirencester.

'Sounds very stressful, Cat. And luckily I have just the thing.'

'As long as it involves chocolate – count me in. Just not now.'

Glen's still a hundred yards ahead; he may only be five foot nine but he's moving like a racehorse while I feel rather more like a donkey.

'No, not now, Cat. Later this afternoon. I'm going to take you wild swimming. You'll love it.'

It's amazing how quickly my breath comes back in a mad panic. I need to knock this swiftly on the head. 'Absolutely not, Skye. Water, swimming and me, we just don't mix. Besides, I don't have a costume.'

'Says the girl who's just come back from a cruise ship. Last time I looked, they depend on water. And don't tell me that after three months onboard you don't have a complete wardrobe of swimming costumes. Besides, where we go, costumes are optional...'

I'm sure I can actually hear her grinning as my mad panic turns to into Hitchcock horror. My legs go weak and I'm not sure if it's the prospect of what Skye's dangling before me (and dangling is just the word) or the lack of air in my lungs, but it does occur to me, that if was I to die on the spot, it would be the perfect excuse to avoid wild swimming. Which has just replaced snakes as the greatest horror I can imagine. Even worse than the wretched business plan that keeps haunting me.

'I'm closing at three, I'll pick you up at three-fifteen. I promise you, Cat, you'll love it.' The phone goes dead.

'I promise I won't,' I mutter at a startled passer-by.

Chapter 6

I loved it! Whoever thought that wading into freezing cold water in the depths of March, wearing only a scanty covering of thin cotton, could be so invigorating. The jolt of ice-cold water touching warm, bare flesh. The tingle as you duck your shoulders under the water, ignoring every single cell of your body crying out for you not to do this. The jolt of adrenaline as seconds later you run screaming back up the bank and slide into the delightful heated towelling robe awaiting you, thoughtfully provided by Skye's previous experience.

The lake is only a few miles from our village, in the midst of an estate. The landowner has erected a few half-hearted warnings about NO SWIMMING but shows little inclination to enforce the prohibition. The handful of today's swimmers, for their part, seem to read and ignore – although the only way you'd know it was there was if you knew an enthusiast.

Dagenham was not of the same mind. He stood immovable on the muddy bank, his look as clear as any spoken words. He obviously thought every last one of us was completely bonkers. Especially me, almost as if he expected better from his owner. He's clearly got a lot to learn. And nothing I could say or do, including my playful splashing from the shallows, was going to sway him.

From now on, I'm going to be a devotee of a daily cold shower.

Although, admittedly, this morning's new regime lasted no longer than yesterday's brief skirmish before, with frozen mind and body, I relented and turned the heat back to almost scalding. One day at a time.

My rather euphoric state of mind might explain why, when Boothby rings as I'm vigorously attempting to towel myself dry and warm, I easily agree to accompany him over to St Iggy's to talk to Dale without questioning why we're meeting him there.

Downstairs, dressed in enough clothes for a Cotswold January rather than a spring morning in March, I call Dag and rattle his lead. I'm halfway out the door before I realise he's not joined me. That rarely happens so my heart's beating a little faster as I scoot into the kitchen. His cushion bed is empty. Again, unheard of. I rattle his food bowl, but all to no avail. Only as

I'm swinging round to search elsewhere do I spot his mournful eyes glaring out from under the kitchen table.

'Come on, boy. Time to go.'

Unbelievably he still doesn't move. Whoever's heard of a Golden Retriever refusing a walk? It just doesn't... Oh, hang on a minute. I get down on my haunches, and Daggers tries to move even further away. 'It's alright, my lovely.' He makes it abundantly clear he doesn't think it is and I suddenly laugh. 'We're not going to the lake.' Dag still looks far from convinced. 'I promise. We're just off to St Iggy's. With Booth-by.'

At the mention of the wing commander's name, Dagenham's tail starts wagging and he slowly inches forward, while still making it perfectly clear that one false move on my part or one slight hint of muddy banks and the deal's off.

***

A couple of minutes later, the moustachioed man himself draws up outside the once-more peaceful Wisteria Cottage in his glistening black Rover. Dag has bounded into the back seat and is curled up on the tan leather upholstery before I've managed to get one leg in and he stares at me reproachfully as if to say, 'Now this is how a dog of class should travel. Not like that rusty old banger I usually have to endure.'

Boothby winces as I slam my door, a vital necessity in my old banger but clearly close to a capital offence in his car. Then, without any obvious sound, the world outside seems to move and we glide away. Before we've gone even a hundred yards, I've sided with Dagenham and I have an almost uncontrollable desire to wave Queen-like at passers-by.

As we glide out of Much Slaughter, Boothby half turns in my direction. 'Catherine, thanks for agreeing to this, I've been undertaking some research about what's been happening in St Cyril's and St Iggy's, although I knew some of it from my fellow warden up at St Iggy's. I must say, I've found it all fascinating. And I think you'll find my information useful for your investigation.'

'But I'm not...'

He grins. 'Of course you're not. Even so... I should explain, that wearing my local history buff hat. I've been doing some preliminary checking up.' He pauses to swerve round a pheasant with a kamikaze death wish as it ambles across the road.

I nod, intrigued. 'Yes, but first, what exactly is a pyx? I mean, all I know is that it's a kind of bowl for bread.'

Boothby winces. 'Not exactly. Traditionally, a pyx was a small round container a vicar used to take the consecrated wafers to the sick or those who couldn't come to church. One unusual thing about St Iggy's pyx is, it was silver. They were sometimes wood but more often brass, silver, or even gold. Which is where it starts to get interesting.'

He pauses again, this time because we've reached a T-junction, and twists to squint and stare left, then right, before pulling out left with a squeal of tyres. I realise I'm holding onto the door handle so hard it's likely to come off in my hand and I make a conscious effort to relax. Not an easy matter with this heady combination of scary driving and tantalising mystery so I'm inordinately relieved when a couple of minutes later we pull onto the grass verge behind a very smart looking silver van, the medieval church of St Ignatius of the Vault looming over the Cotswold stone wall.

But before we're out of the car, the van door springs open and Dale jumps out, looking, I have to say, perkier than I've seen him before.

He shakes hands warmly with Boothby and gives me a decorous peck on each cheek. 'Thank you both so much for coming.' He's positively bouncing up and down on the spot, his cheeks ruddy and his face glowing with a warm smile. It's such a stark contrast to the pale figure I've met before. Even his latest Pringle sweater is louder – bright blue diamonds on a light brown background with red/orange lines, cuffs and neck. He nods at the church. 'I thought it might be more exciting to do this in situ.'

He then bounds off up the pathway, looking every inch like a human Golden Retriever. Daggers gives me a filthy look but bounds after him all the same, so I'm even more convinced of the similarity.

As they reach the church, the door's thrown open and out steps a tall imposing woman with short greying hair, who looks to be around fifty. Even at this distance I can tell she's muscular – something I can't claim to be. What's even more intimidating is that, despite a temperature bordering on freezing, she's wearing a thin-strapped athlete's vest. She greets us with a warm smile and an extended hand which, when I shake it, is surprisingly gentle, despite the calluses. Intriguing.

Her voice is equally arresting. 'Welcome to St Iggy's. I'm Major Anna Valley, church warden.'

Ah, now her bearing makes sense, the military background. She swings round and marches into the church then down to the vestry which, like St Cyril's, is separated out from the body of the church by a somewhat rickety carved wooden screen, although here the screen's been filled in, so the room is closed off and much more cosy. And warm.

The major mops her brow with a large handkerchief. 'Sorry about the heat. Reverend Cross insists, insisted. It's warmth not cleanliness that's next to godliness.'

Personally, I'm hugely grateful.

There are four wooden folding chairs set out in a tight circle and we each settle into one. Boothby clears his throat and takes the lead, so I wonder for a moment if the fact that a wing commander outranks a major means he feels he must do so. 'I've been explaining to Catherine on the way over what a pyx is.'

'Indeed.' The major smiles at me warmly, although the warmth seems to peter out before it reaches her eyes. 'I'd never heard of one either until I became a warden. And it turns out that the one we've got is more ornate than usual, in fact. We don't use it nowadays, but I happened to see one similar in *Country Life* magazine, which seemed to suggest it might be sixteenth century. And since ours is also silver, and inlaid with jewels, and theirs is apparently worth quite a few thousand pounds I thought we should check, if only for insurance purposes. Reverend Cross said he'd ask the diocese but ended up consulting Dale, who very kindly said he'd research its provenance.'

The warm smile is transferred to Dale, who nods and beams. 'Indeed. Although the reverend was so cagy and dismissive about it, I nearly didn't bother. He wouldn't even show me the real thing, just photos. But what a good job I did.'

My heart leaps and Boothby twirls his huge moustache as if he's priming propellers ready for take-off. Even the major stiffens and leans forward.

Dale smiles and slowly gazes from one to the other of us. *Come on, man, stop milking it.* 'There's a possibility the pyx could, conceivably, be more significant than we realised. That's why I was going to see Reverend Cross, to tell him I needed to see the actual artefact as soon as possible.'

'And?' We're all leaning forward now, hooked on his every word.

'Well, since the reverend's death I've carried on checking. Assuming the photographs are accurate, what we're about to see in the safe here is of national significance, probably international.'

The major turns pale and perspiration beads on her brow.

'According to what I uncovered, it's likely to have been a personal gift from the Archbishop of Canterbury, Thomas Cranmer, when the diocese of Gloucester was set up in 1541.'

Now it's my turn to be staggered. Even I've heard of Thomas Cranmer and know how important a historical figure he was, not just in the Church of England but in the whole of English history.

Our antiques expert is clearly revelling in every second of the impact he's having. He stands and paces the room like a lecturer addressing a class of students. But then I suppose this is exactly what every dealer and collector dreams of, the hidden reveal and the spotlight of fame.

'And that's what gives the pyx its real value, the story attached to it. I just couldn't figure out how it ended up at St Iggy's. So a couple of days after the murder – and swearing him to the utmost secrecy – I sent an email to the wing commander here to see if he could shed any more light on it, given that he seems to know the history of everything within a ten-mile radius.'

Boothby puffs himself up to even greater volume, reaches inside his bulky jacket and extracts a single sheet of typewritten paper which he slowly unfurls as if reading a royal proclamation. Which I suppose in a sense he is.

'Indeed you did, Dale. And indeed, I did!' Oh good grief, these two should go on the stage, they're so theatrical. And to think on our journey here, the cheeky blighter hadn't given me the slightest hint.

'And, as it turns out, I *can* help you. The first Bishop of Gloucester and hence recipient custodian of said pyx was one John Wakeman, who wasn't exactly averse to a bit of ecclesiastical skulduggery. He died in 1549 and his son cashed in the family jewels or rather the church jewels and came to live in the village here on the ill-gotten gains. When Elizabeth I came to the throne, he suddenly 'saw the light' and to cement his status donated large sums to the church. Seemingly including this pyx.'

He pauses, somewhat out of breath after all that puffing and panting, looks around at each of our faces and slowly announces, 'I think it's time we took a look. What say you?'

We're so caught up in the theatricals we simultaneous cluck our agreement.

But Boothby hasn't finished his performance yet. He raises his hand and we turn to stare at him. 'Just one more thing. We need to have your tame police inspector here, Cat. I called him earlier and arranged for him to meet us up here. Mind you, he took some persuading. He's really not your strongest supporter, is he?'

I'm about to protest – even though he does have a point – but before I can, he makes an over-the-top show of cupping his hand to his ear. 'And unless I'm very much mistaken, that crashing door will be him now.'

He nods to the major who crosses and unlocks the safe (with a key, I notice – my detection skills are clearly improving) then sits down with the air of an actor who knows he's just given the consummate, immaculately timed performance and awaits the roar of audience approval. We don't oblige.

Moments later, Chief Inspector Parva launches into the room. He's closely followed by a short woman, maybe late thirties or early forties, sporting short, spiky, black hair. She's carrying another folding chair which she flicks open and drops down between Boothby and myself. Glen plonks himself on it. She's on the point of leaving again when a single look from the major halts her in her tracks. 'Why don't you stay, Pixie? You're part of this, you know.'

The woman hesitates and hovers near the door. Anna turns to the rest of us. 'Pixie's our administrator. I've known her for years and I can tell you without fear of contradiction, she knows more about the paperwork in this place than anyone I've ever met.'

Glen jots down a brief note before fixing her with his best police stare, as Pixie tries to blend into the wooden panelling and away from our combined gaze. 'Seems a little extravagant?' says Glen, 'A paid administrator for somewhere as small as St Ignatius? St Cyril's doesn't seem to need one.'

Harsh, I think. But then it's a police officer's job to provoke with difficult questions.

Anna winces. 'Her family's been part of St Iggy's for decades. We saw it as a way of helping them as well.'

If Pixie had looked uncomfortable before, she now looks positively – what? I'm not quite sure.

Embarrassed? Certainly that. But there's something else. Anger? Resentment? Or maybe she just hates being the centre of attention.

Dale coughs, drawing my attention back to the group. 'If I may continue?'

Our self-appointed national treasure, Boothby Graffoe, graciously nods his approval.

'The good news is that there are quite a few photographs of the pyx from over the past hundred years or so, one of which you can see on the wall around us.'

He pauses as we all gaze at them. Then something catches my eye, a large, framed photo, next to a black and white one of the pyx on the altar surrounded by half a dozen men in formal Victorian clerical robes, some sort of church celebration with a very formal Bishop centre stage.

The contrast between the two photos couldn't be greater. And it's the other that fascinates me, two adults in battered working clothes and a young girl of about four or five are standing in front of a tiny, dilapidated cottage, a wisp of smoke rising from the chimney. Even from a quick glance, I can tell that the child is Pixie.

Dale clears his throat in the manner of the professor who's decided his students now need to concentrate on *his* pearls of wisdom. 'After close examination, and beyond all doubt, I can tell you that the whole set of photos supplied for my research all feature the same item.' He scatters half a dozen pictures across the vestry table like a lecturer revealing his star specimens, then nods to Anna, who walks over to the safe, reaches inside and draws out a small purple velvet bag and shows the lumpy bag to each of us in turn, like a magician plying her trade. She hands it to Dale.

He unties the ribbon holding the bag closed and reaches inside. We're all transfixed.

The unveiled artefact looks beautiful, although much smaller than I'd imagined. I suppose I'd expected something the size of a soup bowl, not something that sits snugly in Dale's palm.

Which is when I realise that Dale is staring at it with a very strange expression. He swallows heavily and mops his brow with his sleeve, as if his performance is taking its toll. He's suddenly deathly pale, as he stares wordlessly at Anna and Glen.

Chapter 7

'It's a fake.' He shakes his head and studies the silver box closely, glancing between it and the photos on the wall. 'There's no doubt, I'm afraid. It's smaller than the one in the photos and the jewels are a slightly different shape.'

There's a stunned silence before Parva growls, 'Couldn't that just be distortion – they are old snaps?'

'Really Inspector, credit me with some expertise.' Dale, despite his ashen appearance, looks deeply offended.

I'm puzzled. 'Does that mean there wasn't a real one or just that this one isn't it?'

Dale scratches his head. 'Now that's a very good question, Catherine. Maybe someone thought it might give the church some prominence to invent the story and produce some cheap imitation. But I suspect the truth is, it *was* real and now it isn't. It's been swapped.'

Glen is scribbling in his official notebook as if there's no tomorrow. The dealer glances at him before adding, 'I have to say, Inspector, it could have happened anytime in the last twenty years since that's when the last of the photos was taken. Assuming they were even taken here and not copied from some magazine.'

Glen crosses for a closer inspection of the pictures, returning seconds later. 'In my opinion, they were taken here. You can see different parts of the church in the background.'

I turn to the warden, Major Valley. 'So, when was the last time you authenticated it?'

She stares at me for a split second before glancing at her administrator in the corner, who looks even smaller now, and just shrugs, leaving Anna to answer. 'I honestly don't remember it being brought out for a service for years. If it's been out for anything else, well, you'll have to ask Pixie to check through the records.' She glares at her, and the woman looks desperate for the floor to open up and swallow her.

The major suddenly sits bolt upright. 'Inspector, couldn't this mean there's likely to be a link with Mark's murder, and that it wasn't just a chance encounter?'

Glen glances across at me, just as I'm trying to mask a look of *I told you so*, before he fixes his angry stare on the warden and demands, in his best police interrogator voice, 'For the record, where were you when the reverend was killed, Major?'

Goodness, where did that come from? The major also seems thrown by the question, so maybe that was the point, to get her off-balance. But then her military training seems to come out because she stares defiantly at him and announces, 'Tending to a young filly, Inspector, like I do most days around that time, and no, no-one can vouch for me. Unless of course you're a horse whisperer.'

Glen looks horrified and I want to giggle.

'Chief Inspector Parva, I can tell you that the warden is honest as they come.' Boothby turns towards her and wiggles his moustache as she reddens. 'Now, are we sure this young filly can't shed some light on our discussions?' He turns towards Pixie, who winces and glares at him.

'It's certainly not been valued in my time, Chief Inspector, and I started in 2013. I can't help you.' She fondles a small medallion on a chain around her neck, and it glitters in the gloomy light, emphasising the depth of her glare. Glen snaps back.

'Nevertheless, I'll thank you to check the blasted books.' *Oh dear, the man is definitely riled.*

Pixie, however, sticks her chin out and fixes him with a cold stare. 'Well, yes, I suppose I can. But there's no guarantee, Inspector... the admin was a bit higgledy-piggledy when I arrived.' The two stare at each other.

'Maybe we should all just take a look, shall we?' I've seen Glen when he's riled and it's not a pretty sight so I'm keen to move on.

Pixie pointedly holds the police stare a few seconds longer, then shrugs and crosses to the safe, where she extracts half a dozen leather-bound books and a handful of notebooks. Then she grabs a large bunch of keys, marches across to the desk drawer and bangs another few books on the vestry table. 'If we've got anything, it'll be in here somewhere.' She starts flicking through the pages.

A sudden thought strikes me. 'When was it last used?'

Momentarily, a flash of what looks like fear crosses her face, only to be replaced by a not-quite-convincing thoughtful expression. *Interesting*. 'That's a very good question. Apparently it used to be brought out literally every high day and holiday, as regular as clockwork. Then when the Reverend Cross swanned in, well, he wasn't into all that stuff, he thought it was hideous, so it stayed in the safe and we bought a plain silver chalice and paten. He arrived maybe ten or twelve years ago, I reckon.'

I stare at the wall photos for a few seconds, an idea fluttering around in my brain. 'In that case, a thief would have to have known it was there, then they'd have to have had a replica made and then they'd have to have been able to make a switch. And, given its provenance, they'd have to have known some pretty dark contacts to sell it on. And how does all that tie in with the murder in Much Slaughter?' Ha! Amateur sleuth – one, police inspector – nil.

Before the Inspector can attempt to level the score, and he certainly looks as if he's about to try, Pixie announces in a rather triumphant voice, 'There's no record of it, whatsoever in the last ten years, as far as I can see.'

Glen grunts. 'It's a total waste of my time, this, there's a specialist investigation team for missing jewellery. And now, if you'll excuse me, I have two very strong leads to follow up in my *unconnected* murder enquiry. Rather than waste any more time, I'm off to track down a thieving little rat who'll no doubt be hiding in some festering sewer nearby.' He storms out of the vestry and moments later, the heavy wooden church door crashes shut behind him.

We look around in stunned silence. I need a change of scenery. Time to slip into my swimming cozzie.

Thankfully it's a dull Saturday afternoon so Skye is able to slip away early from her coffee shop duties. Daggers is no more enamoured of my wild water exploits than he was previously. But at least this time he consents to remain cosily on a rug in the back of Skye's car rather than stare at me the whole time from the bank like a disapproving parent.

Once again the shock of the water washes everything out of my mind, leaving me free to revel in the carefully monitored three minutes of immersion and wild splashing and deafening squeals with my young friend. She's a natural in water, a total mermaid in her surprisingly restrained silver-grey costume.

My allowed time passes far too quickly but even so, when I emerge and start rapidly towelling off, I feel so much better; my mind is so much clearer and my resolution is stronger... and my goosebumps are mountainous.

Skye has insisted I have a proper schedule for building up my endurance rather than just hurtling myself, well, inching myself, into the freezing water and then pretty much immediately turning tail to bolt out. Who knew it was so complicated? She's promised to help me set up a complete training regime on her computer once we're back in the village, so I suppose that's alright then. Personally, I prefer spontaneous madness, but as she rightly points out, it's a safety matter and no-one in their right mind puts their body through such shakes without a degree of care.

As warmth slowly seeps back into my body courtesy of the heated towelling robe I've now invested in and the heated car, the world looks a much better place. Especially with a supper booking with Linton in a few hours.

As we swing into Much Slaughter I'm surprised to spot Chief Inspector Parva standing on the Green in front of three huge film trucks. He appears to be in deep conversation with a stocky figure dressed head to toe in black leather. It seems the most natural thing in the world for me to hop out of Skye's car and make a surreptitious attempt to eavesdrop. The fact I'm towelling my damp, bedraggled hair while still wrapped in a large towelling coat doesn't help anonymity, though, and they both turn to stare.

If anything, Glen looks even more angry and frustrated than earlier and I feel really sorry for him. We have our differences but I genuinely thought we'd been getting on better when I left for the cruise ships. And despite our different approaches I do believe that underneath all the bluster, he cares deeply about his job. 'Glen, are you okay?' I say. 'You look...'

His head snaps round. 'Thwarted at every turn? Yes. The day's not getting any better.' He glares at the young woman, who looks pleadingly at him and is finally dismissed with the briefest of nods as he announces in a tired voice, 'Another lead gone up in smoke.'

'Inspector?'

'She's our dark figure in the churchyard. Seems she's a runner with the TV crew. Says she was grabbing a few minutes to check out the church as a possible venue for her wedding, then got called back for filming because a ewe was birthing, or some such thing. After that, she was so involved she missed all the kerfuffle taking place just a few metres away in the church.'

I nod. 'I've always been intrigued by filming. Not that I've ever been involved, but it seems so exciting.'

Glen looks at me in disbelief. 'They're filming an episode of that sheepdog competition, *One Dog and his Sheep*.'

'But when I got back on Wednesday, it looked as if they were filming a Victorian farmyard.'

Again, he looks at me pityingly. 'Each show has a segment based around a local farm, either something they make like fancy local beer or gourmet burgers, or something to do with the wool trade or Victorian farm life . That's going to be our angle.'

Suddenly, he looks across at the caravans. The young woman is staring over at us but talking to a handful of others and she makes the mistake of catching his eye so he summons her back with yet another curt nod.

'I don't suppose you happened to see anyone else during your romantic interlude, did you?'

The girl shakes her head, her eyes darting longingly back at one of the caravans. 'To be honest, I was only concerned not to delay the shoot.' Her voice is thin and reedy. 'The director gets right snarky if he has to wait.' She stares at Glen who pauses for just a moment before giving her the briefest of nods.

Dismissed again, she sets off eagerly towards the caravans but after a few paces, stops and half turns. 'Although, now you mention it, I did get the sense there was someone watching from the shadows, but it was sense not see. It only struck me because there was a momentary glint, like the flash from a phone or a torch.'

'Male? Female? Age? Build? Hair?'

The young woman shakes her head. 'Sorry, mate, I didn't really notice. I was more concerned with keeping my job.'

The inspector waves her away then glances across The Green and up at the church clock . 'I'm off home, while there's anything remotely resembling a weekend to enjoy.'

Good point. Even though *he* says it with some sadness, I'm looking forward to mine. I'm looking forward to doing some internet research for companies who can do a fast turnaround on making moulds for Wickham's Easter eggs, followed by preparation for Linton arriving for our Saturday evening rendezvous. And since this will be my first opportunity to cook in my lovely kitchen since I got back from, no, *left* for the high seas, I intend to make the most of it. And I expect the doc to be suitably impressed.

On the walk back to Wisteria Cottage I enjoying planning the supper menu, diverting briefly to Rackem & Stackem's excellent fresh meat counter for their best lamb roasting joint.

Once we're back, Daggers slinks off to his bed making it abundantly clear he hasn't forgiven me for forcing on him my watery expedition. Good job I'm starting early because it takes me twice my usual time to compile pots, pans and ingredients since my brain has inexplicably dumped all recollection of what lives where. But at last cake tins are lined up alongside half a dozen eggs and the carefully measured and twice-checked 200g caster sugar, 35g of cocoa, litre tubs of chocolate and vanilla ice cream (also taste-tested) and a packet of chocolate biscuits (sadly not taste-tested – a girl has to be careful what she eats). Luckily, just before I start mixing I realise there's something missing and, after a quick recipe scan and only one trip to an incorrect cupboard, I locate the flour and measure out 130g. Phew, that was close.

I should have got the hint. Maybe if I had, the rest of the evening would have taken on a very different flavour. But I didn't. Instead, I chose to work on one of my more complicated chocolate recipes for dessert while the joint of lamp sizzled away in the oven. Okay, I admit it, I was going for the showy: a gentle reminder of all the little extras Linton can enjoy with me. And a Chocolate Bombe Cake isn't really that difficult, not for a fully functioning Catherine.

Unfortunately...

As the clock hands creep round to 7.15, I open the oven door to be confronted by a soggy mass of sticky goo that looks more suitable for adding to wallpaper. And even worse, the cake tin has generously shared its contents with the meat tray below, so that I now have neither a delicious chocolate dessert nor a delectable roast lamb main course.

I sink to the floor, sobbing, and Daggers takes pity, poking his soft head between my arms so he can lick my face. I curl my arms round his head and sob into his ear. 'All I wanted was to show him what I can do. And all he'll see is how useless I am.'

Dagenham clearly thinks differently as he continues nuzzling, and slowly my sobs calm down. Finally, I reach into my pocket, extract my mobile phone and type in a number from my kitchen notice board.

Moments later, a deep voice booms out, 'Friar Tuck's Fish and Chips. Austin Friars speaking. How may I help?'

A few minutes later, make-up reapplied to red-rimmed eyes, the wonderful Austin Friars hands over my wrapped packages as I give thanks for village facilities and shuttle back home with barely enough time to stow them in the microwave and do a quick internet search before the knock at my door heralds the arrival of my lovely doctor.

'I hear you've got a surprise for me,' he announces cheerily, stepping inside and kissing me heartily.

Slightly taken aback by how he's heard so quickly, I stutter, 'How do you know? I'm so sorry, I really wanted to...'

He holds me at arm's length, looking at me as if I've gone mad. 'You texted me! Promised me the treat of my life. So here I am, to collect.'

'Yes, well, about that. You see, things didn't go quite according to plan.' My eyes water and I can feel my bottom lip quivering.

The lovely man leans in and kisses me again, much more softly this time.

'My dear girl, do you think it even remotely matters to me if our romantic supper in celebration of your return is with, if I'm not mistaken,' he pauses for a brief sniff 'fish and chips. My favourite.' I smile.

This is going to be a wonderful evening.

Chapter 8

Chief Inspector Parva's use of police yellow tape is as enthusiastic as his pursuit of red herrings. In my humble opinion. Anyway, it's a further week before it's removed and we're allowed back into the Cotswold stone edifice of St Cyril the Obtuse. The delay might explain why the church is unusually full on this third Sunday in Lent, not to mention the presence of the hugely popular Bishop of Burford, Bishop Norton. Or so Wickham informs me, and since he seems to have trimmed his hair and his beard and replaced his habitual necktie with a silk cravat beneath his check suit I'm inclined to agree.

There's certainly an air of appreciation as I inspect the full pews at suitable moments during the service, and when the bishop assures us he's on hand for any support we need 'in your unfortunate circumstances' the ripple of approval threatens to break out into applause although, this being the Church of England, it's soon dampened down. Nevertheless, his light-hearted insights about the follies of human behaviour produce ripples of laughter and his huge grin certainly lifts the atmosphere. Quite a tonic in the middle of Lent.

I will, however, admit to a degree of apprehension overshadowing the service as the bishop has requested a few moments in the vestry after the service with those of us who'd witnessed the 'unfortunate circumstances'.

When my turn comes round, I'm in a cold sweat pushing the vestry door open. Not only is this the first time I've been up close to a real bishop, it's also the first time I've been back in the vestry and I half expect to see the proverbial chalk outline of the body etched on the floor.

Bishop Norton looks much taller close up, although he's probably only about five foot ten. His broad shoulders stretch his purple cassock and, now he's removed his mitre, the bushy white hair proves to extend no further than the outline of the hat. The rest of his head is bald and shiny. His huge smile remains firmly in place as he extends his hand towards me and for a moment I wonder if I'm meant to shake it or kiss it. He answers this by turning his large hand sideways and the ensuing handshake is warm and firm.

'Ah, Catherine, we meet again.' His blue eye twinkle and I feel as if I'm in the presence of a grandfather figure, much as when we'd previously briefly met some months back on Scott's driveway. Very reassuring. He indicates a wooden chair to his right while he settles into the padded chair near the desk. 'How are you coping after your shock?'

I'm about to say dead bodies are rapidly becoming the norm for me but thankfully I realise just in time how that might sound so I simply stutter, 'Fine, thank you.'

His eyes twinkle again. 'I gather this is becoming quite a habit of yours. The third time in not much more than twelve months.'

The guy does his homework.

'I'm very sorry, Bishop,' I splutter, producing a loud guffaw which echoes around the empty room.

'Ms de Barnes, I don't hold you personally responsible! I'm merely suggesting it probably wasn't the reason you came here?'

It's my turn to laugh. 'No, indeed. I came for a fresh start, but not as an amateur sleuth.'

His bushy eyebrows rise as he leans forward slightly. 'And what exactly did you come here to escape?'

'Pretty much everything really. A job I'd begun to hate. A marriage that was sucking me dry. Pollution. Constant noise...' Good grief, this makes me sound like a real moaner.

'That sounds like a lot of escaping. And what fresh start did you think you were coming to?'

'Honestly? I'd no idea. It was all about what I was putting behind me. Especially working all the hours under the sun – and under the moon as well – for a boss who expected me to do literally anything necessary to get a deal, no matter how unethical.'

'Good for you then.' He looks thoughtful. 'And your marriage?'

I sigh. 'Oh, the complete cliché, I'm afraid.' I feel my shoulders tighten. 'He ran off with his business partner after several other affairs.' I stare out through the carved wooden partition into the weak sunshine flooding through the opaque glass window opposite.

The bishop sits motionless, his eyes fixed on me and I have the oddest feeling he's praying. My spine tingles, I don't think I've ever had anyone pray for me before.

'To be honest, now I look back, it was a relief. Even before his betrayal it was never a great relationship. I should have listened to my dad.' I continue staring at the window hearing Dad's voice across the decades asking me how sure I was, while my cocky twenty-year-old reply thunders in my ears: 'I know what I'm doing, I'm not a child anymore.' Even now, a decade after his death, I can see the pain in my dad's eyes. Not once did I ever admit to him how bad things had become, but he knew, he was my dad. I glance at the bishop.

'My ex- was always strong-minded. I think that's what attracted me to him: he knew what he wanted and he was determined to get it. It took me five years to realise that the expensive gifts he showered on me weren't to woo me, they were an investment to buy me. Once he'd done that, got his pearl, he expected me to be grateful and to fall in with his plans and ways of doing things. He'd get more and more angry if I didn't, so I took the easy route and gave in.'

We sit in silence, me fixed on the window, the bishop deep in thought, or maybe in prayer. Then he looks up, puts a hand gently on my arm and says in a voice so soft I can barely hear it, 'That sounds like abuse to me, Catherine.'

Moments later I'm sobbing loudly as I feel a huge weight lift off my shoulders. I'd not thought about it that way but now the words are uttered I see that I'd felt it and having someone else acknowledge it, say the words out loud, was a huge relief.

Bishop Norton reaches into his cassock and hands me an immaculately ironed pristine cotton handkerchief which I promptly stain with eyeliner and mascara.

'Sorry.'

He waves his hand as if ruined hankies are an everyday part of life, which I suppose for a bishop they might well be.

He waits a little while longer, before his grip tightens on my arm. 'And how are you feeling now you're in Much Slaughter?'

'Not as free as I'd hoped. I mean, the financial security helps, of course. And being able to go home to my cottage without being afraid of what's waiting for me. But, sometimes, it feels empty, even with my lovely Dagenham.'

'Ah yes, the famous Dagenham. Your neighbour told me how good he's been for you.'

I nod. Right now, I'd give half my kingdom just to be able to hang my arms round Dag's soft neck and bury my face in his fur.

'Is there anyone else in your life, Catherine?'

I feel myself go bright red and tingly, and the bishop smiles. Of course he knows.

He then looks rather serious. 'And how will this relationship be different? What have you learnt about yourself?'

God, this guy's good!

'I need freedom, I suppose. To be myself and to make my own decisions and have my own opinions.'

He nods. 'Anything else?'

I shake my head, but as he keeps up the eye contact I realise there's more. Then the penny drops. 'I need to learn how to trust people again, especially those closest to me.'

The bishop breathes out deeply and nods several times, before suddenly announcing, 'Stand over there and tell me what you see.' He points to the full-length mirror leaning against the wooden partition.

Glad to be getting the focus back on the murder investigation, I readily comply. Except, I've jumped to the wrong conclusion. *I thought that was Glen's problem, not yours, Cat?*

He turns his back to me and announces in what feels like a truly episcopal voice, 'What do you see?'

I shiver. I don't like looking at myself in a mirror at the best of times. To be quizzed about it feels even more difficult. But I feel as if a corner's been turned this morning so I take a deep breath.

'A middle-aged woman, with a not bad figure. A good dress sense. Wayward frizzy hair and nice shoes. Someone who could do with losing a few pounds but overall, not too bad.' I turn to face him, relieved and actually quite impressed with myself.

The bishop however has other ideas as he raises his eyebrows, still gazing intently at me. 'And? If you look deeper?'

A long pause and a gulp. 'I see a woman who's a survivor. More than that, who's capable of getting what she wants. And now actually knows what that is.' I pause for a moment, my heart beating faster as pieces fall into place. 'I know what I need from Linton, mostly to be able to trust him. And I know that'll be hard. I know that

I have the skills and the business ability to make my chocolate business work. And, I've got the best friends in the world who'll be there for me. And – a murder to solve.'

'Excellent. That's my girl.' From anyone else it might sound patronising, but he's earned my gratitude and from him it feels right. I'm not so sure about the sign of the cross he makes in my direction, though, but I suppose he *is* a bishop.

'Now, walk me to my car, will you? Even an octogenarian needs some help sometimes.' He grins and passes me a heavy suitcase while he trots off through the church at a speed that would challenge someone half his age. Including me.

By the time I catch up with him he's lounging against a bright red van that's complete with a striking black bonnet, fenders and radiator. If memory serves me correctly, they used to be post office vans almost fifty years ago: absolutely beautiful. And oddly fitting.

He nods towards the rear of the van. 'Drop my bag in there, will you, please?' And then folds himself almost in half to ease into the driving seat before pulling the window down and waving heartily as he drives off in only a small cloud of exhaust gasses.

I grin, feeling better than I've felt in months, and I'm still grinning as I settle on the wooden bench in the churchyard. After all, as I've just said, I've a murder to solve.

Before I can get any further, though, Cherry drops down beside me. 'Has Bishop Norton gone, then? I thought I saw him from the vicarage window.'

I nod, luxuriating in the afterglow of the conversation.

'How did it go?'

It takes several seconds before I can get to the words through my emotion and be sure I'm not going to tear up again. 'Cherry, I told him things I haven't even told myself. He's quite amazing, isn't he?'

She laughs. 'Scott always says he's the best thing that's happened to this diocese in a long time.'

I nod. 'I remember Scott saying that one of the privileges of a clerical collar was how quickly people you'd never met before trusted you and shared their deepest secrets. Guess I'm the living proof. I'll fill you in when I'm feeling less exhausted.'

'Come and join me for Sunday lunch, then, you look as if you need it. The Holy One is still wrapped up on his retreat.'

Just as I thought the day couldn't get better, this angel dangles food in front of me. 'Lead on. And while we do, let's see if we can work out who's responsible for the murderous shadow over Much Slaughter.'

The steep vicarage driveway renders conversation impossible for anyone less than an Olympic athlete and since neither of us is in that category (although in fairness Cherry, as a rugby coach, is significantly nearer to it than me), our deliberations are paused until we reach the house and I finish wheezing and panting. By which time the excellent Cherry has produced two generous glasses of sherry and perched me on a kitchen stool while she clatters pans and produces a pile of potatoes for me to peel, followed by peas, cauliflower and broccoli to prepare. 'Shepherd's pie with veg okay?'

I nod enthusiastically while taking a generous sip of the amber liquid, savouring it as it burns down my throat.

'So, where are we on the murder front, Cat?'

'Right, well, the way I see it… it's all as clear as mud! Let's start with Glen's idea, which I admit is the most obvious, that it was just a passing chancer. That would mean he or she was checking the place out, maybe saw Mark leave the safe open and took their chance to grab a few things of value. Then when they were confronted by the returning cleric the thief struck out with the nearest thing to hand, one of the candelabras. Except, if that's the case, would they have had the presence of mind to close the safe, which must have been open since Mark was preparing for the midweek communion service?' I shake my head. 'It makes no sense. And besides, my gut doesn't like it.'

Cherry shakes her head as if I'm mad so I decide not to tell her that after the last two murders I'm learning to listen to my gut more and more.

'Doesn't the inspector have any suspects then, Cat?' She pauses for a moment before resuming her vigorous chopping of cauliflower florets as if they were murderers.

'Well yes. Two. Dale thought he saw someone moving in the shadows outside the church but that turned out to be a runner from the television company. She claimed she was checking out St Cyril's as a possible place for her wedding then got called back before she even looked inside. We've interviewed her...' Cherry's eyebrows shoot up. 'What? I just happened to be passing and saw him talking to her so I thought I'd join in.'

'Of course you did. Carry on.'

'Well, I have to say, she seemed genuine and Glen seems to think the runner's out of the running – sorry, no pun intended – so she's off the list. Which only leaves the sports car driver someone on the Green reported screeching away from the scene. And, as far as I can tell, Glen's got no more idea who that was than I have. And there's no CCTV once they leave the village.'

I take the opportunity for another sip of my drink, feeling frustration take over from euphoria. Nothing makes sense about this murder. And that's before we even consider the theft at St Iggy's, which my gut and I are convinced are linked.

Then I remember seeing myself in the vestry window, a confident, competent woman waltzing into her new life. And I remember feeling the same frustration in the other murder investigations I was sucked into – and they both turned out well. Third time – well, I'll certainly need to be lucky as things stand.

Chapter 9

My fourth and final culinary attempts cover my work surface, and my patience is at an all-time low, as are my chocolate stocks, despite next-day deliveries – and it's still barely nine in the morning. The church bell tolls, reminding us it's almost time for Thursday communion, and I shudder. It's only a fortnight since our grim discovery and although the church services are now back in full swing and the wonderful Bishop Norton is proving a universal hit, it still feels too soon, even as a distraction from kitchen disasters. There's work to be done. And it's not going well.

Two of the new moulds will have to be sent straight back as they don't match my spec; the other three have proved as keen to hold onto my chocolate as I've been to get it out (my first attempt). The next mould proved it would be very effective as a pond liner when, to avoid repeating my first failed attempt, I immersed it in warm water to ease the chocolate out and ended up turning the chocolate contents into melted goo (attempt two). My third attempt was going fine until Dag decided it was time to nuzzle me to remind me it was time to feed him, just as I was balancing the tray between sink and worktop.

If I'd known it was going to be this much trouble, I'd never have agreed to Wickham's idea. Or maybe I'd have gone for standard moulds. Oliver Twist's Mr Bumble was, frankly, a doddle to design and make. William Shakespeare less so, his pointed beard making him look rather like a sinister Father Christmas. And don't get me started on the problems with Superwoman who, according to the purist Wickham, shouldn't even be considered a literary figure anyway.

I'd thought my idea of individual soft mint chocolate creams in paper wrappers printed with famous book titles and slipped in to a 'library' chocolate box was genius – until I'd tried to fix five sticky chocolate slabs together at anything approaching right angles, so perhaps I'll save that one for the Christmas Fair, along with Superwoman. After all, Easter's for eggs. Even if they are in the shape of a rotund workhouse manager and Stratford's prolific quill-wielder.

The now fed Dagenham chances his luck again by nudging me and pawing at the door. I glance at the kitchen clock and my heart quickens. I suppose mass production can wait while I exercise the hound. It'll give the prototypes a chance to fully cool down, along with their creator.

Daggers and I wander down High Street just as the delicious doc comes out of Bedside Manor. Pure coincidence that we happen to be there, just as he takes his daily pre-surgery constitutional, of course. He spots us immediately – anyone would think he'd been looking out specially – then waves and hurries to join us.

Oh, wow, he's holding my hand as we walk. First time ever in public. It's official! I pretend not to notice, even though every fibre of my being wants me to dance around the Green as if it's the maypole.

'How's the baking going, gorgeous?' My hand tenses and he glances at me in some concern.

'Great. If you ignore all the disasters.'

He turns towards me and, after only the merest hint of looking around, kisses me lightly, full on my lips. My heart leaps as my face reddens. The Green's residents are famous (infamous) for their curtain-twitching and I swear half of them only live there in anticipation of all the gossip and scandal they'll be privy to. But actually, who cares? The whole village will know within the hour and I couldn't care less. We've worked hard for this.

I realise Linton is still looking at me with some concern, so I smile before kissing him back. 'It's fine. Honestly. I've left the first set to settle because I wanted to, erm, because Daggers wanted a walk.'

My pet looks at me as if to say, 'Don't blame me,' and then shows his approval by trotting up to Linton and enthusiastically wagging his tail. Linton stoops to stroke his head, and he looks in absolute ecstasy. That's Daggers, not Linton. Although, come to think of it, Linton's rather partial to a bit of head-stroking as well and I squeeze his hand.

My daydream is rudely interrupted as a small black car swings into the Green. It's unusual to see any kind of car here as all the residents have garages at the back of their properties, and tend to make their displeasure obvious to anyone blocking their view. And I can't imagine any of them owning the ancient rust-box that's now beginning its second circuit. Which is even more odd. What if...

I drop Dagenham's lead and Linton's hand and leap out in front of the vehicle, my hand held up in the classic cop-STOP gesture. The tiny car swerves and skids slightly before coming to a halt just in front of me. Even more scarily, the door's flung open and a huge, muscular tattooed arm is thrust out, quickly followed by a dark-haired man in blue overalls whose broad shoulders and furious expression make him seem like a character in *The Godfather*.

Linton, however, bounds across and gets between the two of us – my hero – then starts to shake his hand. 'Culkerton Ashley, great to see you.'

The 'gangster' is momentarily thrown, then his face lights up with the most amazing smile as he drops Linton's hand and gives him an enormous hug. 'A'rite, mate?'

My now-official boyfriend slowly extricates himself, puts his arm around the man's shoulders and turns to me. 'To think you were nearly flattened by my old mate Culkerton Ashley.'

I just stare, open-mouthed. I'm completely lost for words, as his mate smiles warmly at me. 'Ashley Culkerton. Pleased to meet you.'

Now I'm confused. Linton notices and lets out an uncharacteristic bellow of laughter. 'Long story short – when Ashley set up his car repair service, he took over an old railway goods shed about four miles from here. And when we went over for the official unveiling, the signwriter had got his name wrong and painted CULKERTON ASHLEY on the doors.'

The mechanic grins ruefully. 'And it's kinda stuck ever since.'

'Culk, meet my girlfriend, Catherine de Barnes, Cat.'

Ashley/Culkerton/Culk rubs his rather hands down the front of his overalls and plants gentle a kiss on each of my cheeks, then drops on his haunches to make a fuss of Daggers, who senses a new friend and has hurtled across at top speed.

'He's the perfect man for keeping your old banger on the road, Cat.' Linton shakes his head, obviously thinking he's bestowed praise on his mate, at the expense of my poor little car. Although, to be fair, he has a point.

I turn to the mechanic. 'What brings you to Much Slaughter. Mr Culkerton?'

'Please, call me Ashley – or Culk.' He stares at me for a few moments, his face tense, before he jerks his thumb at the car and mutters almost under his breath, 'Test drive. I sometimes need a run to make sure everything's working before I hand the car back. Why?'

A sudden, horrible thought springs into my mind. 'What about on the day of the murder?'

His face looks even more grim, and there's a slight tick under his eye. 'Murder? What murder?'

'Reverend Cross, our locum vicar. You must have heard about it, surely?'

He shakes his head. 'Been keeping me 'ead down last few days. Gippy tummy. So, no, I've no idea what you're talking about.'

'It happened a fortnight ago. He was struck with one of our candlesticks in the vestry. It was a nasty job. Someone reported seeing a car racing away from the Green.'

Ashley stares at me for several seconds. 'What exactly are you getting at, Ms de Barnes?' His voice is cold.

'I was wondering if it might have been you. On a test run, I mean. I wondered if you might have seen anything?' No point in telling him he's the inspector's new prime suspect.

Linton is looking far from happy with me as the mechanic pulls out his phone and scans it. 'As it happens, yes, I was.'

I look him up and down for a fraction of a second. Significantly, my gut is silent so I reckon it's time to do some defusing. 'So it was you treating the Green as if it was Brands Hatch racetrack?' I grin.

He looks briefly embarrassed, but then he glances across at Linton and a mischievous grin spreads across his face. 'Been doing some extensive repairs on that sports car, I just couldn't resist it! Plus, there was some old biddy staring at me from behind her lace curtains so I thought I'd give her something to tut about.'

'So you didn't see anything suspicious, then?' Good grief, I sound like some film cliché.

'To be honest, I needed every bit of concentration to keep the car on the road. Funnily enough, my customers don't take kindly to me pranging their cars when I'm supposed to be preparing them. I didn't even stop in the village, I wanted to keep the engine fully warmed up, and I'd been on the run, as it were...' he gives me a pointed stare, 'for at least an hour running in the new engine. You can check on my workshop CCTV.'

'Sorry, Culk, I wasn't accusing you, just asking you as a witness.'

Ashley shrugs, nods at Linton, and moments later drives away, at a noticeably slower speed than before.

We turn and watch him disappear, then my lovely boyfriend swings round and grabs me by the shoulders. 'What on earth were you thinking of, Catherine? He was only inches away from flattening you.'

'Rubbish, it was at least a foot.' I glare my defiance back at him.

'And as if that wasn't bad enough, you then all but accuse him of murder. You really need to stop this sleuthing hobby taking over. It's becoming an obsession.'

I shrug. 'At least now we know we can eliminate him from our enquiries,' I say. I can feel steam rising.

'You've done that, all right. And probably eliminated his friendship as well. I've yet to come across anyone less likely to commit a murder than Culk.' He sighs and reaches for my hand, reluctantly.

I ignore it. 'Linton, there's something we need to get straight. It's really important.' I turn to face him full on, my hands on my hips, willing myself not to look into those gorgeous blue eyes. 'If this relationship is going to work, you have to let me be myself. I've had too many years of men telling me what to do.'

He looks taken aback and I feel sick. 'But I just saved your life.'

'No, Linton, you didn't. He was never that close that I couldn't get out of the way. What you did was decide was that you'd take on the role of my protector, and then decide what was best for me. This "sleuthing hobby", as you so charmingly put it, is important to me. And if you can't understand that, and if you can't let me be my own person, well…'

We stare at each other for a few moments, my breath coming in short bursts and my heart pounding in my ears. Linton's mouth keeps opening and shutting like a fish. But he says nothing.

'Oh for goodness' sake, I don't have time for this,' I say. 'I need to make a phone call.'

I stomp off up the Green towards the ancient stone Cross at its centre, while I find my phone in my jacket pocket and, turning towards the church as if begging it for support, I dial.

'Ah, Inspector. Catherine de Banes. I have some information for you about our murder suspect… Alright, *your* murder suspect. I can tell you who the mystery rally driver is.'

I'd like to think the silence greeting this revelation is due to how impressed the chief inspector is, but I fear it's due to him rolling his eyes and preparing to lambast me for what he insists is interference, and I insist is help.

'The driver was Ashley Culkerton who runs a garage nearby. And he was simply testing a car repair. Apparently his workshop cameras will prove what time he left and what time he got back.'

There's another long silence, followed by a click, and the line goes dead. What cheek. Here I am making his life easier and all the wretched man can do is put the phone down on me. That's gratitude for you.

Cat, has it occurred to you that your good news is actually bad news for him? His list of suspects is now non-existent.

Rubbish. Coming up with suspects, however unlikely, has never been one of Glen's problems. All I've done is stop him wasting time by accusing innocent Ashley. I've done him a favour. This is clearly a day of being misunderstood by men.

I plonk myself down on the stone base of the cross and stare at the window of St Cyril's vestry, trying to piece together in my mind the possible sequence of events. And especially who might have had both the motive and the opportunity to extinguish the life of Reverend Mark Cross, late locum vicar of the parish, in such a bloody way. And seemingly over such a trivial treasure as two items of cheap brass. No, it makes much more sense if it's connected with a four-hundred-year-old church relic.

Okay, I acknowledge I'm being rather overdramatic. It's just that I find sometimes the more creative I am with the re-enactment the more creative my mind can be with finding the suspects. My gut rumbles agreement. Or maybe it's simply rumbling with hunger.

However, before I have chance to get up, a list of my own begins to form, at least for the theft. I figure, if I can work out who did that, I'll be well on the way to solving the murder as well.

Top of the list is Major Anna Valley. I recall that look of almost fear when I asked her when the pyx had last been used. There's something about her that doesn't ring true. Plus, she'd have known about the pyx, and as church warden, if there's a hope it might be valuable, well, she'd certainly be interested in that.

Or maybe her financial interest might be rather more personal. After all, from a church perspective it wouldn't be an easy process to raise cash from selling it. But proceeds going into her own pocket, well, that might be a different story. After all, horse riding isn't cheap and when I arrive at the address given on the church noticeboard, her pokey cottage suggests she's not exactly flush with cash. Plus, she'd obviously have ample opportunities to remove the pyx from St Iggy's safe and slide in a replacement without anyone knowing. So, what if the Reverend Cross was checking in preparation for the Archdeacon's official Visitation and discovered the pyx was fake, and Anna took the opportunity of him being out of the parish to silence him, knowing it would focus enquiries on Much Slaughter? Especially if she removed a couple of items from St Cyril's safe, while she was there. My gut rumbles again, and I feel cold.

I turn to share my thoughts, but Linton has gone. Dag looks at me accusingly and whines. That's all I need, a stroppy dog and a stroppy doctor. Ah well, time to set up a meeting.

Chapter 10

Friday morning turns out to be one of those amazing warm, sunny mid-March days in the Cotswolds where you can finally believe spring has sprung. There's a cloudless blue sky, with no hint of wind, as Dagenham and I pull into the lay-by or passing place. We're in my sweet little car – 'old banger' indeed, how rude. We've still got a few minutes before we're due to meet Major Anna Valley, and my gut clenches at the thought so, as Daggers stretches his leg and sniffs happily in the verge, I lean on the Cotswold stone wall and appreciate the skill needed to build something so level and strong with such an array of different-sized stones, all without cement. I can't help smiling as I remember the scandalised horror of most of the villagers when, a few months after I arrived, a DFL (Down From London) newcomer patched up their stone wall with colour-matched cement and then bragged about it. One of the few major faux pas I've managed to avoid, thankfully.

In the field beyond, a dozen new-born lambs huddle close to their mothers, while a couple of the more adventurous skip around, just beyond the fringes of the flock, yet still under watchful maternal eyes. The world feels silent and still, with only the sound of an occasion lamb bleat. Within moments my soul feels calm and nourished as I make myself breathe deeply and slowly, inhaling one of the richest blessings of country living, once muck-spreading season has ended.

It's barely ten o'clock, but the warmth of the sunshine means I'm sweating – perspiring – and I peel off my jumper before tying it around my waist and pulling the bottom of my shirt out from my trouser waistband. Daggers is also panting and giving me frequent puzzled looks as to why we've come on a walk that doesn't involve any walking.

'Don't worry, boy, we'll be off shortly.'

And bang on cue, a shiny black Rover 2000, just like one my parents owned, lumbers into view. Like theirs, it's belching black smoke, the engine rattling as if it's full of ball bearings. For some reason, my gut suddenly rumbles in sympathy as if it's got its own share of ball bearings, and my muscles tense as the nearest sheep cock their heads and scurry across the field, bleating for their offspring to follow. A gloved hand waves out the window and the major pulls in, her car dwarfing mine. *What on earth are you worried about, Cat? She's no reason to think you suspect her of anything. Just tread with your usual carefulness. Oh!*

Major Anna Valley emerges from the car, wearing a sleeveless sky-blue t-shirt and black, calf-length trousers above trainers without socks. She peels off her driving gloves, tosses them into the car and grabs a walking pole. Then she slams the car door and descends on me with open arms.

'Catherine, how lovely to see you. This was such a good idea.'

I blush, wondering whether she'd be quite as gushing if she knew my real agenda was to grill her on her current position, as top of my Suspects League. Nevertheless, I do manage to put my arms around her as we hug, even though every one of my muscles tenses at her touch. 'Major, it's my pleasure.'

She jumps back and fixes me with an amused grin. 'Drop the major, please. Offsite, it's Anna.'

I nod and smile weakly. 'Anna.' It feels very odd to be so familiar. *You mean, with a possible murderer?* Actually, everything about this feels rather odd, from her attitude to her clothing. I know I shouldn't have expected military jodhpurs and spurs, but trainers and cut-offs? Really? For a major? And another odd thing: she's obviously closer to mid-sixties than mid-fifties. Nothing about this woman is as it seems.

Anna stares up and down the road. 'How well do you know this area, Catherine?'

'Not at all. And it's Cat.'

Then it suddenly dawns on me. I'm about to set off alone into the wilds of the countryside with a woman who could be a murderer. And I've just admitted that I don't know the area. Plus, after the upset with Linton, I haven't even been able to tell him where I'm going. Dagenham lets out a short sharp bark as if to say, you're okay, you've got me. True, although his biggest threat is he might lick an attacker to death. He looks offended, as if he'd read my mind, and resumes sniffing.

Anna throws back her shoulders, points her stick to the sky and sets off at a brisk trot, as if she's leading a group of cadets on a march, an image reinforced when her parade-group voice floats back, 'A couple of hours okay, Cat?' Clearly no answer is expected as she's already out of hearing range, and shows no signs of slowing down, or even checking whether I'm following.

Dag is bounding after her so I pick up the pace as my lungs start to protest and my heart begins to thump. I'm not sure whether her speed is due to her being used to much fitter companions or simply walking alone, but thankfully after another few hundred yards she does finally look back and wait for me to catch up. If she's planning to do me in, then rendering me breathless and weak has worked disturbingly well.

She's now standing in the middle of the road, her feet apart and her hands on hips, looking me up and down as if appraising a prime cow for slaughter. As I near her, she demands, 'Tell me, how's your murder investigation going?'

Straight to the point, I'll give her that.

I gulp and glance around for Dag but my so-called protector is at least a hundred yards ahead, his nose deep in the verge and his tail wagging, totally absorbed in the multiple scents which must be doggy heaven. 'Dag, here, boy.' I say, feebly.

He looks up for the briefest of moments before disappearing into undergrowth. I can almost hear him saying, 'Lick them to death? Really? Moi?' No help from that direction then.

But moments later, his head shoots up, and he turns towards the major with his nose twitching in the air and lets out a single, loud bark, before bounding to my side, his ears and tail down and staring back the way he's come.

My companion looks towards us both, startled, then swings round and a look of terror crosses her face.

Moments later, a single horse and rider appear round the corner. Dag growls and I quickly click his lead back on. Horses always spook him. But nowhere near as much as they seem to have spooked the major. She's bolted to the side of the road so rapidly she's startled the horse who skits sideways, tossing its head up and back as its front legs lift.

The young woman rider leans down to pat her horse's neck, whispering into its ear. Seconds later they skirt us, the rider throwing a furious look in our direction before nudging her mount into a fast trot. Only then does Daggers emerge from behind my legs to growl at the receding figures.

Anna, meanwhile, carefully checks they're a safe distance away. Seemingly satisfied, and as colour returns to her cheeks, she thrusts her arm through mine and moves us off as if nothing had happened. Except, now she's leading us back the way we came and there's a slight tremor pulsing in her arm. Gosh, that encounter really has spooked her. Which is enough to unsettle me and I'm not disappointed to be heading back.

'Now, Cat, you were about to tell me how the investigation's going. Do you think our vile vicar stole our pyx and then met his untimely end when he was trying to fence it?'

The speed of change in her startles me so completely I can only mumble, 'I've no idea. Hang on, did you just describe Reverend Cross as vile? I thought he was popular?'

She snorts and I'm reminded of an angry bull. 'Whatever gave you that idea? Goodness, that man had a rare talent for putting people's backs up. He even seemed to enjoy doing it, if you ask me.'

'But the service I went to, he seemed to be having a whale of a time.'

'If it was a traditional language service, with everyone's eyes on him and doing what he wanted, yes he'd be in his element. I've never met anyone so old-fashioned. He seemed to think everything good stopped sometime in the seventeenth century. Which was why I thought it was strange when he took so violently against that pyx.'

'What do you mean?'

She snorts again. 'It was his very first Sunday in the parish. We'd been using it from time to time, for important services. I mean, with all those jewels and polished silver, it did look special, so we thought it would honour his arrival. Well, as soon as the service was over and the bishop had left, he grabbed it and shouted at the top of his voice, "That comes out again over my dead body," then literally threw it into the back of the safe and stormed out. We were speechless. After that, if anyone tried to mention it, he'd snap their head off. And that's not the only time we've seen the rough edge of his anger. Nowadays, people treat him with kid gloves. Or, at least, they did. So, frankly, I imagine there are any number of people who'd be glad to see the back of him.'

'You included?' I really must stop my inner investigator accessing my mouth and bypassing my brain. Especially when I'm alone on a country road.

But Anna laughs. 'You might think. But no, to be honest, he treated me better than most. Maybe because I was taller and broader than him.' She grins and flexes her muscles, which are equally impressive and intimidating. 'No, I reckon if you do learn who did for Crass Cross, you'll solve both crimes. And given his gambling reputation, you might do worse than start there.' She halts and I'm sure there's more she's not saying.

We've arrived back at our starting point and Anna leans heavily on the roof of her car to stare intently at me. I'm not sure if she's considering whether to trust me or kill me and my gut knots again. I swallow hard, willing it to relax.

'He was a gambler?'

'Far too fond of the gee-gees, if you ask me. He reckoned he'd visited every racecourse in the UK and he could certainly name every Grand National winner, plus the seconds and thirds. He'd got even more obsessive recently, he was desperate to get any extra information from the trainers or the stable hands. There was even talk he'd been banned from Lambourn, he spent so much time there.' She pauses for a few moments before climbing into her car and adding, 'That's pure gossip, of course.'

Moments later, the car engine fires and belches out more blue smoke as she swings round and leaves, in a scattering of gravel.

My legs suddenly feel like jelly and every other muscle aches from the tension of the past few minutes. This is ridiculous: all I've done is take a short ramble with a suspect and encountered a lively horse. Yet I feel so sick I need to put my head between my legs as I sink onto my car seat, the door open and Daggers nudging uncertainly at me. The nausea soon passes but despite the warm day I feel chilled and shaky. Worse still, try as I might, I can't put my finger on why Anna's left me feeling disturbed. She had every opportunity to attack me if she'd wanted to but she was perfectly pleasant and the most tangible thing I have against her is driving the same make of car as my dad. Which is probably not enough to get her convicted of theft, never mind murder. And yet... There's something, I know there is. As another bout of faintness rolls over me. I know I must do the unthinkable and I reach for my phone.

My call is answered almost immediately, although the voice is decidedly cool and cautious. 'Linton, I need to meet up. I...'

The lovely man has picked up something in my voice. 'Give me fifteen minutes. Where are you?'

'I've been out for a walk so I'll meet you at my cottage.' I can't put any of this into words yet so a slow drive back is just what I need.

***

Linton must have been worried. As I park my car he's already at my cottage staring in through my sitting room window, his leather medical bag prominent in front of my door. As my engine splutters to a halt he swings round and positively gallops towards me, so I step out of the car straight into the most massive embrace. 'Darling, are you okay?'

Wow, I've achieved darling status. I guess our previous contretemps must be forgotten. Which is fine by me. At the moment I want nothing more than the warm security of his strong arms around me.

I reach into my bag for my keys. There are no keys. But they must be, I haven't forgotten them in months. It's the final straw, my legs sag, and I sob into Linton's shoulder, vaguely aware of the smell of the surgery on his jacket. Right now, an anaesthetic would be very welcome.

'Come on,' he says. He puts his right arm around my shoulders and guides me carefully down the path and across the Square.

The surgery area of Bedside Manor consists of two low-ceilinged oak-beamed rooms in what, centuries ago, would have been two separate cottages. It's everything you might imagine a cottage to be: small windows, gloomy and with more oak beams than you could shake a stick at. When I first came to Much Slaughter and sat here waiting to register, I tried to count the heavy black beams criss-crossing all four walls and continuing into the ceiling. I'd given up at thirty-eight.

Today, it's as gloomy as ever and already filling up with patients. Linton, however, marches me straight through, Daggers trotting protectively by my side. The doctor mutters 'medical emergency' in his best professional tone, and the disbelief is palpable. I can't blame their scepticism; there can't be a single villager who doesn't know we're an item.

The consulting room is large and light, airy even, with glazed double doors opening out onto a long, terraced garden. Linton lowers me onto the leather couch like a floppy rag doll, which is exactly how I feel, and busies himself checking my pulse with his lovely long fingers. He may be in full professional medic role but it doesn't stop a wonderful bolt of energy shooting up my arm and tingling my spine, especially when he unbuttons the top of my shirt and, having magically conjured up a stethoscope, places its freezing cold bell on my chest.

'Sorry,' Linton winces and smiles. 'I always forget to warm it. Same with my hands.'

Even in my parlous state, I disagree. That's not been my experience. I'm obviously feeling better. 'Sorry, doctor, I don't know what came over me. I'm not usually an hysterical wimp.'

He raises an eyebrow and smiles but seems satisfied with both my explanation and his examination as he scoots his wheeled chair across to the side of the couch, still the consummate professional. He does, however, reach for my hand, rubbing his fingers gently across the top, causing my heart to flutter even more. Good job I'm not on a monitor.

'What happened, Cat? Did you fall? Oh my God.' He looks horrified. 'Did someone attack you, darling?'

'No, no, nothing like that.' I pause, not sure how to explain. Now I'm back in the village, in the safe warmth of Linton's protection, it all seems faintly ridiculous. 'I just... it's silly.'

Linton's brow furrows and his fingers press painfully into the back of my hand. There's a definite edge of anger in his voice. 'I saw the state you were in, Catherine, and it definitely wasn't silly.'

He scurries across the room and pours a glass of water. I'm not sure whether it's medicinal or his way of giving me time to get my thoughts straight. As it happens, I appreciate both.

'It sounds silly. I mean, it was only a walk with the major. I wanted to check out her alibi for the murder and whether she had a motive for the theft.'

I feel him tense again. 'And you did that on your own? In the open countryside?'

'I had Dagenham with me.' Goodness, I do sound defensive. After all, Linton's only showing concern. I stare at him. 'There's nothing I can put my finger on but there's something she's not letting on about. Apart from the fact that she got so spooked by a horse that she finished the walk. And she did say that the saintly Mark Cross was far from being as popular as they'd have us believe. Something doesn't feel right. But I'm probably just being ridiculous.'

'No, you're not.' Linton smiles. 'But, medically, you're fine. Get your spare keys from Wickham, pour yourself a stiff brandy, and as soon as I've finished here I'll come across. I might even cook you supper, if you play your cards right.'

Now there's a prospect I want to dwell on. And what shall I wear...

Chapter 11

Heavy rain rattles on the roof. My eyes sting and I rub them, which makes them worse. Somewhere beyond my blurry vision an argument is raging but I can't make out the words or the people. An elderly man with a shock of white hair falls at my feet, blood oozing from a head wound and he turns to me with a look of acute disappointment. The drumming rain gets worse and the raised voices continue until, with a supreme effort, I manage to force myself awake.

My darkened bedroom is terribly hot and I fling the bedclothes back before taking a large gulp of water from the glass on my bedside table. My phone informs me it's two-thirty, not even halfway through the night. I listen for the sound of the rain, but there's nothing. Yet only minutes ago, it had woken me up. Maybe what I heard was some animal feet or other, paddling around in my roof; thatch is always going to attract insects and despite its wire covering, all sorts of birds still try to transfer bits from my nest to theirs. The peculiar noises had alarmed me for my first few nights here until Wickham slowly and carefully explained the thatch facts-of-life to the naive city-dweller, after which my mind was satisfied and my ears heard nothing.

Maybe I'd been dreaming? But the rattle had seemed so real, so close. I try to focus my sleepy brain and gradually the details seep back. Of course, I'd been inside Dad's old car on the way to a summer break in Skegness, or Nottingham-by-Sea, as it was often known. What I could hear was the summer rain hammering on the car roof. And the smell was from the exhaust pipe, which had collapsed into pieces and brought us to a clattering halt, barely an hour after we'd left our Nottingham home. And with all the patience of a nine-year-old, I was about to have the meltdown of all meltdowns.

I shudder at the memory. And at my behaviour. But, hey, I'd been a little girl. More significantly, I tell myself, if dreams are meant to be your brain's way of making sense of important data, what on earth had brought this back? I'm never at my best in the early hours so it takes a while. First step: the body in the dream. So, if this is all about the crimes, the body must be Reverend Cross, who unsurprisingly was looking disappointed after sixteen days of unsolved crime.

Step two: the car: Dad drove the same model as Anna, a Rover 2000, it was his pride and joy. Except, on this occasion, his pride and joy has become Mum's useless-pile-of-old-junk and stranded us on the A46 neatly between villages. But what on earth is my gut trying to tell me?

I groan and sink back onto my pillow, suddenly wishing I'd not been quite so hasty about banishing my knight in shining armour. Having delivered on his half-promise of cooking us supper (a very delicious prawn macaroni in a rich cheese sauce served with lettuce from his garden) Linton had offered to spend the night with me. But I'd reluctantly declined: given the tempestuous nature of our fledgling relationship in recent days, days of swinging emotions, I sensed we both needed to take stock. Not in a bad way though, we'd agreed we were back on firm ground. And, maybe it was also me underlining that I'm an independent woman. None of which stops me imaging his warm arms comfortingly around me, stroking my hair as I fall asleep. Plus I should probably email an update to Glen.

Saturday morning is usually one of the busiest times in the Crimson Courgette Coffee Emporium and I see, when I wander in at almost eleven o'clock, that today is no exception. Every table is full and there's even a small queue. Regular Customer status can earn you quicker service but it doesn't confer queue-jumping rights so I lean against the counter and look around. There are a few faces I recognise and we exchange nods.

Skye is buzzing around like a very colourful maroon-haired bee so we manage nothing more than quick smiles. I'm pleased for her: she so committed to keeping this place going, almost single-handedly. Then I check her counter and my display of chocolates, making a mental note to book in kitchen time tomorrow, ready for the new week. Maybe I'll try a new line, possibly something with salted caramel.

I'm in the middle of making a mental shopping list of ingredients while examining my stock cupboards when Cherry bursts through the door, almost flattening me. She stares pointedly across the room at a middle-aged man with a single, empty coffee cup in front of him, alongside his laptop and mobile phone. *Really, how can people be so inconsiderate?* He's probably been there for ages and that single cup will be all he's ordered.

The man catches her eye, looks around and takes the hint to pack away. He's barely out of his seat before I dive in (some people have no idea about queuing, and it wouldn't have been the first time my place had been usurped by a new arrival). So speedy am I that I can still feel his warmth as my bare legs meet the chair.

Cherry giggles as she slides into the seat opposite me. 'Worthy of a fly-half, that was, Cat.' Cherry coaches young people in rugby, as well as running the village pre-school, as well as being the vicar's partner, all of which makes her an interesting individual.

However, none of that stops her also being a total busybody, which she instantly proves. 'Come on, Cat, spill the beans. You're looking decidedly peaky.' She moves in closer across the table and for a moment it feels as if she's going to pinch my cheek. Just as Skye arrives with hot chocolate, coffee and buns.

'I'm fine, Mum, don't fret.'

Cherry grins. 'Point taken.'

Skye isn't so easily put off. 'Doesn't get you off the hook, though. This is what friends are for. Finally dreaming up your business plan?'

I wince. 'It's nothing. Just a bad night and bad dreams.'

'Oooh, intriguing. Tell me more.' Skye slips into the third chair, totally ignoring a large-hatted woman who's beckoning to her. The woman tuts loudly.

'Skye, you've got...'

'The sooner you tell me, the sooner I can get back to them.' She folds her arms across her chest.

'Alright, alright. It's no big deal. I just had a dream about when my dad's car broke down in the rain when we were off on holiday to Skegness.'

'What – *Welcome to Skegness – it's so bracing*?'

'We spent every summer there, so don't knock it. It had some of the best amusement arcades you'll ever find. And some half-decent lads.'

'So why's that a bad dream?'

'Well, that's the odd thing. I mean, I know we'd broken down miles from anywhere, and it was raining, and I flung my proverbially dollies out of the pram, but I'd never had it down as particularly horrible.'

'So why now?' Cherry's face is a mixture of puzzlement and excitement.

'That's easy. It was Dad's cherished Rover 2000.'

'Oh well, that explains everything – not.' Skye shakes her head, tossing her hair back.

'Sorry, I should have said, I went for a walk yesterday with Anna Valley, the church warden at St Iggy's.' I glance around and lower my voice. 'And I'm wondering if she should be one of our suspects.'

'What, the major? One of your suspects?'

I nod, reluctantly, knowing what's coming next. I'm not disappointed.

'And you went for a walk with her? Alone. Without telling anyone?' Cherry looks angry.

'Don't you start. I've had enough of that from Linton.'

'And quite right too.'

I hold up my hand. 'Okay, I get it, I really do. And I have texted Inspector Parva. The point is, the major drives a Rover 2000, just like my dad did. Although his was an original.'

They both look puzzled, but with a forest of waving arms trying to get her attention, Skye reluctantly takes to her feet. 'Call in, tonight.'

Cherry takes hold of both my hands and looks me straight in the eye. 'Cat, why would the major and your dad driving the same model of car give you a nightmare?'

I swallow and nod. 'Well, she left me feeling very disturbed, which is why I called Linton. I just can't put my finger on what it was, she was perfectly pleasant, and apart from being frightened by a horse and ending the walk early, she behaved normally. But something doesn't sit right, and I *will* get to the bottom of it.'

Cherry's phone buzzes and she glances at it quickly before resuming her stare. 'I need to go, Cat. And you need another hot chocolate.'

Never has a truer word been spoken, and bless my lovely friend Cherry, she soon passes those words to Skye, who moments later arrives with the promised steaming beverage.

***

'I hear things are back on track with the doc, then?'

As an opener, you've got to give Skye due credit. Faithful to her comment from this morning, I'm reporting for our evening catch-up and I'm barely over the threshold of her flat above the village store when she grills me. I grin.

'"Hello, Cat." "How are you feeling?" "Would you like a drink?" "Please have a seat."'

'Yeah, yeah, all of that.'

My café-running pal opens the door, bare-footed and wearing nothing but a rather grey towel. 'Sorry, Cat, I've only just got back. I've been catching up on some paperwork and I'm about to have a quick shower. Come on in, make yourself at home and join you in a tick. You can pour the wine.'

Skye's sitting room is awash with stuff. A huge mound of clothing near an ironing board has given up the unequal struggle and toppled over onto the floor. There are half a dozen dirty plates on a large mahogany coffee table suggesting her last few meals have consisted of pizza, half a cannelloni (the other half is congealed on the plate), an almost untouched plate of fish, chips and mushy peas, and a mass of something totally unidentifiable. All of which, I suspect, have been bought from the village shop underneath where I'm standing. There must be a dozen Crimson Courgette coffee cups scattered on any available flat surface, so it's a wonder she's got any left in the café.

But, more importantly, a bottle of red wine has been uncorked and rests on a small table while two rather splendid and slightly incongruous art deco wine glasses sparkle in the flickering light.

I grab a pile of clothes from one of the armchairs and search for somewhere to put them, before giving up and dumping them underneath the dining table and I settle into the cleared upholstery. Skye will have to sort out her own perch.

The sound of running water filters through as I pour two generous helpings of wine and, and in the absence of anything else to do, rather than give my brain an excuse to recall the murder investigation, I gather up as many cups as I can manage and load them into the dishwasher. It takes three trips to complete the task and I'm just pondering whether to start on the plates when Skye reappears, wrapped in a huge black and gold kimono, her maroon hair tightly wrapped in a blue towel, although a few damp strands dangle down her neck. As she sinks into an armchair (on top of the clothes rather than trying to find somewhere to move them to) she tucks her legs underneath her and rearranges the robe to restore decency.

'So, Cat, fill me in on all the gossip. And how did the great detective respond to your update, did he swoon at your brilliance and frame your words as an example?'

We giggle. 'Hardly. Although I get the impression from his reply he's rather hoping I might have miraculously pulled something out the bag.'

'And did you?'

'Well, I actually thought I did, Skye. Unfortunately, our super-detective wasn't exactly impressed. I was trying to convince him there's much more to that Anna Valley, than meets the eye.'

'The major?' Skye looks rather taken aback. 'I've met her a couple of times when she's come in for coffee. Or at least, peppermint tea. She seemed very pleasant, actually. I liked her.'

'Oh, I'm not suggesting she's some cold-blooded killer. But perhaps something more innocent just got out of hand.'

'What, you mean – let's meet for a cuppa – oh dear, I've accidentally murdered you?'

'That's not what I mean and you know it. And in my experience, murderers can be quite pleasant to everyone else.' Except, in fairness, out of the two I've encountered over the last year, one was odd and the other was creepy. *Okay, maybe Skye has a point. And tonight's meant to be a distraction, so – let's distract.* 'How's business going?'

Skye winces. 'Actually, business is fine. More than fine. Auntie Rose reckons I'm doing better than she did. It's not that.' She dabs her eyes on her billowing sleeves and I perch on her chair arm so I can hug her. She smells of coconut body lotion and a lemony shampoo. 'When I moved here, all I thought about was making a new start, a clean sheet where nobody knew me. And it was. And people have been absolutely lovely. So many of them make a point of coming in regularly, even if it's only for a quick cup of tea.'

She reaches for her wine, empties a third of the glass and splutters as she swallows. 'Frankly, Cat, I'm lonely.'

Now that's something I never expected to hear. Skye always seems to be chatting to someone, even out in the village. Except, come to think of it, I've never seen her out with a group, apart from one time, when a bunch of us went over to Cirencester's Mop Fair.

'And working all the hours God sends doesn't help.'

I tighten my hug. 'We definitely need to do something about that, then, Ms Green.'

She turns round and grins at me. 'We do. But that can wait. More importantly, how are you? It can't have been easy for you either, settling back in a second time. At least I've only had to do it once.'

I consider for a moment. 'In some ways, no, it hasn't been easy. In others, there's been rather a lot happening, to take my mind off that.'

She nods, looking pensive. 'Cat, there's something really important I need to ask.'

Chapter 12

'Ye-es.' *This doesn't sound good.*

'Why did you choose to move here, of all places? I'm assuming it wasn't the old chestnut about being closer to family since we've neither seen nor heard of any. I mean, I'm really glad you did, but why Much Slaughter? Of all the places in the world...'

At this point, I notice that both our glasses are empty and I reach over to the coffee table to refill them. Once our drinks are replenished, I lean back and this time I do hook my legs over the chair arm.

'Simple answer? I drew a ninety-minute commute circle out from London and visited a handful of nice places, north, south and east. And when west brought me to the Cotswolds, I knew this was it. Then it was just a simple matter of deciding where. The Oxfordshire side felt a bit too busy and when I saw my cottage in the window of an estate agent in Cirencester, I instantly fell in love with it. And the rest, as they say in the films, is history.'

'So it wasn't even that someone from your family lived here, like, a hundred years ago?'

I wince and shake my head.

'Not a good topic?' This time *she* squeezes me.

'Well, I suppose I *am* nearer my parents, geographically at least. Just not in travel times.'

'So why haven't I met them? Mind you, I haven't seen mine since I moved here, either.'

'No good reason, really. There was no big disagreement or anything like that. We're just very different people gradually moving apart, I suppose.'

Skye regards me carefully for a few seconds and I can almost hear the cogs in her brain turning.

I grin at her. 'Come on, young lady, spit it out. We are friends, after all.'

'Well, I guess I was wondering, if that was the simple answer, what's the deeper reason for moving here?'

I sigh and swing my feet onto the floor. I should have seen that coming. 'Okay, Skye, here's the Catherine de Barnes family history in two minutes flat. My dad was born and brought up in Birmingham. My mum was born in Leicester, so when they got married, Nottingham seemed a good compromise. My father was a solicitor and my mother worked in a bank until she got pregnant with me, after which she became a housewife. They've been married, let's see, for almost fifty years. We email every month or so and I visit them from time to time. End of story.' *Good grief. I'm glad that's finished, and now it's my turn to take a large slurp of wine.*

Skye, however, isn't finished. Her intense stare fixes on me and she shakes her head. 'Cat, those are just facts. What are your parents like? What's *their* story? Why do you see so little of them?'

'Well, if you really want to know, my dad's as pedantic as you'd expect from an old-school solicitor. He's also super-critical. He doesn't mean to be. And part of me knows it's only because he cares and wants the best for his only child. But whenever anything goes wrong, it's his voice I hear telling me what I should have done and how I need to try harder. Plus he was inordinately fond of my ex-husband because he was a successful businessman and promised the world. My father still can't really understand why I divorced him. I mean, he knows about the affairs but my dad's from a bygone age and although he'd never say it out loud, I'm sure he thinks that's just what men do and if I'd tried harder, well, he wouldn't need to stray.' I blow my nose.

'That's unforgivable. If I...' Skye squirms on her chair, huffing and puffing and I have a sudden glimpse of her in full campaigning mode. It's impressive.

'He's not that bad. I don't doubt he loves me. It's just the way he was brought up and he's never seen the need to change.'

'But what about your mum? Surely she's more enlightened?'

'She tried to be. And when I said I was going to do something creative rather than pore over boring law books every day, like my dad, she was supportive. And I suppose I should be grateful that they wanted me to have a good career: a lot of that generation still assume the woman works until she marries, then has children and dedicates herself to running the home, except for the occasional coffee morning. But she was never going to defy her husband, so her support was all whispers and squeezes, and *"he only wants what's best for you, darling, like he does for me"*. It made me so angry, for her as well as for me. Even when I was MD of the advertising agency in the City with a staff of twenty under me, he still couldn't tell me I'd done well. It was the same however hard I tried. It was only when my ex traded me in for a younger model and set up home with her that I finally thought, why on earth am I putting myself through all this?'

Skye crosses over and hugs me and I sniff loudly into her top. 'That must have been a difficult upbringing.'

'To be fair, Skye, most of it was fine. Compared with a lot of families around us, it was good. My father brought in a decent, regular income. My mum took huge pride in a comfortable home, they didn't fight and I was well clothed. They even got me into the amazingly prestigious Nottingham High School. I really can't complain.'

Skye doesn't look convinced but wisely opts not to pursue it. 'When you were in my coffee shop, you said something about being freaked out by a car. What was that about?'

'Ah, yes. Anna Valley drives a Rover 2000, which is the same model my father drove. It was his pride and joy. His father worked as a manager with British Leyland in Birmingham and when the model first came out, and my father passed his driving test at the first attempt, it was his reward, a brand new white one, and he drove it for the next forty-odd years. He was such a careful driver, I don't think he ever pranged it. Mind you, he's a nightmare to have in the passenger seat, he always keeps up a running commentary on things to watch out for. It's like driving with an angry driving instructor. In the end, I stopped driving him around. But I still hear his voice when I'm driving. And at other times as well.' I sigh and stare at the floor.

Skye sounds impatient. 'Yes, but what did I miss this morning? What on earth did that woman do to spark such a meltdown?'

I wince.

'Sorry, not tactful.' Skye pushes a thick mop of hair out of her eyes.

'Actually, that's the whole point. It doesn't make sense to me, either. It's just that Anna's car reminded me of my dad's.'

'You didn't inherit the car?'

'I didn't pass my driving test first time. Or second, either, for that matter.'

Skye raises her eyebrows questioningly.

'It was the fourth time. And I still didn't get a car. Mind you, I was twenty-two by then, about to leave Cambridge and move to London, and move in with my now ex.'

Skye looks shocked. 'You're Oxbridge?'

I wished the sofa would swallow me up. 'It's not something I like to publicise. Girton. English.'

Skye giggles. 'You sound like the intro to University Challenge: Girton. De Barnes. Reading English.'

Little does she know, I was actually put forward for the programme but failed the college try-out. Thank goodness. I can't think of much worse than having my lack of knowledge exposed in front of millions of viewers.

Skye gazes out of the window for a while before turning back to me. 'Is this about the car? Or the major? Or your dad?'

I shrug.

'If I was a therapist...' we both laugh at the idea, 'I'd say, "Tell me more about your dad." And I'm not. But – tell me more about your dad!'

'Not a lot to say, really. He and my mum still live in Nottingham. He's retired now. Spends his winters supporting Nottingham Forest football team and his summers on the allotment, or watching cricket at Trent Bridge.' I lean back on the sofa exhausted.

Skye shakes her head. 'That's what he *does*. Tell me who he is.'

I have to think quite hard, it's not something I've considered much. 'He's a stickler for detail. I guess that goes with the job. Or, maybe he was successful because of it. I don't know what more I can say. He was proud of being the provider.'

'And were you a daddy's girl?'

'Probably.' I blush.

'Yet I've never met him and you never talk about him. When did you last see him?

I blush again, squirming on her suddenly uncomfortable chair and I wish she would stop. It's none of her business. *Except that's what friends do, Cat, they talk about things, even personal things.* It's true, I suppose.

'Just before I moved here.' Skye looks shocked. 'What? When did you last speak to your parents?'

'Last week, actually.'

'Well, we WhatsApp most weeks. At least, Mum and I do. Dad doesn't often join in. But he's still a huge part of my life. I often ask, what would Dad think about this?'

'And what does he think?'

'He just wants the best for me. And I want to make him proud of me, at last.'

At last? Oh for goodness' sake, I really must think more carefully before I open my big mouth. Time to change the subject. 'That's more than enough of the soul-searching. We need to discuss a great business plan for my chocolates and your cafe.'

Skye stares at me for a few moments and just as I'm congratulating myself on a successful diversion she reverts to the previous subject. 'So why haven't they visited you here?'

I sigh. 'Look, I'll say this and then let's drop it. As I said, they were both fond of my ex, who was very successful and told them what they wanted to hear. Even when he moved out, Dad was convinced it was just to make me come to my senses. So I told them they weren't welcome until they, at least, tried to see my side. Now...' I dab my eyes inelegantly, 'can we please change the subject?'

Skye squeezes my hand and pours us more wine, emptying the bottle, and for a few minutes we both stare into our wine glasses, punctuated by the occasional sips.

But finally Skye can't bear any more, and after a few seconds squirming in her chair, she blurts out, 'You've still not updated me about Linton. I hear it's going well again now, after the hiccup.'

You've got to be in awe of the village grapevine. Not only have they picked up on my latest spat with Linton, it's barely a day since my distress call paved the way for our delicious making up. But clearly the village is fully abreast of both. Although I suppose being half-carried through a busy surgery waiting room is a drama always likely to spread like wildfire.

Skye grins. 'Apparently you're now labelled Much Slaughter's most romantic couple.'

If you can't beat 'em join 'em – and you certainly can't beat the village gossip machine, so I wiggle my eyebrows and blush modestly.

Chapter 13

My Monday morning phone call from Chief Inspector Parva is as unexpected as his request to 'pop in and see me at my cottage'. Not only does the chief inspector rarely 'pop in' anywhere, that would be far too informal, but he talks about seeking my advice. Which leaves me both shaken and stirred. Shaken because it's so unlike him to actually seek help from someone he once called an interfering busybody, let alone twice in ten days, so I'm deeply suspicious that there might be more to this than meets the eye. And stirred because, whatever his ulterior motives might be, he's reached out an olive branch to me, again.

The request also poses a sartorial dilemma. Left to myself, today would be tracksuit bottoms, a t-shirt and a huge, knitted jumper together with my ankle-high furry slippers. But Glen is on duty and coming for an official visit, and if he's offering the olive branch of collegiality or at least co-operation, I probably need something smarter. Without looking as if I'm scrubbed up for royalty.

To scrunch my frizzy hair back from my face in any vaguely smart style is a time-consuming and frustrating experience, but after half an hour it's combed and tightly held in a scrunchy and Alice band that shows off my light make-up properly. After a similar time selecting and discarding wardrobe items, I settle for a loose calf-length printed cotton dress in a flattering shade of dark red that's tight at the waist and then flows out over the hips. The v-neck is rather deeper than I'd like, for this occasion but, set off with a simple platinum necklace, it makes me feel good. I sigh as the final touch is to reject my comfy, fluffy slippers and settle for tight black leather boots.

I punch out a quick early morning text to Linton to reassure him that all's well, medically and romantically, and I've just poured hot water into the cafetière and arranged the chocolate macaroons on a plate when there's a hearty knock on my door. Dagenham raises his head, sniffs for danger and sinks back into snoring.

When I open the door, Glen marches in, stamping his feet and rubbing his hands, before sliding his familiar sunglasses up onto his grey hair. 'Colder than I thought,' he mutters, reaching out his hand in greeting before changing his mind and unbelievably leaning in to kiss my cheek.

Momentarily, my body tingles until I feel guilty about Linton, redden and turn away.

Luckily he doesn't seem to notice or is too gentlemanly to comment, he just slides out of his coat and hands it to me. By the time I've hung it on the peg by the door I'm relieved to see he's already made his way into my sitting room and is standing in front of the embers of a fire, still blowing on his hands as if he's trying to inflate a balloon. I take the hint and open the fire's vents before tossing on a handful of twigs to waken it up. Moments later, there's a roaring inferno which I feed with a couple of larger logs.

'Coffee?'

He nods. 'Black, no sugar. Please.'

When I return with the tray he's graduated to the sofa and sits stiffly upright oozing an air of authority and reliability. He's dressed in a dark blue waistcoated suit that's beginning to look more than a little creased and shiny, but I notice that it sits comfortably across his broad shoulders and slim waist and I'm content that my own choice of clothes was spot on.

Hooking my foot around the leg of a small coffee table, I ease the table out and across the carpet, deposit the tray on it and drop into an armchair. I'm at the point of swinging my legs over the arm towards the fire when I remember I'm supposed to be radiating professional propriety, so I quickly adjust my dress over my knees and draw my legs back against the front of the chair. 'So, Inspector, what can I do for you?'

'For a start, today you can call me Glen, Catherine.' His gaze wanders around the room seemingly intent on avoiding my gaze as he shuffles on the sofa. Oh dear, I know from past experience with numerous men where this is leading to. And although Glen had briefly flitted across my romantic radar as a person of interest, that role is now well and truly taken.

I'm about to explain all this when Glen clears his throat. 'This is very difficult for me. I want to ask you… erm, for your help with this case.'

I'm sure the trained officer must see my relief from the little beads of perspiration on my forehead. If he does, he's too polite to let it show. Or maybe he's just too uncomfortable to notice. Either way, he extracts his black police notebook, licks his pen in the familiar police throw-back gesture, and skim reads a few pages as I pour us both a steaming hot cup of coffee.

'It seems to me, Catherine – or may I call you Cat?' I nod, yes. 'It seems to me, Cat, we've got a list of four potential suspects for the murder of Reverend Cross. Firstly…' He raises his forefinger as his voice takes on a tone I can imagine addressing a hushed courtroom. 'Dale Hill, who found the body. They're always one of the first we look at, especially since in the reverend's case he had no immediate family. Maybe Dale's distress in the vestry was shock because it had all gone horribly wrong. Perhaps the reverend's gambling habit meant he owed Dale money and he'd come to collect, perhaps threatened to "take" something in lieu and when the cleric refused or fought back, well, you saw the outcome.' Glen nods in self-approval.

'That's all very well,' I say, 'apart from...' I raise my hand to count on my fingers. 'First, the missing items are pretty much worthless. Second, they're hardly something to kill over. Third, why would Dale lend Mark money, anyway? They're hardly likely to come across each other. Fourth, as far as we can tell, Dale wouldn't have had time to dispose of the items before we arrived. Unless, of course, he hid them quickly and intended to come back later. Fifth...'

'Yes, alright, I take your point. The other theory I'm working is that the vicar tried to sell something to Dale, maybe the proverbial family silver...'

'Which, if the two cases *are* linked, Glen, it could have been the pyx. But since you keep insisting the two cases aren't linked, that won't work as a motive.'

'Well, I don't want to have a closed mind...'

You? A closed mind? Perish the thought, Inspector.'

He grins.

But our last exchange has had the opposite effect on me. Could I really have been duped so easily by our antiques expert? A horrible thought floats into my mind. 'If you're right, Glen…'

'If?' He grins again and I'm suddenly not sure if I don't prefer the normal grouchy version, it's less disconcerting.

'*If* you're right – and I'm not admitting you are yet, but if you are – supposing Mark Cross offered the pyx to Dale in payment for his debt and Dale realised it was a copy. Maybe he was at St Cyril's to confront Mark. And it came to blows…'

Now it's Glen's turn to look sceptical. 'But the replica was in the safe at St Ignatius' vestry. And I can't believe Cross had the time and the contacts to produce a fake like that.'

'Suppose he didn't know it was fake? He wasn't an expert after all, not like Dale. Maybe Dale had arranged to view it previously, with the major or even Pixie?'

'But, Dale would've recognised straight away it was a fake.'

'Maybe he did, Glen. Or perhaps he had his suspicions but didn't want to say anything until he'd done some more research.'

Glen licks his pen with the relish of a schoolboy licking melting ice-cream and scribbles busily in his notebook. 'I'll check.' He looks up again, and I smile.

'Now, in the interest of being thorough, who else have you got on your list?'

There's a long pause while he stares anywhere other than at his notes, and once again I wonder if there's a different agenda behind all this. Which, I have to admit, I find very disconcerting, not so much because of the agenda, if there is one, but because, for the life of me, I can't work out what it is.

But finally, he sighs and flicks back a couple of pages. 'Well, there's our film runner. We've checked her phone records and she definitely got a phone call at the right time, which seems to give her an alibi. Although…' he pauses, 'we do need to check she went back straight away. She claims she only got as far as the churchyard. But what if she was already inside? It's possible her phone went off as she was rifling the safe and that's what alerted the vicar. I'll get someone to check. She's not fully out of the frame yet.'

I nod, picturing the girl we'd spoken to on the Green. I suppose, if she was used to lugging heavy film equipment around she'd be able to wield the candlestick with enough venom. And it would explain why she kept staring back at us once Glen had let her go: she was checking to see if we'd believed her.

'I'm still not ruling out my local petty crook.' Glen's enthusiasm has evaporated like morning mist and he's beginning to sound quite petulant, as if I've been stealing his favourite toys. And there was me thinking he'd come to me for the voice of reason. 'Maybe some chancer came in, looking for shelter, and saw the open safe. One of your local lads or lasses, maybe. As I keep saying, nothing to do with the pyx.'

Glen's forehead seems to have concertinaed into deep creases to match his suit, his rich baritone voice seeping into a dull bass, then he sighs, as if he's got all the woes of the world on his shoulders. Poor man. Nothing about this case seems clear-cut at the moment. I pause to consult my gut, but it's silent.

'Well, at least we can rule out Ashley.' I smile at the note-scribbling police officer, who pauses, looks up and then flips back a few pages.

'I'm not sure we can.'

'Oh come on, Glen. He gave a perfectly reasonable explanation, backed up by his own CCTV footage.'

'He's got form, that one.'

'For stealing church property?'

'Well, no. But he was a right little tearaway in his youth. Always in and out of mischief.'

'And recently?'

'Not in the last few years. I reckon he doesn't have time these days. But that doesn't mean anything.'

'Once a villain, always a villain, is that it? No chance he's a reformed character?'

'In my experience, Cat, there's no such...'

'Okay, I get it. Let's move on. Anyone else on your list of subjects? Maybe someone plausible this time?'

I know I sound sarcastic, but Glen doesn't seem to care, he simply rolls his eyes and announces in a tone of deep defeat, 'Pretty much anyone who might have come in early for the Thursday morning service.'

I laugh. 'No one comes early for services here, Inspector.' Rather than getting a reciprocal laugh, this produces a ferocious scowl. 'To be honest, Glen, every single person arrives five minutes either side of the advertised time. This would need someone to be at least thrifty minutes early. So I think you can safely rule out that line of enquiry.'

He snorts and seems about to mutter something – probably along the lines of it being up to him who he rules in or rules out – but then he shrugs instead. This is getting rather heated, so I nip out to the kitchen to refill the cafetière.

On my return, Glen doesn't seem to have moved. It's only as I refill his cup and offer the plate of macaroons, that I see he's eaten one while I've been out, so he's obviously managed to do that. Which doesn't stop him taking another one, as he smiles weakly.

I take a deep breath. 'Glen, can I try out an idea on you?'

He raises an eyebrow before nodding almost imperceptibly.

'I think we should probably reconsider the major.'

I pause, waiting for the explosion, but it seems the inspector is trying to accommodate me. So I plough on. 'She knew about the pyx, and she'd have had any number of opportunities to switch them. It probably wouldn't be too hard for her to get a replica made either, with plenty of photos around. She just needed to find the right people.'

I might almost have thought that Glen believed I'd come up with a novel idea, if it hadn't been for the fact that he'd written none of this down. And for an officer whose middle name would be Procedures, that's damning. Instead, he stares into the flames of my fire for several seconds, not even bothering to turn back to me before announcing, in a bored tone, 'What's the motive? To put against the fact that she's a church warden, a pillar of the village community and shows no sign of being short of money.'

'Glen, you don't need me to tell you that appearances can be deceptive. The looks as if she might need money but there could be other motives. Maybe a love interest?'

'And who exactly did you have in mind? Reverend Cross?' He shakes his head as if pitying the amateur sleuth who's way out of her depth but needs humouring.

'Why not?' I say. Glen's scorn riles me. After all, he wanted to ask *my* advice, not the other way round.

'You mean, apart from the fact that he was at least ten years older?' He still isn't looking at me.

'What if they were planning something together? Maybe not running off, maybe one of them had an expensive medical need? Or maybe she needed the money because she was being blackmailed. So she stole the pyx, then Mark found out and threatened to go to the police.

Glen gives me a patronising look and speaks slowly, as if to a small child. 'Has it occurred to you, Catherine, that perhaps your determination to link the theft and the murder is blinkering you to other possibilities?'

'And has it occurred to you, Chief Inspector, that your determination that they aren't, is blinkering you?'

We stare at each other, both breathing heavily, horns locked, while the fire crackles as if it's feeding off the angry atmosphere.

'Sorry, Cat.' Glen leans forward. 'This case is really starting to annoy me. Which is not a good reason to take it out on you. Especially since you're only trying to help.'

I bristle.

Glen sighs. 'Sorry, that came out wrong. I mean, I recognise your suggestions are made because you're trying to help. After all this time, I feel no further forward than day one.'

'I understand,' I say, grateful I haven't got any number of superior officers breathing down my neck and moaning about valuable resources and 'our public image'. 'Was there something else?'

He shakes his head, no. 'I really do appreciate your perspective, Cat. And I promise I'll get someone to look into the major's background.'

'Thank you.' My gut gurgles, so I must be onto something. But what, exactly?

Chapter 14

My brain works best when left to do its own thing in its own time. At least, that's what I'm telling myself as I march across the Green. Daggers only too keen to lead the way – although his keenness noticeably vanishes when we veer away from the recreation ground and climb the steps to Skye's apartment.

Mind you, my brain has already been left to marinate for three days, with no discernible outcome or fresh insights on the theft or the murder as regards suspects, or even a motive. Three days since my fractious yet oddly congenial session with that bastion of Gloucestershire constabulary, Glen Parva. Who, incidentally, has also been noticeably silent.

So what better way to take a break from my mental machinations than to have an evening with my favourite coffee shop proprietor? And perhaps a drop of something alcoholic. Or chocolatey. Or both.

Skye flings open the door and enfolds me in a huge hug while Daggers darts in to select the warmest spot in the room. After her daily labours, she's now out of her work clothes and wearing a thin-strapped, black ribbed top that makes little attempt to reach her grey tracksuit bottoms. Her feet are thrust into giant furry bunny slippers that make me wish I'd brought my own; they'd look great together.

As I'm crossing the room, my phone buzzes, causing us both to jump. I fumble in my bag, glance at the screen, then hit the IGNORE button and shudder. 'It was my mum. I'll maybe call her back later.'

Skye grins. 'I thought they never contacted you?'

'They don't. Well, apart from Christmas and birthdays.'

'Hang on.' Skye's eyes have lit up like spotlights. 'I'm pretty sure it's not Christmas – so that must mean…?'

Oops, I'd meant to keep that quiet.

'Today?'

I nod, grinning sheepishly.

'How come…? Does…? Wait here.'

She leaps out of the chair, races out of the door and within two minutes is back with an enormous, boxed, chocolate cake. I guess it's one of the advantages of living above a shop. In no time at all, she's unpacked it, produced blue willow-patterned plates and actual cake forks – which presumably is one of the perks of running a coffee shop.

She's just started cutting into the amazing gooey gateau, causing a rich cream filling to ooze out from the middle, when there's a brief knock on her door and in marches my lovely doctor, grinning broadly before planting a juicy kiss on my lips that's every bit as nice as the cake before me, definitely the icing on the cake. And moments later, the cherry on the icing on the cake arrives when in marches Cherry herself, with Scott's young dog Barking – much to Dagenham's delight – closely followed by Boothby and Wickham, to *my* delight.

Suddenly, everything's right with the world, and this might just turn out to be the best birthday ever. I think it probably did. Except that I have absolutely no memory of it...

Chapter 15

After my aborted meeting with Anna Valley, the last thing I expected was an invite to Saturday pre-lunch 'drinks' at her cottage. But the chance to find out more about my suspect is too good to miss.

Now, as I stand suitably scrubbed and buffed in front of her cottage, it strikes me all the majors I've even known have lived in a grand mansion, or at least a substantial smallholding, befitting their rank and status. *Oh, come on, Cat, be honest. The only ones you've ever 'known' have been in magazines or on TV.* Anna's house is, shall we say, modest. A two-up two-down at the end of a Victorian terrace of four other, identical frontages. Identical, apart from Anna's bright green door which stands out amongst the other modest black ones. Her small front garden consists of a neatly-clipped lawn bordered by flowerbeds which, now, in early spring, contain only daffodils, a few hardy snowdrops and some budding rose bushes. A few brave green shoots suggest a whole lot of other plants just waiting for warmer weather before they venture forth.

Against the neat stone wall is a weathered wooden trellis interleaved with boughs of what I think is Virginia Creeper, judging by the way it clings. The path to the door is a jigsaw of irregular stone slabs interspersed with greenery which I imagine in summer will be scented wildflowers so that walking over them will send amazing aromas into the air.

As I climb out of my car, my ears ring with a cacophony of my friends' voices pointing out the foolhardiness of venturing yet again into the presence of a possible murderer without the backup of even a solitary companion, never mind a whole battalion of cavalry. I shake my head vigorously, displacing both the voices and my barely-contained curls, and head for the Last Chance Saloon otherwise known rather disappointingly as End Cottage.

Anna stands at the front door beaming. If she has the slightest memory of the horse encounter at our last meeting she doesn't show it. Once again I'm wondering why a horsewoman would be upset by a sudden encounter with a horse. Or maybe she didn't like the direction our conversation was taking; but that would need her to be an outstanding actor. Or me to be off on another of my dead ends.

It's hard to pursue a line of thought when you're drawn into a warm embrace and then escorted arm into a cosy sitting room. Her welcome is as warm as any I've received in Much Slaughter. The room is as modern as the outside is traditional. All the chairs have polished metal tubular frames, as does the magnificent glass-topped dining table and three small matching tables. The floor looks like original floorboards, polished to make the grain stand out, and there's just one exquisite plain cream rug in front of a huge, enclosed log burner.

My host produces two huge, soft sheepskin throws which she drapes across a couple of armchairs either side of the fire and waves me into the one on the left. 'Red? White? Bubbles? Whisky? Soft drink? What's your poison?'

'Red, please.'

She nods, disappears, and returns moments later with a large glass of red wine and a large glass of orange juice, setting the latter on the table beside her, the ice cubes clinking. She's wearing another sleeveless vest, white this time, with a printed logo from a local gym. She's paired this with green tea-dyed cargo pants that show off her muscles when she walks. She's definitely not someone you'd want to cross in a dark alley. Thankfully, however, she's smiling now, and waves her hand to indicate nuts, crisps and olives on the table between us. I grab a wooden cocktail stick to buy time and pop several olives consecutively into my mouth.

'Catherine, thank you so much for coming, after I was so discombobulated last time.' In fairness, she does look embarrassed, fiddling with a strand of her short hair and looking from me to the fireplace and back several times. 'I guess this business with Mark and the pyx has got to me more than I realised. I was just spooked.'

'It's absolutely fine, honestly. I was just surprised, that's all. I'd have thought that as a major in the army you'd have been used to all sorts of sudden encounters.'

A huge guffaw echoes round the room. 'Lordy, no, bless you. I'm Salvation Army not regular army.'

I feel my face turn red with embarrassment. 'Anna, I'm *so* sorry. I just assumed... And you don't exactly look like a Salvation... I mean, you look much more like a ...' *When you're in a hole, Cat, stop digging*.

She guffaws again and wipes her eyes. 'Sorry, Cat, it's me, I just assumed you knew. It's common knowledge round here so I sometimes forget to explain to outsiders.'

I wince at being called an outsider but I suppose in the villages everyone else is an

'Oh my,' says Anna, 'I'm so glad we've cleared that up. Now perhaps we can move on to more serious things. How's the sleuthing going now, any developments?'

Is this a trap? Is she trying to find out whether I know enough to pose a threat? And if so, what's she going to do about it? With muscles like hers, I don't stand a chance. If only I'd brought Dagenham, at least he might distract her.

'Cat?'

'Sorry, just trying to gather my thoughts. Not very well, to be honest. The chief inspector is adamant they're separate crimes and he's the professional, so I guess he's right.'

Oh come on, girl, that's pushing it, even for you.

'I must admit, this business with the pyx has got my interest,' Anna says.

No need to tell her that my gut reckons if I solve that riddle, I'll have solved the murder. I hurry on. 'So, tell me, Anna, who would have known where the pyx was kept, or its value, and would have had access to St Iggy's safe?'

'Well now, had I been in the regular army and told you that secret information, Ms de Barnes, I'd have to kill you.'

My blood runs cold before she guffaws yet again and announces in a much more cheerful voice, 'But as it's the Salvation Army, I'll simply have to pray for you. To solve the case, that is.' She chortles, while I desperately try to calm my panicking heart rate. 'To be serious again, surprisingly few people, actually. Once it had been stowed away, I don't think many people even remembered we had it. Me, of course. I've been in post for almost 20 years now, despite the diocese trying to get rid of me.'

She breaks off to throw a couple of logs onto the fire, opening the vent, so it bursts into flames. Despite the uncomfortable atmosphere, or maybe because of it, I can't help asking, 'Why would the diocese want to get rid of you? I thought churches were desperate to fill that role?'

Ooops, that's more of a backhanded compliment than I'd intended. Anna glares at me for a moment, then glances back to the fire.

Finally, she mutters, 'It all kicked off not long after Reverend Cross arrived and, up to his death, he'd been here about 15 years.'

'According to the chart in the vestry, he arrived in 2013.'

'Really? It feels much longer than ten years.' She sighs and shakes her head and I hear the anger and frustration behind her words, which I add to my mental notes.

'Does anyone else have access?'

'That's a good question, Cat. Well, more recently, Pixie, our administrator has. Of course, she'd have needed access for her job, but Cross always insisted on being there when she accessed any keys or opened the safe. She often said, "How am I supposed to do my job properly when he doesn't trust me with anything, without him being there, breathing down my neck? And then he's never around when I need him!" I felt quite sorry for her. I even tried to raise it with him, but he was having none of it.'

'And other than her?'

'Well, the reverend was fanatical about who knew where the keys were kept. He had serious trust issues, that one, particularly for a cleric. Anyone would think he had the crown jewels in there. It caused no end of ill will, especially with Pixie.'

Something clicks in my memory, the way Pixie stood on the outside of the group when Glen, Dale and I were in the vestry, and the way she fingered her necklace. I replay the scene in my mind, making myself study the contents of the vestry: desk, chairs, safe, old crumbling boxes. Nothing resonates, so I move on to visualising the walls, panning slowly around from the ornately-framed list of vicars going back nearly a thousand years, to the beautifully illustrated list of names of those who'd been Christened, to the much less ornate list of church wardens, the numerous photos of the wretched pyx which has caused so much anguish, and finally to one particular photo that sets my gut rumbling like an approaching storm – a dilapidated shack with three people, presumably a family, posed in front of it. The man is stooped, grimy, and gnarled, sporting enough grey beard to almost obscure his face. Beside him stands a frazzled woman in a tatty shapeless work dress. On closer inspection, she's quite a bit younger than the man but it's as if she's been infected with his old age. And between them, in contrast, is a carefree young child grinning at the camera, a locket around her neck and holding it out so that the light glints off it, almost as if it was alight, while the other hand twirls what appears to be one of St Iggy's church warden staves.

'Anna, that photo of the young girl in the vestry, isn't that Pixie?'

'It is. You did well to spot the likeness.' She sighs. 'We don't see much of that fun in her these days. Her mother was a warden here for years. My predecessor, in fact.'

'Ah, that explains the child's cheerleader stick – a warden's stave.

'The grumpy old codger's her father, Roby Mill. He was our verger at the time. And our grave digger. And down at St Cyril's too.'

'So would Roby have had access to the safe?'

'Yes, before Reverend Cross arrived. He'd have needed to get the burial registers out. And the service register. That photo must've been taken about thirty or thity-five years ago. Let's see, Pixie would have been about five and she's nearly forty, so, yes, I reckon somewhere round about 1988.' She stares into the fire for several seconds.

'Sad story, really. We had to pension him off, even though he was, what, only in his sixties. But the drink had aged him, made him unreliable. He used to wander off and leave the doors and the safe open, then forget to come back and lock up. Eventually, he'd forget to turn up for a service. Looking back, it'd been coming on for some time but I suppose you don't really notice when it creeps up slowly. Or maybe you just don't want to see it. He could be such a lovely man. But when Reverend Cross arrived, well poor old Roby was soon out on his ear. I remember the reverend moaning that the old bounder was just as likely to fall into the grave as fill it in. There was some row about paying Roby off, but I can't recall what it was. I do remember though, that it wasn't long before Much Slaughter dispensed with his grave-digging services as well. Poor Roby, he never really recovered from that and, sad to say, he became very bitter, always keen to share stories of his unjust treatment to anyone who'd buy him a drink. And quite a few who wouldn't.'

'You say Roby wandered off and left the safe open. Could the pyx have been stolen then and replaced with the replica later?'

'Good thought. I'll have to check. I'm pretty sure it was after we let him go, though, so probably not. It was a difficult time for us all. The church was Roby's life, you see, when he wasn't drunk. But the final straw was when he started getting his wife to cover his duties. On top of all the forgetting.'

She breaks off to stare into the fire and I have the distinct impression she's wondering how to express something quite difficult.

'The thing about a village is, you try to take care of your own, especially when they've got problems. But it turns out, we couldn't do much for Roby, he was well past it by that stage. So we did what we could for Pixie. That's why we were so happy when she settled down and married Milton Combe.'

'I didn't realise she was married.' It crosses my mind that we might just have found another suspect and I make a mental note to do some discrete asking around. *Discrete, Cat, when did you ever do anything discrete*?

'Oh, Milton's a lovely man. He started off as a miner, somewhere down in the southwest, then moved here a few years ago to manage the police offices over in Gloucester.'

Okay, not a likely suspect, then.

'They married back in, let's see, 2017, I reckon, few years after Pixie settled into her job. Surprised you've not come across him via your police inspector, Cat.' She glances across and a smile plays around the corners of her mouth as I blush. Is she trying to put me off, I wonder.

With the merest heartbeat of a pause, the major picks up where she'd left off. 'Mind you, he does seem to work long hours. Which is tough on Pixie.'

'Did you hint that Pixie has, shall we say, a chequered past?'

'Oh no.' Anna's voice is sharp, with a hint of anger. 'At least, no more than you'd expect with such a hard family life and a constant struggle to make ends meet. There were a couple of thefts, but only ever food. And once some clothes for her mother. But, as I say, we're a village, we dealt with it ourselves and from time to time they'd find a box of groceries or a bag of hand-me-down clothes on their doorstep when they got up in the morning. Roby used to gripe about it to anyone who'd listen, but we all knew it made a world of difference to Pixie and her mum.'

'It might be useful to talk to Pixie's parents in that case. See what light they can shed on all this. Are they still around?'

'Well, yes and no.'

I frown. *Oh for goodness' sake!* I really don't need any more complications in this case.

Anna must have caught my look of irritation because she quickly clarifies, 'Yes, they're both around. But no, you can't speak to them.'

'And why not?'

'They're both buried in Much Slaughter. She died two or three years ago; he died last year from liver failure. Mind you, for all the shenanigans, trust Roby to have had the last laugh. It turns out he used a false name to book a family plot in St Cyril's. He knew they wouldn't want him here, even though he'd dug plots for half the village. Not a forgiving place, this. "There's no rest for the wicked," he'd complain, "even though you've devoted the best years of your life to giving *their* loved ones their final place of rest."'

'Oh dear, another dead end. Oops, sorry, that wasn't exactly appropriate.'

But the major is grinning. 'A very good summary, though. Now – drink up and let me refill your glass.'

I rapidly place my hand over the rim. 'Sorry, I'm driving. And I should probably be going. It's getting on.'

'Oh well, if you're sure? I mean you're welcome to have another glass.'

'Lovely idea, thanks. But sadly, I'm driving and I've got a few dozen cakes to bake, ready for Skye's cafe.'

A few minutes later, as I near my cottage, the lane is blocked by two huge pantechnicon lorries *Oh no, not again?* Surely if the film crew were back they'd have let me know? I really can't cope with more disruption right now. But as I pull into my parking space, it clearly isn't a film crew.

Chapter 16

Two huge removal vans are being unloaded by a bevy of muscular individuals and their contents transported into the cottage three up from mine. They remind me of ants on the rampage, especially when they're carrying huge pieces of furniture on their backs. The removers, that is, not the ants.

Three Chimneys Cottage has been empty as long as I've been in Much Slaughter and, according to Wickham, much longer than that. Apparently it was a second home owned by a London family who were something to do with the media – nobody seemed to agree on what – but equally, no-one had seen them use the cottage. Speculation was rife and opinion split over whether the house was a means of money laundering, a secret hideaway for spies or a drug factory. Some villagers, those with a more lurid imagination (and no, I don't include myself here), speculated that it housed ladies of the night although, since no-one had ever seen even a light, never mind ladies, that seemed a little fanciful. Even our lovely solicitor, Carlton Curlieu, had been vague, revealing nothing more than they 'Used their own solicitor,' uttering the words with such contempt and a curled lip that we dared asked no more.

Speaking of Carlton, I could have sworn that the figure silhouetted against the window just now was the legal legend. It's hard to mistake his flowing locks, cultivated moustache and sideburns. So I'm not too surprised when he scampers down the path to remonstrate with two hapless workers who are teetering precariously with a heavy wooden table.

Glancing up, he spots me approaching and waves me over. 'Catherine, I'm glad I've caught you. Say hello to your new neighbour.' I look over his shoulder but I can't see anyone. Carlton roars with laughter. 'It's me, dear girl. I'm your new neighbour.'

'But what about your lovely bungalow behind Linton?'

'Not enough ground. You see...' He looks around furtively, twiddles his sideburns and lowers his voice to a whisper. 'I've bought myself an old gypsy traveller caravan. I need space to park it and space while I'm doing the renovations. This place is perfect. And it keeps me in the village with my friends...' He grabs my hand like an excited schoolboy, with a (very expensive) new toy. 'The workshops out the back are spot on. Pit and hoist and everything. I even managed to buy all their equipment.'

I've no idea what he's talking about but it's impossible not to be infected by his enthusiasm. And in any case, he's such a lovely man, it'd be hard to begrudge him his pleasure. 'Carlton, that's wonderful news. But I didn't even know that Three Chimneys was up for sale.'

'It isn't, or wasn't. I just made them the proverbial offer they couldn't refuse. And they didn't. So, here I am, your new neighbour. And hopefully these guys will be finished in the next hour, so we can all get some peace and sleep tonight.' He swivels to check and stares intently at one of the men, who I assume must be the boss. He's paused momentarily to mop his brow with a large rag that I really hope hasn't come into contact with any of Carlton's belongings.

The man nods at him and returns to work, tossing the rag into the back of the van.

'Drinks tomorrow lunchtime, after the service?' Carlton mimes imbibing some wine, as if I, of all people, wouldn't understand what he meant.

'Wild horses wouldn't keep me away, Carlton. What can I bring?'

'Just your lovely self. And the lovely doctor, of course.'

'I think that's within my abilities. But, you're cutting it a bit fine aren't you, for a party tomorrow? I'm amazed you could even get these guys to move you on a Saturday. When I suggested it to my removers, they pretty much laughed in my face.'

'You clearly weren't doing legal work for their boss then.' He grins. 'Now, if you'll excuse me, I might have been able to pull strings to get them here but that doesn't guarantee my stuff will stay in one piece.'

I catch his arm as he sets off in pursuit of some hapless workman. 'Pop in later, if you'd like a break. I'm inviting Linton over. You'd be most welcome.'

'What, and interrupt Much Slaughter's most romantic couple? I don't think so. I'm a party-giver not a party-pooper. Besides, I've got about a hundred boxes to unpack and, tonight, an hour less to do it in. I really don't understand where all this stuff's come from. I even asked them if they were doubling up on someone else's move. Didn't have anywhere near so much stuff when I moved in.'

'I didn't realise you were a newcomer too, Carlton.'

'Oh, yes, thirty years ago. Still, so much clutter. I'll need a mega garage sale as soon as I've unpacked.'

I smile at his now receding barrel-shape. From what I know of our solicitor, the chances of Carlton Curlieu holding a garage sale are about as likely as Princess Anne holding one down the road at Gatcombe Park.

A frantic barking from my cottage reminds me that my lovely Dagenham is due his evening constitutional. Only now, as I'm walking up my path, does something Carlton said register. What on earth did he mean by having an hour less to unpack? Oh good grief, don't tell me the clocks go forward tonight?

I pull out my phone and it takes only moments to confirm that today is indeed the last Saturday in March, highlighting the impending arrival of British Summer Time. Now all that's left is to work out is whether the clocks go forward or back. Even that takes only moments on my phone, before up flashes the old adage, *spring forward, fall back*. Ah well, at least that's settled. I find these twice yearly time changes really irritating. Every time, I'm determined to alter every timepiece. And every time, twice a year, I forget one. You'd think Wi-Fi and the like would improve matters but my car is far too old, my watch hasn't heard of digital and my cooker takes almost the whole six months for me to remember how to reset it, then how to get it accurate to within twelve hours. My ex would make regular sarcastic comments about me cooking his supper at seven am.

By the time I've finished lamenting my time woes to myself, I've collected Daggers, clipped his lead on and we're two-thirds of the way round the Green, ready to head off up Cowley Road for a circuit of the Recreation Ground. My mind has been so preoccupied with my new near-neighbour and my horological frustrations that I forgot to grab a sweater and with the moon now high and clear with an ominously fuzzy edge that threatens a stiff frost, I'm starting to feel uncomfortably cold.

It seems that I might not be the only chilly one because when I don't veer left towards The Rec and instead turn right, Daggers doesn't hesitate. He doesn't even look back to check with me before bounding up the path to Bedside Manor and yelping loudly. This has the benefit of ensuring that by the time I arrive Linton has opened the door and is ready to welcome us both. He jumps as I place my hand on his cheek causing my puckered lips to miss him entirely and plant the kiss onto fresh air. But it's worth it because his skin is so soft and warm to my icy fingers.

Then he grabs my shoulders and propels me directly and speedily into his wonderful furnace of a sitting room with a magnificent roaring fire.

As I lean towards the fire in a frantic effort to restore warmth to my hands, he reaches over and kisses my hair. 'An unexpectedly early surprise, Cat. To what do I owe the pleasure?'

Even I know better than to say because his warm house is a darn sight nearer than mine. 'Couldn't bear to be separated from you any longer, my love.' I tear myself away from the warmth of the fire to enjoy the warmth of his hug and the heat of his lips as we kiss.

When we both surface for air, I look up into his eyes. 'Have you heard the news, Doc?'

'And which bit of news in particular might that be, O light of my life?' He grins mischievously.

'I've got a new neighbour. You'll never guess who.'

'Would it by any chance be Carlton Curlieu?'

I shouldn't be surprised, though how Linton manages to be the lifeblood of village gossip without ever starting or passing on any, I'll never understand.

He brushes a strand of hair back from my face, tucks it behind my ear and kisses the tip of my nose. And just like that, winter's a much warmer place, almost tropical. 'My love, we've known that for weeks. Although,' he pauses for a moment, 'I guess it was while you were serving your sentence of hard labour on the High Seas.'

I wince at the memory, but one long, luxurious kiss later, my mind has cleared amazingly. Well, actually, it's been wiped as clean as a computer with a major hard drive failure.

Sometime during the kissing, I've ended up on the sofa, with Linton curled up next to me and Daggers with his head on my feet, a million miles away from thoughts of murder suspects and chocolate éclairs. Decidedly homey and romantic.

Unfortunately, the same can't be said for Linton. As he runs his fingers through my knotted curls, he whispers, 'How are you getting on with your business plan?'

How he thinks I can even remember what a business plan is, with him massaging my scalp and his breath caressing my ears I really don't know.

The love of my life unwinds himself from me and the sofa and gently slides into an armchair, where, unfortunately, he can see me better.

I sigh and swing my legs to the floor. 'Now that's a very good question, Doctor!'

He grins. 'In other words, you've done nothing.'

'I wouldn't say that, exactly.'

Then what would you say – exactly?'

'Well, I've got a mental plan.' He looks dubious. 'And I've finally managed to get Wickham's moulds working properly. Now I just need to boost my supplies to Skye, and everything's in place.'

'That's it? That's the sole scale of your ambition? You surprise me, Ms de Barnes.'

Goodness, I swear there's a note of disappointment in there. Which, as it turns out, is an excellent way to get my attention. Linton goes on.

'If that's the limit of your ambition, Cat, then all you'll ever do is break even. At best. And I was convinced you were heading for world domination as the Queen of Cocoa.' He shakes his head.

'I guess I could put some cards on Skye's counter and get something in the parish magazine.'

'And?' Linton looks deeply unimpressed.

'I don't know. Sell my chocs on the street corner?' My tetchiness leaves him totally unmoved.

'You need more outlets, my love. And not just our village summer and Christmas fairs. You might think about taking them to events around the Cotswolds. I reckon they'd go down a storm at the Badminton Horse Trials or even the Cheltenham Literary Festival.'

Hmm, he has a point. 'Buut...' *Oh good grief, I sound like a spoilt school kid.* 'I need to manage expectations. My kitchen isn't on the scale of Harrods, you know.'

'True. You'd need to build up some stocks. But with good planning and a good fridge, you might store quite a lot. Plus, once you sell out, you pack up. It's called scarcity value! You'd soon be able to double your prices.'

I like the sound of that. 'Maybe I could talk to the bank about a start-up loan, get some bigger equipment and even a dedicated cold store.'

'That's my girl.'

'I'm not your... Sorry. You're doing well.'

'No, *I'm* sorry. I was being flippant but it wasn't appropriate.'

I give him a big hug. 'It's fine. Just remember I'm my own woman.'

'I wouldn't dare forget.'

He gets up, catches my hand and pulls me to my feet, then enfolds me in another blissful hug.

'Social media?' he mutters into my hair.

'You want to put our hugs on social media? I'm not sure what the General Medical Council would think about that.'

Linton laughs, his warm breath fluttering my curls as well as my stomach. 'No, silly. I meant, build your chocolate presence on social media. That way, you get more time and control over orders. Maybe we could even film you at work in your kitchen: the artist creates. I can see it now – the Delia Smith of Chocolate.'

I can see it now too, the biggest disaster movie of all time as the goo refuses to set, the macaroons refuse to rise and I'm right there in the midst of all the chaos, with more chocolate on my face and hands than in my moulds.

Unfortunately, Linton is determined. His hands shape a camera and he mimes filming me from all sorts of angles, stopping only when he trips over a coffee table and rattles his shins to the accompaniment of a tirade of expletives that most definitely wouldn't be allowed online, even from Gordon Ramsay.

I help him back to the sofa and perch on his lap, then kiss his forehead. 'You know, for a doctor, you can have some surprisingly good ideas.'

He pouts. 'And for an entrepreneur, you can have some surprisingly unimaginative ones. So, how about I jot some ideas down, and we meet again tomorrow after Carlton's drinks reception to discuss them?'

'Am I being dismissed, then?'

He stares at me for several seconds, then grins. 'Certainly not. While we're here, I have some very definite plans for you, young lady.'

Chapter 17

Three Chimneys turns out to be every inch the picture postcard its name and outside suggests it should be. The front door opens straight into a large sitting room, low-ceilinged with a huge open log fire blazing in an inglenook fireplace, its red bricks glittering in the light from the flames. The room is generously oak-beamed, each beam a rich pattern of deep grooves, uneven surfaces and jagged edges, with a fair number of deep holes and chiselled insets, suggesting they were in use before they were brought to the cottage, which itself is probably seventeenth century. The equally uneven walls are painted a bright white, and on the floor is a white woollen carpet that's greying along the sides and partly protected by an amazing embroidered Indian rug whose reds and blues and golds glitter in the firelight. Of Carlton's supposed hundred packing boxes there's not a sign. However, there is a long four-seater sofa with three matching armchairs, upholstered in a Harris Tweed herringbone, the colour of Peatland. (I know this because not long ago I considered having my pieces re-upholstered, and this had been my favoured option until materials costs alone took it well beyond my budget.)

Like many cottages of this vintage, the steep narrow wooden staircase rises from the main room, behind a lovely pine door with huge, black-painted hinges and a latch. A similar door, slightly ajar, allows me a glimpse of the dining room and a huge wooden table covered with a stiff white linen tablecloth, roughly the size of a transatlantic ship's sail. Four carved wooden legs with carved feet peep out from under the cloth like demure ladies' legs. The table is laden with snacks, glasses, cutlery and crockery, candles and goodness knows what else.

In these first moments, the other thing that catches my eye is a huge black and white cat lying in front of another door. It's only when Carlton slides it to one side with his foot so he can open the door, to reveal a to-die-for garden room, that I realise it's not real but a mightily impressive draught excluder. It's a good job Daggers wasn't invited, it would have freaked him out for days.

The front door is pushed open and in marches Linton (be still my beating heart), Wickham, Cherry and Skye, followed moments later by

Boothby and Martin Dales. That's the thing about our villagers, they're like London buses: you wait for ages to see one and then six come along in a convoy.

They usher in a draught of cold air and the fire sizzles just as Carlton emerges from the kitchen sporting a blue and white butcher's apron and a gigantic white chef's hat. And, much more importantly, carrying a gleaming silver tray of tall, slender flutes brimming with champagne.

Linton crosses to me and we kiss briefly, mindful that we're in public and the doctor has strict protocols on suitable behaviour. The rest of the newcomers hurry to warm themselves as the previous cohort of arrivals moves away from the fire (that's another strict protocol). Handholding is allowed and we interlace fingers and squeeze, while I wince only inwardly at the chill.

Linton nods around the room. 'Nice place.'

'And a good turnout.'

We laugh as he whispers, 'Anymore clichés we can rustle up?'

'You new here?'

'Get your coat, you've...'

'Linton, behave yourself!'

Our giggles cause the fire-facing party to swing round and shake their heads despairingly as Skye mutters, 'What are they like?' loud enough for me to hear her. She grins at me, warmly. I really do have the best friends.

Speaking of best friends, my very best bestie squeezes my hand just as the champers arrives and we have to briefly break apart. Once we have a glass in hand and our host has moved across the room, I stand on tiptoe to whisper to my lover, 'I thought these churchy-types gave up alcohol for Lent? Is it starting to wear off by the fifth Sunday?'

'Carlton's not as churchy as he might like you to think. Besides, traditionally, Sundays and Saints days are exempt from the abstinences, days off.'

'Now that's definitely worth knowing.'

'Because you've given up so much this Lent, Cat?'

'Well, no, to be honest. I mean this year it just kind of crept up on me and to be fair it started before I got back here. And with the murder, it was another a week before it even dawned on me to think about what I might give up. So, let's just say, this year instead of giving something up, I've decided to add something.'

'Which is? Other than to eat more chocolate?'

'How rude, but true. But let's just say I've been doing more thinking and praying.'

For one lovely moment, Linton looks impressed. Then he grins and shakes his head. 'You mean about these crimes, don't you?'

'No comment, officer!' I reward his cheekiness with a playful punch to his arm, and as he reacts as if I'd nearly severed it at the shoulder, Wickham and Skye glance across, decide they must be missing out on the fun and wander across to join us.

'It seems I've got competition in the favourite neighbour stakes now, Cat.'

I put an affectionate arm around him. 'Wickham, you still have the Number 1 Neighbour crown. Even Carlton can't dislodge that.'

'Hmm, crown, eh. Might need a selfie of that, young lady.' He chortles as Skye whips out her phone.

'Allow me, King Skeith.' We both put on the typical Instagram face and she clicks a couple of angles, presses a button and announces, 'Done.' These Gen Z youngsters!

'While I've got you here, King of the Neighbours, can I ask you something'?

He mimes adjusting his crown, then taking it off and handing it to Skye, who does an impressive mock curtsy before mime-tossing it over her shoulder. Wickham tries to look horrified but can't because he's laughing too much and spluttering, 'The peasants truly are revolting today.'

'Come on, you two, be serious for a moment,' I mutter through my own laughter.

However, I don't get chance to pose my question as Carlton rattles a spoon against his glass and we all fall respectfully silent.

'Fellow Slaughterers...' He pauses as we giggle at our new nomenclature. 'Welcome to my humble abode.' Did I ever say, Carlton is the master of irony? He's also an eclectic dresser. Today, beneath his apron, he's wearing a dogtooth tweed three-piece suit trimmed with tangerine velvet over a white ruffed shirt, popular with the costume directors on Poldark. His black horn-rimmed glasses hang from a gold chain around his neck and as he lifts his glass to the crowd I can see he's even got personalised cufflinks with a picture of Three Chimneys on them. He really is quite something. But the toastmaster hasn't finished with us yet. 'There are some people who think I was hasty over buying this place, who think I paid over the odds.'

Inevitably, there are cries of disagreement.

Predictably, Carlton ignores them. 'Yes, there were. I know who you are.' He slowly scans the room trying hard to look fierce but failing miserably, not least because he's also grinning. 'And to you I say...' he raises his glass, 'I couldn't care less.' This produces a cacophony of foot-stamping, table-thumping cheers. 'For me, it's far more important that I'm able to stay in this lovely village, with you lovely people...' more pounding, 'and that's worth far more to me than money.'

The ensuing roar echoes around the low-ceilinged room much as it must have done in the past with the gladiators in the Roman amphitheatre up the road in Cirencester.

'All that remains, old friends and new neighbours, is for you to eat me out of house and home.'

'We rise to the challenge.' Linton lifts his glass in a toast we all follow before he links his arm through mine and steers me and the other eager beavers into the neighbouring room, which, within seconds, echoes to the clatter of cutlery and plates.

Impressively, we're at the front of the queue. 'Where did you learn to do that, doctor?'

'A quarter of a century of coffee mornings, cocktail evenings and far too many buffets, Agatha.'

'Christie or Raisin, Doc?'

'Which would you prefer?'

'Now that's a tough one. How about Christie for the brains and Raisin for the style and fun?'

Scintillating as our banter may be, a higher priority takes over. Both our plates are now suitably laden with fresh cold salmon, gammon slices and more salads than you could shake a fork at, so for the next few minutes our mouths are needed for a higher calling than speech.

During our munchinations, we're joined by Wickham, Skye and Martin so we constitute a cluster by the window overlooking the back garden. Over to the left I can see the wooden harness spars of Carlton's traveller caravan, looking bereft without the horse between them. By craning my neck can see the flaking paint of the main body so I make a mental note to book in for the full tour. How romantic, spending your days ambling around the countryside behind a pair of beautiful horses.

Linton follows my gaze and, disconcertingly, my train of thought. 'Not quite so romantic in the rain and mud.'

Wickham and Martin laugh.

Skye wiggles her eyebrows and digs me in the ribs. 'Lots of fun keeping warm though, eh Cat?'

I blush. Can everyone read my thoughts?

We're about to join the queue for seconds when Linton's phone bleeps. He glances at the screen. 'I need to take this.'

Which is the last I see of him, although a few minutes later, a text arrives full of sorry emojis. A little of the light fades from the room, although I know I need to get used to this now that I'm the doctor's official girlfriend. Which sounds so good it's all worthwhile.

Skye nudges me and points to the desert trolley. 'Where are your chocolate dishes, Cat? Missed an opportunity there, didn't you?'

She's right. I need to get cards printed and post them around the village. Maybe I should have brought a chocolate tart or something. I know he said not to, but I'd noticed Skye and a couple of others had been disobedient. I really need to buck my ideas up if I'm going to make a success of my business. Not if, I will. And the same with this wretched case – ideas will be bucked up.

'I'll help you design some flyers, Cat.' Once again she's reading my mind. Has my forehead suddenly become a computer screen? 'Let's fix an evening for you to come round. Once I've replenished my wine stocks.' She giggles.

'My turn with the wine, Skye. And, to show my intent, I'll also provide something chocolatey. So we can audition them for your cafe.'

She smiles, then whispers, 'Need the loo,' then hurries out, leaving me to sidle back to Martin and Wickham who are now deep into some highly technical debate about the best way to preserve oak beams. I suggest Rentokil and they giggle. I need all the Brownie points I can get with Martin after I all but accused him of murder. But then he nods and peels off to join the throng in the sitting room, so perhaps I'm still very much in deficit.

Martin's departure presents me with an opportunity I'm not going to miss. I grab Wickham's arm and steer him into a quiet corner.

'I've been thinking.'

Wickham, half-drained glass in hand, glances over his shoulder but he does it so furtively we might as well have asked Carlton to announce, along with his toast, that Catherine and Wickham are about to slope off to discuss the murder-theft.

I lean in slightly and lower my voice. 'The candelabra.'

He cups his ear. 'What?' It's easy to forget that Wickham's in his late sixties and, as he recently confided, his hearing in groups isn't always great.

I shake my head and determine to annunciate a little better. 'I'm talking about Mark's murder and the candlesticks. Something's been nagging at me, and I can't put my finger on it. Why would the reverend have got them out? We know it wasn't to have them valued. And we use the wooden ones during Lent, don't we?'

'Indeed we do, Cat. I imagine it was to do with the archdeacon. It's time for the annual visitation, he's doing a clutch of them in this area and he's got a reputation for being a hell of a stickler for detail. Plus he's new to archdeaconing, so I imagine he's feeling the need to make his mark, as it were.'

'Poor Mark would have been up for a double dose, then, wouldn't he? Here *and* in his beloved base at St Ignatius of the Vault. Do you think he was he was simply checking the inventory, then?'

'It's possible, I suppose. But the archdeacon is normally only expected to check that the records have been completed properly and look at the state of the building, not the value of the assets. Or indeed, whether we still have them.'

'Maybe Mark was taking no chances and was determined to get his ducks in a row. Or rather, his candlesticks?'

Our church warden considers for a moment then shakes his head. 'I didn't get the impression that the reverend had much time or respect for the authorities, even though an archdeacon spurned could have made life very difficult.'

Well, that's food for thought. 'There's something else bothering me. How did the murderer get in without Mark seeing or hearing them? The only explanation I can think of is that Mark knew them!'

'Perhaps if you know you're going to steal from a church, you wear soft-soled shoes rather than clunky boots? And you avoid slamming doors or whistling a merry tune? That'll be apart from Inspector Parva's view that the killer was already in the vestry and was caught in the act.'

All perfectly valid points, I begrudgingly admit. Which means I'm even more determined to prove Glen wrong. But how?

Chapter 18

At precisely five o'clock on a blustery Wednesday evening that epitomises late March perfectly, the vestry door of St Ignatius of the Vault swings silently open (which is quite a feat) and in walks a surprisingly small man in his thirties, with a mass of jet-black hair and intense blue eyes. He smiles benignly as his gaze sweeps the room but there's steel in those eyes and I have no doubt he's taking in every detail as his fingers massage a large cross that sits on his chest. The atmosphere tenses.

Anna Valley gets to her feet and announces in an unusually formal voice, 'Welcome, Archdeacon.'

He nods acknowledgement as the rest of us follow the warden's example. Anna continues.

'Unfortunately, our treasurer can only join us later, along with the PCC (Parochial Church Council). So for now, allow me to introduce Catherine de Barnes.'

'Ah yes, Ms de Barnes.' He throws out a hand for shaking and when I take it he lifts my fingers and formally kisses them, though it's hardly a kiss because he drops them almost the moment we make contact, as if they've burnt him. 'I thought you'd like to be here since I know you're being such a help to both parishes in investigating their unfortunate circumstances.'

So that explains it. All the major let on when she rang me with the invite was that it was a special request, which she didn't seem overly pleased about. And since archdeacon visitations don't normally feature on my social calendar, I even had to ask exactly what I'd be letting myself in for. Her voice didn't sound any the less irritated as she painstakingly explained that the visit fulfilled legal requirements under the Care of Churches and Ecclesiastical Jurisdiction Measure 1991, the Parochial Registers and Records Measure 1978 and the Inspection of Churches Measures 1955. Who knew? Plus, apparently eight different folders of policies ranging from insurance to employee contracts. 'As if we're some international corporation,' she'd muttered angrily.

After her diatribe ended and she'd put the phone down, I'd been left with two thoughts: one: why me? and two: how can I break both my legs and be spared the ordeal? Sadly, no answers appeared.

The archdeacon rubs his hands together as if he's trying to get rid of some sticky residue and instinctively I check mine before I realise it's just one of his habits. 'Bear with me a few minutes, Ms de Barnes, and then we'll take a stroll around the church and grounds and you can fill me in on where you think our treasures might be and who murdered our dearly beloved brother.' He crosses himself and bows his head, but something in his manner suggests to me that Reverend Cross wasn't quite as dearly beloved as he'd suggested. If we're going to promenade together, I'll need to learn what lies behind that. Who knows what light it might shed on the theft and murder?

By this time, the archdeacon has seated himself at the desk and is making his way through the registers and folders as quickly as I make my way through chocolate macaroons. It hardly seems fair after all the effort Anna has put in and I'm on the point of feeling sorry for the warden when the archdeacon, without even looking up, announces rapidly and with only cursory reference to his iPad, 'Inventory and logbook fine. Minutes Book up to date, but there's no officiant's signature from a service of Holy Communion held on the first Sunday in Lent. That's February 26th, in lay person's terms.'

'It was Reverend Cross's habit to sign everything on a Friday morning when the records were put in front of him.'

The venerable cleric turns with a rapidity that would leave me dizzy, a look of horror on his face. 'But church rules say...'

'Unfortunately, and rather inconveniently for you, Archdeacon, he died the Thursday before the next signing.'

The archdeacon, unsurprisingly, rises to the occasion and in a gruff voice announces, 'Then, Madam Church Warden, it's within your power, and indeed it's your solemn duty, to sign it *per procurationem* and make a suitable note in the margin.'

Good grief! This pretentious pr... prelate is the first person I've ever heard use pp in full. Despite myself, I'm impressed.

The remaining documents are despatched with similar speed whereupon the investigator produces a gold-ringed fountain pen from his cassock and signs one of the documents in front of him. Even at a distance I can see it's a florid signature, all swirls and loops.

As he stretches arms and legs in an elaborate and obviously habitual routine, I take a few moments to practise my observation. My strongest impression is of a perpetual motion machine: every movement is fast and precise, practised, even. Yes, that's it exactly – practised. It's as if he's learnt how to do and be all this. I note that along with his prim black clerical stock. I've learnt from Scott that stock is the proper term for the clerical garb that isn't a shirt and only covers the chest, before being tied behind the back. But what about the large silver cross he keeps fingering, what's that about?

Right then, great detective, what do you surmise from what you observe?

Well, the archdeacon certainly seems to know his stuff well for one so young. He's also perceptive, he doesn't miss much. He's keen to make a good impression and be liked, look at how he kissed my hand. I've only ever seen royalty and bishops do that. So ambitious for high office perhaps? And yet there's also something else about him, is he trying too hard? Or desperate to overcome something, some past failure? Which would certainly explain his restless fingers. And his foot constantly bouncing when he sits, legs crossed.

At that moment, he looks up, catches me staring at him and raises a questioning eyebrow. As I say, he doesn't miss much.

He rises from the chair, all five foot four of him, and nods to Anna. 'That'll be all, Church Warden, you may stand down. Ms de Barnes and I will take our constitutional and then I'll meet with the PCC when I've finished with her.'

Which manages to make both Anna and me cross. But the archdeacon seems to be oblivious and sails out into the church, leaving the door open behind him, obviously expecting me to follow. Which, after an exchange of mutual sympathy with the major, I do.

The church feels pleasantly cool after the oppressiveness in the vestry and the archdeacon is already halfway down the aisle, occasionally darting into a wooden pew, to tidy the kneelers into symmetry.

When I finally catch up with him he swings into one of the pews, thus ending one of the shortest constitutionals I've ever taken, and indicates for me to set in the row in front, and waits for Anna to clomp noisily through the church and out into the fresh air.

'Now, tell me how you're getting on with finding the person who stole our pyx, Ms de Barnes.'

It's an order rather than a question and I bristle at his use of the possessive pronoun.

'Well, Archdeacon, perhaps I can explain simply...' he raises an eyebrow, 'erm, clearly, if I take it chronologically.'

He nods.

'I was at my neighbour Wickham Skeith's cottage, having just returned from being chief chocolatier on a series of cruise ships.' Okay, slightly overstating it but if the man wants to be officious, I'll show him I can do better. And judging by his expression, I've made a good start. 'I was having breakfast with our local doctor, Linton Heath...' I stop and blush. Drat, that doesn't do my officiousness any good at all.

'Ah, yes, Dr Heath is your young man, I understand.' Again, it's a statement, not a question.

I struggle to suppress a giggle, because I know Linton would be tickled pink to be referred to as 'young' anything, especially by a man who is himself only in his, what, thirties?

'He got an emergency call from our very distressed local antiques dealer Dale Hill. Linton, Dr Heath, I mean…, I feel myself blush again, 'thought it would be helpful to have Wickham there too, since he's one of our church wardens. And I tagged along. I went in a support role, to see if I could help.'

'Which had absolutely nothing to do with you investigating two previous murders, of course.'

Goodness, he's well informed.

As if reading my thoughts, he smiles. 'I believe in being thoroughly briefed before I go into any tricky situation, Ms de Barnes. I do not like being caught unawares. About anything.' Those deep blue eyes practise their laser precision again.

'Quite, Archdeacon. It only took a couple of minutes to reach the church and Dale was so distraught that Linton, Dr Heath, rushed straight past him and found Reverend Cross spreadeagled on the vestry floor with a candlestick beside him.'

'Ah yes, the candlestick. One of a pair, I believe. Yet strangely overlooked in favour of two pieces of ecclesiastical trivia.'

Heavens, does this man eat liturgical dictionaries for breakfast? 'Indeed. Which was strange because...'

'The safe was closed and locked. Why, if Cross was getting ready for a service? And why were those particular candlesticks even out? Cross would know it must be wooden ones during Lent.'

'Yes, that's one of the few things Chief Inspector Parva and I agree on.'

His face is the epitome of disbelief. 'You presume to disagree with a police officer with more than thirty years' experience? Interesting.'

Indeed it is, since the archdeacon's briefing is suddenly not as comprehensive as I'd thought. I know for a fact, because Glen told me in an unguarded moment of friendliness, that he's fifty-four and didn't join until he was thirty. Which leaves me wondering what other facts spoken by the archdeacon with so much ecclesiastical certainty aren't as they seem.

'The chief inspector and I don't disagree over the facts of this case,' I say, giving him a hard stare and hoping to make him realise he's been rumbled. Of course I fail miserably as he simply stares back. 'We may, however,' I go on, 'disagree over interpretation, on occasion.'

'You mean over whether the murder and the theft of our pyx are related?'

'Exactly. He thinks I'm widening the possible suspects too far by linking them. I think he's narrowing them too much by insisting they're not.'

'And his experience...?'

'Might blind him to different possibilities.'

'Interesting.' The archdeacon stretches both hands before lacing them again, then rubs the side of his nose. 'And why exactly are you convinced they're linked, Ms de Barnes?'

'Well, firstly, there's the obvious fact that two crimes being committed within a few days of each other would, if they're not linked, be a massive coincidence. And detectives don't usually believe in coincidences.'

'But it seems this one does.' *Okay, he wins that point.*

'And, as far as I'm aware, you only know when the theft was discovered, not when it took place, and not even when the copy was made? Or am I mistaken?'

Don't you just hate it when know-it-alls like this man know they're right but still ask, patronisingly, whether their brilliant mind could perhaps have been bettered by an inferior one? But he is right, so he wins that point too. Time to move on.

'Secondly,' I say, 'it seems highly unlikely that an opportunist would come in at exactly the right time to discover the open safe, would then be willing to murder the person who discovers him, especially a vicar, and *then* not grab the more valuable items, i.e. the candlesticks, especially when one of them is the murder weapon, but instead take two small things from the safe. *And*, with the unplanned dead body lying at his feet in a pool of blood, have the presence of mind to close and lock the safe. To say nothing of displaying the body.'

'What do you mean, displaying the body?'

'Oh, didn't your briefing say, Archdeacon?' *Two-one to me.* 'Mark had been splayed out in the shape of a cross. Glen, Inspector Parva insists it's the way he fell. But Linton believes that's highly unlikely. So who would stage him like that, and why?'

'Those are indeed good questions, Ms de Barnes.' He shifts in the pew to face me more directly and, I'm sure, with more respect. 'Go on.'

'Clearly Reverend Cross is the link between the two. Otherwise we have yet another coincidence. So, what if, with all due respect, your reverence, Reverend Cross was being blackmailed over some indiscretion or other?' Probably best not to let on that I know about the gambling habit, although the merest hint of a shadow then passes over the archdeacon's eyes, and I can tell he knows. *Two-all.* 'Is there any light you might be able to shed on that, Archdeacon?'

The cleric looks so startled I can only think no-one's ever been so upfront before and it certainly wasn't in his briefing. Of course, being the consummate professional, he recovers in moments. 'You know as well as I do, Ms de Barnes, that I can't possibly comment. It would be most inappropriate.'

'As is murder, don't you agree?'

The clerical mask is firmly back in place so all I get is a curt, 'Quite. Proceed.'

For a moment, it feels as if I'm addressing a High Court judge rather than a mid-rank Anglican clergyman. But nothing else is forthcoming so, with a sigh, I press on. 'What if the blackmailer came to collect and it went wrong?'

He nods, thoughtfully. 'This is all very well for why, but what about who? According to my obviously fallible sources...' I swear the hint of a smile crosses his face, 'it would seem that between you and the chief inspector all you've achieved is to know who *isn't* involved, while having no clue as to who is.'

Ouch, that's some sting in the scorpion-archdeacon tail.

'It's true that we've both ruled Dale Hill out. He had an appointment with Mark, which made him the most obvious suspect, but he claimed he arrived late and the body was already on the floor. Plus, Glen traced a customer who accounted for his movements before he arrived late at the vestry. Glen's still convinced it's a local petty crook and maybe that it's our local car mechanic, Ashley Culkerton. He was seen driving a sports car, speeding away from the Green, around the time of the murder, but his workplace cameras seem to show that the time he left and the time he got back wouldn't have allowed him to stop, go into the vestry, and do everything else in the time he had. Besides, I can't see it, myself. Any more than I can see it being the film runner.'

The archdeacon raises a well-manicured eyebrow.

'When Dale finally recovered enough to make any sense, he admitted he might have seen a shadowy figure running of through the trees as he arrived. It turns out it was one of the crew who were in the village then, filming some programme.'

'I think you'll find it's that rather popular sheepdog competition, *One Dog and his Sheep*.' Not that I watch it, of course, but I find as Archdeacon of Cirencester it pays to know something about those traditional local occupations. I'm just helping you keep the facts straight.'

Of course he is. No thought of a put-down ever entered the holy head. 'Quite. Well, the runner said she was checking out the church as a venue for her upcoming nuptials but got called back on set before she had a chance to get inside. Again, witnesses and phone records seem to bear that out. Although I'm not entirely convinced. Something didn't seem quite right and I'm still following it up.'

'And that's it? That's the sum total of suspects.'

'At the moment, yes.' I've no intention of sharing my suspicions about the major, it would give the archdeacon too much ammunition to use against her. And more importantly, put her on her guard about whatever it is she's hiding.

The archdeacon trains the full power of his blue eyes on me and, when I don't react, he taps his fingers loudly on the pew top, unfurls himself and stretches a few times. He's halfway up the aisle before he turns and calls back to me, 'Do carry on with your investigation, Ms de Barnes. And be sure to let me know what you discover. As I've every faith you will.'

Seconds after the arrogant man departs, Anna scurries in. She must have been waiting to see him go. I'm sure she'd have been desperate to eavesdrop, but the middle pew of a church is far too isolated, unless you've managed to secrete yourself down at the bottom of another pew. Nevertheless, I'll need to be careful I don't let anything slip.

'Well, what did you make of that, Catherine?' She stands a couple of pews back from where I'm perched, her hands on her hips.

I'm still trying to make sense of the encounter when she spits out, 'He's quite something, isn't he?'

'He's certainly a force of nature. I imagine he's having quite an impact on the churches around here?'

'That's the understatement of the year. Which, interestingly, is about the time he's been in post. He's just thirty-eight, you know, one of the youngest archdeacons of modern times. He's definitely seen as a rising star, which hasn't gone down well with his fellow clergy, from what I can gather. Everyone reckons he's a future bishop, if not archbishop, including the good man himself. You know they say you should dress and behave as if you're in your next job? Well, that man's taken it to the nth degree. Mind you, he's had the best preparation: Repton School, then Cambridge – a Blue in fencing, apparently – then on to Cuddesdon Theological College. After which he had a tailor-made curacy and then plum incumbencies somewhere in the Home Counties and Wimbledon Village before arriving out here in the sticks. He'll be a bishop before he's forty, they say.'

'Seems to know his stuff, though, Anna.'

'Oh yes, no doubt about that. He's already promised me he'll email his Visitation Report by ten tomorrow morning. I can't wait.'

A sudden thought strikes me. 'Anna, do archdeacons lose their names like nuns when they're, well whatever you do to turn them into archdeacons?'

Anna's laugh reverberates around the church like a peel of bells. 'Lordy, no, you dear thing. He's officially the venerable Bamber Bridge. Apparently, the title "venerable" means "heroic in virtue". Although I believe his fellow clergy refer to him by an altogether different title. But I couldn't possibly comment. I can't imagine ever calling him Bamber, though, can you? I remember someone once calling him Reverend Bridge, and they were told in no uncertain terms that "reverend refers to junior clergy, I am an *archdeacon*".'

Goodness, she's got his voice pitch-perfect.

'And I swear he said it in capital letters. He's let it be known that he wants to be called *Archdeacon*, just as you'd say, Bishop, rather than his name.'

She links her arm through mine and leads us out of the building, just as a couple of thoughts strike me. The first is, I hope the Venerable Archdeacon didn't find a way to overhear our conversation. And the other is, I can't wait for Scott to get back from his retreat so I can find out what the archdeacon's really called.

Chapter 19

The last day of March, Friday, swings into action with two phone calls in as many minutes, each from men eminent in their respective fields. Such popularity could go to a girl's head. Well, not mine, obviously. But perhaps my éclairs are baked with my head held a little higher that morning and decorated with a little more melted chocolate than is strictly necessary, or commercially justified. I hope Skye will be impressed with her stock.

So, when the third person, my beautiful doctor, waves at me from the surgery window as I'm out on my delivery round, my spirit is so elated I'm sure I must be hovering at least a foot off the ground. I mime 'lunch?' and he signals a thumbs-up and moments later, with a huge grin on my face, I deliver my *chocolates magnifique* to the coffee shop.

Skye has obviously spotted my approach through her shop window, and she smirks at me. 'Good night with the good doctor, I take it, Cat?'

'For your information, he didn't come round. Also, for your information, I'm not the kind of girl whose only excitement comes from the love of her life.'

Skye's mouth drops open in horror before I realise what I've implied. I rush on quickly. 'I don't mean that there are other men in my life apart from Linton. Although, having said that, I am seeing two men later.' I wiggle my eyebrows as suggestively as I can (which is pretty high on the scale), turn on my heels and bolt, while also texting a brief change of venue to Linton. I'd bet my life – or in this case, my reputation – on trusting Skye's discretion for the moment. But in a village, walls really do seem to have ears, and within five minutes Mrs A has heard it from Ms B who heard it directly from Mr C who just happened to be asleep under the table or fixing the plumbing or working next door and coincidentally leaning against the wall with a wine glass to his ear. You get the picture.

Changing our lunch venue proves easier than providing the menu. But thanks to a quick delve into the freezer for bread, the speedy mashing of avocados only a couple of days past their 'Best By...' date and the fortuitous discovery of a hidden pack of feta cheese, Dr Linton's ad hoc lunch is on the table the moment he's cleared his morning list and lets himself into my cottage. Yes, he's now earned his own key: a step of faith for me and a very useful standby next time I forget my own.

As with any good meal, the first mouthfuls are enjoyed in appreciative silence, broken only by the clatter of knives on plates and platter. And Dagenham's Richter-scale snores from the hearth.

I polish off my second attack on the cheese platter, delicately touch the corners of my mouth with my elegant napkin – alright, piece of kitchen roll – and smile contentedly across the table. 'So, my love, how was your morning? Oh, yuk, how married-couple was that!'

Linton grins, before popping his mouth and reaching for his third helping – not that I'm counting helpings or calories. 'Ten patients. Nothing serious. Patient confidentiality.'

'Ah the excitement of dating a doctor.'

His mouth is open to reply, until he spots my grin and nods. 'However, doctor's date, the weekend weather forecast is good so a picnic might be on the cards. Maybe even a spot of camping.'

My own mouth is open until it dawns on me he's teasing as well. 'That would be lovely. Although, given the British weather it's just as likely to be on my front room carpet. And maybe a...'

Linton's diary alert buzzes so he plants a short but very lovely kiss on my upturned lips, mutters, 'hold that thought,' and after the briefest but still knee-buckling cuddle we're both off to our separate responsibilities.

Dagenham is very happy to have his lunchtime constitutional around the village, which strictly speaking should take no more than twenty-five minutes. But we're in a village and it's sunny so the world and his wife are out like bees around a honey pot. They're also desperate for updates on anything and everything from the prices in our local store to the perilous state of so-and-so's marriage, to the shocking state of the government. Suffice to say, it's close to three o'clock by the time we get back home. So, within moments, I'm hastily peeling off my casual clothes, ready to shower, preen and emerge, butterfly-like for my intriguing late afternoon appointments with the two eminencies.

Which explains why, as I walk to my car, I'm not only still feeling elated but I'm also sporting the biggest ear-to-ear grin in living memory, and all seems right with the world. It's the last day of March. The days are getting longer, the sun, in an almost cloudless blue sky, is getting warmer, and every day, new shoots are popping up in soil freed from winter chill. Dagenham's tail seemed to wag more enthusiastically as I took him to 'stretch his legs'. Even my car engine seems to fire up more quickly and confidently as I set off for Cirencester with a CD of Bizet's *Carmen* blasting out full volume, and the windows fully down (although only after I've left the village: a girl has to take care over some things). Daggers curls up on the back seat, his paws over both ears. No taste, that dog.

Late Friday afternoon is never a great time to find parking in our local town and I'm lucky to squeeze into almost the last space, courtesy of some slick and competitive manoeuvring befitting the Daytona racetrack.

Five minutes later, I'm seated in Dale's office. While he deals with a customer, I take the opportunity to scan the photos on his wall, which, on my previous visit to his inner sanctum I'd been too preoccupied to notice. Most of them feature Dale in garish check suits and flamboyant cravats sitting behind a huge auctioneer's podium with a raised gavel or alongside presenters and competitors from the BBC's *Bargain Hunt* television show. A bigger contrast with the incoherent wreck who discovered Mark Cross's body is hard to imagine.

Two sets of footsteps echo down the corridor (yes, two sets, I'm not an investigator for nothing) and Dale ushers in my second eminent man, Chief Inspector Parva, before hopping from foot to foot in the doorway.

The police officer smiles warmly in my direction as he removes his sunglasses and places them in a branded case. Daggers ambles across and Glen tickles him behind his ears as my pooch licks his other hand.

'I'm glad you're here, Catherine. When Mr Hill said he'd like you present, I must admit at first I informed him it was a police matter and I wasn't having any civilians present.'

The antiques expert coughs apologetically. 'Actually, Inspector, you said you weren't having an interfering...'

'Yes, thank you, Mr Hill. I'm well aware of what I said... Anyway, Catherine, I realised it could be quite an education for you. So here you are.'

Hmm, really? An education? Why's that, I wonder? But today he'll get the benefit of the doubt. *Goodness, I am in a good mood.*

Before I can come up with a suitable jovial reply, Dale reaches into the far corner of his office and grabs a muddy supermarket carrier bag from which, with a theatrical flourish worthy of the already mentioned TV programme, he produces something wrapped in black muslin. Only when he passes it to Glen and it rattles, do I realise it's the missing patten and chalice.

The inspector glares at Dale, who shrinks in front of me. 'Did you have to put your fingerprints all over the bag, Mr Hill? I suppose you've plastered them all over the contents as well?'

'I'm sorry Chief Inspector. When the boy brought the bag in I had to open it to see what was in it. That was the only way I could tell him what the contents were worth.'

Glen snorts loudly before turning to me. 'Some urchin brought the bag in first thing this morning. He wanted to know what Mr Hill would give him for the contents. Trouble was, the kid had no idea what the stuff was, other than some fancy bits of brass plate. So when Mr Hill did the right thing, and asked him how he'd come by the things, he became very defensive and swore–'

'On his mother's grave, Inspector.'

'Quite. He swore he'd found the bag a few days ago on the grass verge just outside Cirencester, near the Royal Agricultural University. He reckoned he was out for a walk and saw it glinting in the sunshine. I mean, *come on*, a fifteen-year-old boy out for a walk? Plus, today's the first time we've had sunshine in a week, so he couldn't possibly have seen it glinting in the sun.' Glen nods, contentedly. 'My bet is, we'll find his prints all over this lot, along with the reverend's and now yours, Mr Hill.'

He turns towards me and a huge smile beams across his face. 'A local petty thief in Much Slaughter, up to no good, chanced upon the open safe, grabbed the two items because he thought they'd be easy to conceal and to sell on, got disturbed, hit out and then made a run for it.

He probably thought that the heat would have died down by now. I've got him banged to rights. The Cirencester police are with his parents now and chasing up his record.'

I wasn't having it – it was far too pat. 'Glen, there might be a couple of things you've overlooked.'

'Oh for heaven's sake, you just won't give up, will you?'

'Not when justice is at stake, no.' *Ouch, I didn't mean to say it quite like that.*

The Inspector is reduced to stunned silence so I take my chance.

'Firstly, if he's a Cirencester lad, what was he doing in Much Slaughter? It hardly ranks alongside the local skate park as an attraction, does it? "Oh, I fancy a laugh today, I'll just pop over to that hotbed of teenage entertainment for a few hours." Come on, Inspector.'

Momentarily, Glen looks thoughtful. But only momentarily. 'Unless, Miss Clever Clogs, he fancied some extra pocket money and thought, "Those old biddies in Much Slaughter mean a lot of easy opportunities for a quick-thinking lad like me." No, you come on, Ms de Barnes.'

Oh dear, back on those terms, are we? He may have a point, but I'm not finished yet. 'Then how did he get there, Inspector? He's too young to have a motorbike licence, never mind a car. And

I can't see him cycling along a busy narrow road like that, can you?'

Glen tuts. Always a bad sign. 'You may have noticed those big blue and white things - they're called buses. And, low and behold, they run between Cirencester and Much Slaughter.'

'So what you're saying, Glen, is that he caught a bus over to our village? So he'll be on the bus CCTV, I presume?'

'We're checking even as we speak.'

'And he did that on the off chance that he might find something worth stealing? Then, when he did, and he just happened to kill someone in the process, he calmly hopped on another bus, having, presumably found some way of getting rid of any blood on his clothes, since that sort of thing does tend to get noticed, even in rural parts? Which, presumably would also be on the bus CCTV? I know...' I hold up my hand, 'you're already checking, along with his fingerprints. Which reminds me. Of course you'll find his prints on the chalice and the patten. He's bound to have touched them to see what he'd found.'

'I've no doubt of what we'll find. I hate to say it, but I was right all along.'

This is ridiculous. How can he expect such an implausible set of suppositions to hold water? I jump to my feet, startling both Dagenham and Dale. 'Well, there's clearly nothing more to be said then, is there?'

And with a shake of my head to show my pitying disapproval, I flounce out of the shop, almost garrotting poor Daggers in the door in my haste. He lets out a startled yelp and by the time I bury my head in his fur my face is wet with tears of guilt and frustration. Luckily, Dagenham is a bigger dog than to take it out on me and instead he licks my ear and snuggles up.

Through the fur, I can see both Dale and Glen behind the shop door, hovering with uncertainty. To my relief, next time I look up they've gone, no doubt to exchange views on the fragility of women and their refusal to give up in the face of evidence.

With my eyes still misty and damp, Daggers leads us back to the car.

How can a day which started on a high be descending into such disaster?

Taped to my windscreen and displayed in a prominent position so it can't be missed by either the driver or passers-by, and nestling in a sealed plastic wrapper so it can't get wet, is a parking ticket.

They say pride comes before a fall, but all this? Really? When I was simply full of the joys of spring? I tear the thing off the glass.

Before I've even half-opened the door, Daggers shoots inside like greased lightening, obviously keen to avoid a repeat guillotining. My poor boy.

As I toss the offending package onto the passenger seat and throw myself in behind the steering wheel, he pokes his furry head between the front two seats and somehow manages to lick my ear, which is almost as soothing as if Linton were doing it. Speaking of Dr Heath...

Fifteen minutes later as I approach my beloved village, I pull into a lay-by, amazed. The red-orange ball of the sun straddles the horizon, casting its last rays across a darkening blue-black sky and illuminating a handful of white wispy clouds with a ring of fire.

Throughout my adult life, wherever I've lived, I've had a special place like this one. Often not the most beautiful or even the quietest spot, and usually discovered quite by chance, they've proved themselves so special they'll never be forgotten. And for as long as I live in the area they've been visited frequently. They've shared lovers won and lost, jobs won and lost. They've heard me howl in frustration at pay rises refused and howl with joy at promotions won. They've seen me celebrate my first home of my own, and commiserate on the one I left behind. And the last place was party to many of my views on attractive young sirens who poach other women's husbands. They've been told of my plans for a chocolate business to rival Willy Wonka's, and of my discovery of my dream cottage in my dream village. But more than that, they weren't just places to rant or revel in, they were places where I felt safe, hopeful.

I once told Scott about these special places and he said religious people often call them 'thin spaces', places where God seems extra close and I understand what he meant. Today, it's an opportunity, not so much to review my day, but rather to make my own decision about what I take from that day. I recall the confrontation with Glen and his absurd commitment to the local villain theory. I recall my impetuous and stroppy exit from *Treasures of Corinium*, for which my unfortunate pooch paid the price. I recall the parking fine where *I'll* pay the price of hurrying to the shop without grabbing a ticket. *Fools rush in, Cat*.

As the last segment of the sun dips into the horizon, I gather those things up, uncouple myself from them and dump them in my mental garbage bin.

Then, as the sky washes into purple and gold rays, I pick up on the good things: the look on my wonderful friend Skye's face when I presented her with an extra-special consignment of individual handmade chocolates for her own personal enjoyment, a warm spring morning, a dog so devoted he always senses my need, my fledgling chocolate business and so many opportunities, and the most magnificent sunset over the most magnificent village in the Cotswolds and beyond. These things I couple myself onto, putting them next to my heart. Along with my wonderful doctor. Speaking of whom...

Moments later, the lay-by is exchanged for my lovely man, all freshly showered and smelling of pine when I reach his door.

As I run my fingers through his still damp hair and relax into our hug, he mutters quietly into my ear, 'You sounded so upset when you rang. I thought you needed something special. So...'

He breaks free of my clinch, grabs my hand and leads me towards the sofa in his sitting room. 'Make yourself comfortable, there's a glass of red breathing on the small table, and I'll finish off our meal. The cooking that is, not the eating. Obviously.'

This wonderful man knows just the right thing to say at just the right moment. He grins and beats a hasty retreat, a flurry of amazing flavours wafting over as he opens the kitchen door. I wonder if it's possible to add this place and this moment to my list of magical spots.

More delicious aromas waft across as Linton returns, a white tea towel draped across his arm in best waiter fashion as he deposits bowls of mixed nuts, green and black olives and three different varieties of potato chips next to what has to be the biggest glass of red wine I've ever seen.

By the time I've taken it all in, he's back in the kitchen amid all sorts of clattering and rattling while I do my duty by the nibbles.

With three of the bowls largely depleted and the wine glass level having noticeably dropped, I'm ushered into a candlelit dining room with a crisp, white cotton tablecloth, sparkling silver cutlery and equally sparkling crystal wine goblets. Perfection.

***

A while later, Linton stretches his hands across the remnants of three stunning courses and grasps mine, shooting a bolt of electricity through my whole being. 'How was that, my love?'

The candles are almost exhausted, so Linton's enquiring look is almost lost in the darkness. But even if I can't fully see it, I can feel it, as hot as the coals in the fire.

'Wonderful, sweetheart. There's just one thing missing to make the evening perfect.' And I take him by the hand, leading the way to another banquet.

Chapter 20

Maybe it isn't the most subtle way to welcome the Reverend Scott Willoughby back from his thirty day retreat, but at least it's unusual. Wickham, Rose (back for Easter from her travels), Martin Dales, Boothby, Carlton and May Hill, along with Linton and myself, hand-in-hand, line the vicarage driveway while Scott's Old English Sheepdog, Barking, sits patiently by the front door (my idea) next to a Wi-Fi speaker blasting out *Zadok the Priest* (Wickham's idea). But as Cherry drives him up the steep slope we wave our hand-embroidered flags, complete with the symbol of St Cyril the Obtuse, at the vicar-mobile and Scott every bit as enthusiastically as if he was the pope.

As they pass, Cherry waves as if she was the Queen of England, then climbs out wearing the biggest smile and looking absolutely delighted as she beckons us to join them. She's followed moments later by the reverend, who looks anything but delighted as he stretches his long legs, shakes his head, grabs his luggage and bolts inside, followed by the ignored, puzzled, but absolutely overjoyed Barking.

The door has been left open but we all exchange glances, shrug and remain rooted to the spot until Boothby voices what we've probably all been thinking. 'Reckon we should leave them to it, what?' He twirls his huge moustache and leads the way back, just as Cherry reappears, her face bright red and holding a tissue to her eyes.

'I'm so sorry, everyone. It was a lovely thought. It's just that after thirty days of silence, Scott found it overwhelming.'

'Cherry, I'm *so* sorry.'

How could I have been so stupid? It's obvious now that I think about it that after so long being silent in a coterie of silent, gliding, brown-cowled monks (hey, I've seen the films) the last thing you'd want is a crowd of yowling yokels jumping up and down and waving flags as if you'd just won the World Cup. I nod. 'Don't worry, we'll leave you in peace.'

This isn't the first time I'll be leaving the vicarage with my tail between my legs, I reflect, as I make to join the others.

'Erm, Cat. Scott did ask if you could spare a few moments to update him, please?'

Linton gives me an encouraging shove. It certainly won't take more than a few moments to do that, so I nod and follow her, feeling rather isolated as my friends file off down the drive. Linton blows me a kiss, and with a smile of encouragement sets off to discover what his urgent calls might entail.

I follow Cherry, stepping over two large suitcases sprawled across the hall, through the spotless kitchen she must have spent hours over, and into their garden.

Scott is sprawled in a rickety canvas garden chair, his legs stretched out, his arms hanging loosely over the wooden chair arms while Barking lies across his feet. He runs his hand through his matted black hair and for the first time I can see strands of grey. Even his face looks grey, with crow's feet wrinkles forming around his eyes. In his crumpled open-necked grubby shirt and shapeless chinos (surely even monasteries have a laundry?), he looks the wrong side of middle-aged and I want to give him a huge hug. Except, as I move towards him Barking growls a low, rumbling warning. If that's what a thirty-day silent retreat does for you, give me a thirty-day party any day.

Scott shows absolutely no sign of opening a conversation about recent events, or any other events, for that matter, so I'm reduced to scanning the garden, wondering if there's inspiration I can take for my own patch. The winter hasn't been kind to it. And Cherry told me that one of the conditions of her house-sitting role was that it didn't include responsibility for anything beyond the walls of the house. Consequently, vast seas of brown leaves lie piled up against unpruned rose bushes while dandelions seem to have beaten daffodils to be first out of the soil. The box hedge boundaries sprout tentacles at least a couple of feet in length and the grass is already almost up to Barking's tummy and is liberally interspersed with buttercups.

Cherry arrives with two glasses of rosé wine (a sure sign of spring) and a generous glass of whisky, which she hands to Scott. She and I retire to sit side by side on a nearby garden bench and wait, anxious and silent, as Scott sips his drink.

His glass is almost empty before he turns in our direction. 'Catherine, I'm so sorry. I know you meant well.'

That surely has to be one of the most cutting rebukes ever.

He sighs. 'It's really hard to explain, but after more than four weeks of peace and solitude – even allowing for my unfortunate summons back – all your senses get accustomed to it. They get reprogrammed. Even your mind declutters and gets used to processing just a few things at a time.'

He stares ahead as a magpie swoops in for a landing, realises it's not alone and with a raucous cackle diverts into a nearby tree, where its head flicks around to stare at each of us in turn –intruders into its domain.

'After all...' Scott picks up again so quietly that both Cherry and I lean forward to hear, 'when all your day consists of is early morning prayer lead by someone else (a rare luxury in this job, I can tell you) followed by breakfast, personal devotional reading, Holy Communion, lunch, an afternoon walk or jobs around the monastery, then supper, silent reflection, Compline and bed by nine-thirty, well I guess there are fewer brain circuits in use.' He isn't actually talking to us, he's just thinking out loud. 'Once you get used to it, it's wonderful, heavenly.' His voice trails off.

I nod, but to be honest it sounds more like the other place.

Scott stares into the distance, which seems to be somewhere beyond his box hedge garden boundary and into the fields where the early lambs have all but deserted their mothers and wander away in ever-increasing circles of independence. In as much as you can ever have independence within dry stone walls. I wonder then if this isn't a metaphor for life in a village, and whether there are the equivalent of dry stone walls hemming *us* in: age-old traditions, perhaps? Or maybe clinging onto impossible dreams of the perfect rural idyll? Are these walls somehow blinding me and preventing me from catching a murdering thief - or a thieving murderer? Ah yes, it's never far away, that one. Yet seemingly no closer either. Despite what Glen reckons.

Cherry stirs beside me on the bench. She nods her head towards the house, rises and tiptoes across the grass, beckoning me to follow.

Once inside, she gently closes the kitchen door behind us. 'Best leave him be for the moment. I've never seen him like this before.' She stifles a sob. I'd been thinking exactly the same and we drop into each other's arms.

Little more than half an hour and another glass of rosé later, we emerge into the sunshine arm-in-arm and mutually encouraged. We may not have put the world to rights but we've had a pretty good try, including wondering why men always disappear inside themselves when there's something troubling them and then expect us to know what it is and how to help them? If I ever meet the person who invented the excuse 'feminine intuition', let's just say there'll be another murder to investigate and the culprit won't be anywhere near as hard to find.

At first, there's no sign of Scott and I feel Cherry's fingers dig into my arm as my heart leaps in panic. We're frozen to the spot, scanning the garden and even the fields beyond. As far as I can tell, the sheep seem as nonchalant as before, the lambs just as spread out. But, in fairness, I'm a human investigator, not an animal one.

Then, to our immense relief, Scott comes out of the garden shed, hidden from sight behind the compost heap, staggering slightly as he hauls several large plastic bags into the middle of the lawn. His bodyguard trots behind him, tail wagging, nose sniffing.

'What the f...' Cherry goes to hurry across the lawn but I grab her arm. I'm not sure how welcome our presence might be, even though I'm there by invitation.

Luckily, he catches sight of us and waves, smiling. Not that this gives me much reassurance, to be honest. However, as we get closer, he waves his arm expansively around the garden. 'I couldn't help noticing that while I've been away, the magpies have treated this place like a drive-through fast food outlet.' He glances up at a churchyard elm tree, the branches of which hang over his garden. Three magpies sit in its branches, eying him with suspicion, as if they knew they were being talked about.

'Just to prove I didn't just learn the spiritually useful stuff...' He scans us both, as if inviting us to disagree, before opening one of the bags and emptying a mini-mountain of old CDs onto the grass. 'Picked these up from a church sale – knew they'd come in useful one day.' He grabs one and holds it at shoulder height before twisting and turning it, as if he's a circus act.

Cherry and I look at each other. I'm thinking his odd behaviour might be much more serious than I'd first thought, and from the look on her face, she's probably thinking along the same lines.

Seemingly dissatisfied with his actions, he empties out enough CDs to stock a medium-sized record shop. 'It's a monastery idea to protect what they grow. You string loads of them on sticks in the ground. Apparently they don't like the way the light glitters off the shiny surface. The magpies, that is, not the monks. Although I did hear them refer to the local nuns as magpies so maybe they hope it'll keep them away as well.' He chortles as he bolts back into the shed and Cherry and I return to our bench to do our own reflecting.

This is our second warm spring day with no sign of the infamous April showers, notoriously short and sharp and absolutely drenching. The sky is cloudless blue, the sheep baa gently while contentedly munching juicy new-season grass and all feels right with the world. Of course Much Slaughter isn't walled in, we're here because we love it and choose it. Our traditions give us a solid foundation. But if we need to move on, we do. And as for the murdering thief/ thieving murderer, well, like the Canadian Mounties, Catherine de Barnes has always got her man.

A slight movement on the other side of the wall, in the unmown area of the churchyard catches my eye, although I can hardly believe that eye. It can't be. If I didn't know better, I'd swear the shadowy figure in the gabardine mac and sunglasses, kneeling and scrabbling through the long grass and last year's thistles is the prim and proper Chief Inspector Glen Parva.

'Cherry, excuse me for a few minutes. There's someone in the churchyard I need to speak to.'

She grins. 'I don't think talking to the dead will help you solve the crimes, Cat. Although I suppose it can't hurt.'

She's probably right, I reflect, as I unlatch the small wooden gate between the vicarage and the churchyard. 'Inspector?'

Glen jumps up as if he's been stung, bangs his head on a low yew branch and utters a very un-police officer-like oath. 'Good grief, Catherine, is there anywhere in this village you don't spring up from? A few hundred years ago, I'd have had you condemned as a witch.'

'Well, forgive me, Inspector, but it's not every day I come across an eminent officer on his knees in a muddy churchyard.'

Glen looks embarrassed, stares around furtively and, even though we're alone, takes me by the arm and leads me towards the church, constantly checking as if he expects to find a villain behind every tree trunk. 'I'm looking for clues.'

'Really, Glen? And you expect to find anything after four weeks, and after your own team's been here?'

He shrugs. 'Alright. And if you tell this to anyone else, I'll not only deny that I said it, but I'll lock you up. What I thought was, if I put myself in the same place as the intruder, I might get a feeling of who it was.' He pulls up the collar of his coat and pokes his sunglasses higher up his nose, visibly embarrassed.

I barely manage to swallow a giggle, the forensically pedantic, scientific recorder of any and every detail, kneeling in a churchyard in the hope of inspiration. Oh, hang on, that's what we do, every Sunday, not more than fifty feet away. Best not to point that out, though.

'But Inspector, I thought you had your man – boy – in custody?'

He winces at my barb, and it occurs to me that I probably shouldn't kick a man when he's down. Especially when he literally is down, on his knees. *And* he's a Chief Inspector.

'You'll find out sooner or later, Catherine, so I might as well tell you now. The kid's story checks out. I've heard more believable fairy tales, but no, it was exactly as he said. We've been given dash cam footage from a council refuse collection truck driver who thought the bag looked suspicious. The kid's on foot and, amazingly, you can even see from his face how surprised he is. We've let him go.'

'I don't suppose their cameras picked up who threw it there, did they?'

'Fat chance. We'll put out a message in case some car driver's camera picked it up but since we don't know when it was dumped, day or night, it would take a major miracle. And while you'd think that the divine miracle-worker might have a vested interest in us catching the person who killed one of His own, well, miracles seem thin on the ground.'

'I rather think that's the point of...' *Don't go there, Cat*.

Glen snorts. 'And it could have been thrown from anything from a bicycle to a lorry –we have no way of knowing. There are even ramblers around there. So, in the absence of divine intervention, I'd welcome an intervention from Much Slaughter's favourite *amateur* sleuth.' I note the emphasis on the word 'amateur', but at least it's slightly complimentary.

'Well, Inspector, since you ask.'

He groans. 'You're going to go on about the cases being linked, aren't you? Well, do your worst and let's get it over.'

'Actually, no Glen, not yet. I do have a couple of ideas I want to pursue, though. I'm happy to share, but I need you to promise that you'll let me make some discrete enquiries first.'

'Discrete? You?' He laughs, but this time it's more of a tease than sarcasm.

'You have to admit it, I do get results.'

'Don't push it, Catherine.'

'Sorry. But do I have your approval?'

His sigh seems to last an eternity but finally he nods agreement.

Game on.

Chapter 21

We're a special case.

I mean, I know that, and I'm pretty sure most of the inhabitants of sleepy Much Slaughter (recently twinned with the murder capital of the world) would agree. But I'm surprised to find the diocese does. Anyway, the result is, we're allowed to have Bishop Norton celebrate our Easter Day service, on condition that St Iggy's celebrates the Morning Communion and St Cyril's pulls out all the stops for a bells-and-whistles Evensong. Or should that be bells-and-smells, given we're in church?

Whatever.

In the churchyard, there's a wonderful smell of mown grass and everything feels fresh and clean courtesy of a short sharp rain shower followed by warm sunshine and blue sky. Now the grass is sparkling with drops of water; daffodils have opened to the heady mix of rain and sun and tower over the snowdrops they've recently outgrown. Along with a musical accompaniment of amorous birds tweeting to their mates high in the neighbouring yews. And behind this, the sound of the organ drifting across on the light breeze.

At the church door, I'm greeted by a very demure Pixie, who waves her hand in an arc and invites me to sit 'wherever you can find a space'. There's no doubt that the two parishes have indeed pulled out all the stops.

St Iggy's is packed to the rafters and there's still a full six minutes to go. Even the St Cyril's regulars have not only crossed the Rubicon to join in the service but have also made the supreme sacrifice of being early. Amazing what Special Case status can achieve.

Today's organist, who is literally pulling out all the stops, is none other than Major Anna Valley. She nears the climax of an overture featuring snippets from all of today's hymns and a few more she's probably usurped from her Salvation Army days. I can't help wondering if she's composed a new chorus for today, one perhaps set to a well-known tune, maybe along the lines of '*We're a Special Case and we know it – clap your hands*'. After which I wonder what would be an appropriate tune if the organist turned out to be doubling as a thief and even a murderer?

Behave, Cat, you're supposed to be preparing for a service of worship.

As I make my way down the aisle to where Linton has saved me a space, nodding to familiar faces left, right and centre, there's a hubbub of chatter despite the music. My lovely man is resplendent in a cream linen suit and a lemon shirt, and I settle down onto the thin pew-long cushion, while simultaneously trying to avoid part of the pew back sticking into my spine.

All around us is an amazing display of Easter wear, it's a get-your-glad-rags-out moment. It's oddly uplifting, as if we're gathering together to publicly proclaim winter is beaten and spring has prevailed.

We're now into the silent reflection part, prior to the service starting, and I notice a fair proportion of the congregation have dropped to their knees in prayer. Personally, I've never found it helps any, but I suppose lack of practice doesn't help. I allow my mind and my eyes to wander around the assembled mass.

My attention is drawn to Skye who is hurrying down the church aisle, scanning right and left for a seat. As we're British, the last seats to go will always be nearest the front. As she squeezes past Boothby Graffoe (Wing Commander, RAF, retired), she tosses her long curly hair over her shoulder then sinks into the pew. Today, her hair's its natural ginger-brown and matches the most amazing colourful batik dress: bare-shouldered, low-fronted, fitted at the waist and billowing out down to her ankles.

'Bare shoulders in a church?' Scott mutters from the pew behind as he follows my stare. 'She'll learn.'

'It's hardly indecent, Scott. Good for her, I say, take a stand and leave decency to older people like me.'

'Not actually what I meant,' says Scott. 'I've seen far too many brides and their parties forget that churches are cold and draughty, even in the height of summer.'

As if she's heard him, Skye gives an almighty shudder and the lovely Boothby, gentleman that he is, silently rises, peels off his jacket and drapes it over her shoulders, bright red with embarrassment. I grin. I have amazingly thoughtful, kind friends.

Scott's right. Outside, it's a lovely spring morning but inside, it feels like we've barely left the bleak midwinter, with a howling gale blowing around my bare neck, my swan-like neck, as Linton once described it.

As if in sympathy, I shrink my swan-like down into my white cotton blouse and warm blue cashmere jumper, thankful for my choice. I've dolled up for the occasion but my choice owes more to wanting to look nice for Linton than for God. Or God's congregation.

Naturally, I now have to take a good hard stare at others' choices, which range from fur coats and gloves for the women and green tweed for the men – on those from the upper strata of our society (or those who wish to be there), to a handful of youngsters like Skye who seem to think they've come to a Mediterranean beach. Oh goodness, when did the time go? I must remember that forty-two refers to my age, not the year I was born.

Now, if there's a murderer and/or thief in our midst, what would they choose to wear? Presumably not a black and white striped prison suit, sadly? It would certainly help at the moment. Maybe the bishop has a humdinger of a sermon that'll have him/her rushing to the front in abject confession. The way things are going, it seems like that's the only way they'll be caught.

Well, that's my five minutes of silent prayer, then.

Somehow, St Iggy's has managed to summon up a robed choir (it's amazing what the visit of a bishop can achieve) and as they file out from a tiny room and make their way to the back, the congregation's noise level drops in readiness.

Traditionally our liturgy begins in silence and the final conversations have been shushed just in time as Pixie noisily closes the church door. Most eyes swivel to watch her as she almost sprints to join a handsome man in the third row, probably her husband. The heels of her shoes click-clack on the stone floor as she hurries towards the pew, her hand nervously fingering her familiar pendant necklace. I feel for her.

Just as she sits down, every other member of the congregation rises and for the time it takes her to readjust she's the only one sitting. Even from this distance I can tell she'd give anything for the floor to open up and swallow her, although her husband, who's called, and looks like a Milton, grabs and squeezes her hand, before swiftly and gently kissing her lips, causing a couple of old biddies behind me to tut.

Thankfully, the stentorian voice of Bishop Norton rings out the Easter Proclamation and we turn to face the Norman font near the west door. 'Rejoice, heavenly powers. Sing choirs of angels. O universe, dance around God's throne.'

Goodness me, how imposing he looks in full liturgical dress. Tufts of white hair stick out like balls of cotton wool glued onto a huge, gold embroidered mitre that – I can't help it – looks like a giant oven glove perched on top of his head. I giggle. Linton shushes me until I whisper in his ear, then he giggles as well and we both get shushed. The bishop bangs heavily on the floor three times with his huge curled wooden staff.

As the bishop ends the Exulted, the traditional Easter Day song, he booms out fit to rock the rafters, 'Alleluia. Christ is risen.'

Our equally robust response, 'He is risen indeed, Alleluia,' is the loudest I've heard, even in St Cyril's, and it strikes me that this lovely man has a real way of encouraging people to join him.

As the echo of our voices dies away, the choir bursts into the opening notes of 'Jesus Christ is Risen Today' and we channel everything into the opening hymn as the choir proceeds through our midst and up into their stall. Bishop Norton is only a few paces behind, draped in yards of richly embroidered gold cloth, and looking absolutely magnificent. His broad shoulders make the material hang richly and heavily and his smile as he processes, looking side to side, is warm enough to heat the whole of the draughty building. He catches my eye and nods.

Linton nudges me and whispers, 'Who's a lucky girl, then?'

I've no idea what he's talking about.

'Who just got the biggest smile of the day? And a special wink. I'm so honoured to be in the presence of a Special Case. Ouch.'

Maybe that dig in his ribs was a little harder than I'd intended.

An hour later, the service draws to an end and we're being sent out to 'Go in the peace of Christ'.

With my voice croaky from belting out the hymns with 'more enthusiasm than accuracy' as Linton so nicely put it, it would appear that no-one's conscience has been sufficiently pricked to produce a confession. Even so, I confess I feel lighter. I'm not a religious person but sometimes being part of all this does lift my spirits, or maybe my soul, and the world feels a better place.

I'm about to ask Linton if he feels the same when Anna announces in a loud and rather irritated voice, 'Bishop Norton wondered if you'd be kind enough to spare him a few moments in the vestry?'

The ever-patient doctor smiles. 'You go. I'll see you outside later. I might even save you some champagne, if you're a good girl.'

I start to respond, 'I'm never...' before realising where I am and adding lamely, 'late.'

When I tiptoe into the vestry, the bishop is sitting at a table and bent over a service book, deep in conversation with someone I don't recognise. It seems to be something to do with this year's attendance figures. Shorn of his robes he looks smaller, which is odd because I reckon he must be roughly the same height as Linton, so around 5'10". Plus, of course he's sitting down. But I can't help contrasting the figure of the bishop, who seems so much more normal and approachable out of robes, with my last appearance in the vestry, with the archdeacon, who seemed puffed up with his own self-importance.

The huddled figures are still talking so I take the opportunity to do something useful. Like trying to visualise what went on here in St Iggy's vestry, much as I did down in St Cyril's. Although thankfully here it's only theft rather than... I shudder.

Focusing my attention on one of the photos of the pyx, I screw up my eyes and try to visualise the environment. Unfortunately, all I can imagine is an endless stream of indistinct figures, always with their back to me, always furtive, every one of them reminding me of Fagin in the Oliver Twist film.

The next thing I'm aware of is Anna bounding into the vestry and with a jolt, I realise that all this time I've been locked onto a completely different photograph: Roby Mill and his family.

Across the room, both men at the table jump in surprise. The bishop turns round and sees me leaning against the wall beside the photograph.

'I'm so sorry, Catherine. My hearing isn't as good as it once was. Just one moment.'

While he turns back to the records, I take the opportunity to whisper to Anna, 'May I have a word with you, later? A quick question, it won't take a minute.'

If her nod of agreement had been shorter, I'd have missed it. She turns on her heels, calling over her shoulder, 'Excuse me, Bishop, the parish lunch will be ready in about forty-five minutes.'

He nods, gently. 'If that works for you, my dear, it works for me.'

Anna makes an odd, uncomfortable-looking half-bow. 'Then I need to make sure it's on schedule.'

Very odd, I think. Was that really all she came in to ask? And if so, why make such a dramatic entrance? Or did she think we'd be talking about her? But then, the vestry isn't exactly a private place, its walls are carved wood with open, unglazed panels. It would be easy to hover outside, pretending to clear up after the service.

At this point, I realise that the other man has followed Anna, disappearing as quietly and completely as the morning mist.

'Well, Catherine, now that it's just the two of us…' The bishop's voice is only marginally less boomy in the confines of the vestry as in the vastness of the church, but it's still warm and rich. 'I hear you've had the pleasure of meeting our rising star archdeacon. I hope he didn't leave you too burned in his stellar wake?'

I grin and mutter, 'I couldn't possibly comment, Bishop,' as I wave my hands in front of my face to mime cooling down.

He laughs. 'And is there anything I should know?'

'Well, erm...' How do you tell a bishop that his archdeacon is an egotistical, bombastic, cold... 'He, um, seemed very – efficient.'

Bishop Norton looks at me for a moment before swinging his pectoral cross over his shoulder, neatly decapitating the altar candles on the desk behind him. He scoops the debris into the bin as if it's a common occurrence, which it probably is, before settling the badge of office carefully, methodically and safely down the centre line of his purple cassock. 'Actually, I meant about the case. Or cases, depending on whose side you're on.'

Ooops. That could have been tricky.

Bishop Norton grabs one of the folding chairs and, disconcertingly, drops it in exactly same place as I'd sat previously and a cold chill runs through my body so I remain standing.

'Well, Bishop, it really won't take that long.'

Especially since, at that moment, in what couldn't have been a coincidence, the major returns.

Rapidly revising what I'd been about to say, I take a deep breath. 'To be honest...'

Chapter 22

My report to the bishop lasts for barely five minutes before he excuses himself, looking as disappointed as I feel.

I can't blame him. An update that basically consists of, 'We had a few suspects, but it seems they've all got alibis. I think the theft and murder are linked, but Chief Inspector Parva doesn't,' may be factually accurate but it's hardly going to persuade an ecclesiastical bigwig that an amateur sleuth is anything other than a distraction, in bringing to justice the person who killed one of their own and maybe also ran off with the family silver. And I'm not sure that waiting for divine justice is high on his priorities at the moment. Of course, I hadn't deemed it appropriate to tell him that my number one suspect might turn out to be one of his ecclesiastical colleagues.

The bishop hadn't shown any signs of suspecting I was holding anything back, so it seems I have at least some acting skills. Maybe this investigating lark really isn't for me and I should take up acting instead. After all, in his sermon, the bishop spoke about Easter Day being the opportunity for rising from the grave of past events and embracing new starts.

This would be the same Cat who Linton describes as being like reading an open book? Okay, maybe not.

Maybe I should concentrate on breathing new life into my business. I can see myself now, standing in crisp chef's whites scanning a gleaming new kitchen – maybe part of an extension built onto my garden, so I can feel surrounded by my colourful flowers, shrubs and trees, the outdoor scents drifting in through the open windows and a gentle breeze wafting fresh air through the oven heat? Portuguese blue tiles on the walls. A stone slab floor. On the black and white veined marble work surfaces, all the professional gadgetry any chocolatier could ever dream of. Cardboard boxes piled up by the door waiting for the dutiful courier to send them off around the world. My PA pokes her head around the door to inform me that my online order book is filling up like water in a lake (note to self: swim later), my social media profile has reached Kardashian levels and, by the way, would I like a hot chocolate? On the wall is a framed photo of me in a breath-taking sheer black satin evening gown, with a glittering diamond choker around my neck, holding up an award, as the dinner-jacketed impeccably suave doctor beams proudly from behind me. Strike that, alongside me.

Speaking of the good doctor, what about breathing new life into that? Except that I believe I already have the breath of life with the infinitely patient and wise Linton Heath. I imagine him slipping in unseen through the sliding doors of my dream kitchen and the first I know of it is when his strong brown arms curl round my waist as he whispers in my ear, 'I'm so proud of you.'

A guttural throat clearing startles me back to reality. Anna looks decidedly frosty. Which is odd, considering how friendly she's been recently. And therefore suspicious.

'Anna, I'm so sorry. I got carried away thinking about, erm, the bishop's sermon.'

Anna's face is the epitome of disbelief. Her mouth drops open and she just stands there, her hands on her hips. 'You called me back because you wanted to talk to me about the bishop's sermon?' *Goodness, she has a powerful stare.*

'No, of course not. I wanted to ask you a question, well, check something out, actually. Almost an intuition. Well, no, more a passing thought.'

From the look on her face I'm not doing anything to convince her of my sanity.

'That woman with Roby, his wife...'

'Ah yes, the photo.'

She turns and we both look across the room in silence for several uncomfortable seconds while I try to stare simultaneously at the picture and the major, ready to note her every reaction.

'What is it you want to know?' Her voice is sharp as she swivels to confront me so rapidly, I'm lost for the words I'm not even sure I had in the first place.

I swallow. 'Well, something doesn't seem quite right about it.'

Anna stares at me while I try to work out what's going on behind her blue-green eyes and what doesn't feel quite right about her.

Eventually, she sighs, drops her hands to her side and flops into the recently vacated chair. 'In fact, Catherine, you're right. It's interesting how a photo can hide so much. But it can't hide everything. The trouble with most photos is that we look at them and see what we expect or want to see. Or even what the photographer wants us to see. But if you stand back, if you block all of that out, and wait, until you can see behind what you see, well...'

Now we're both staring at it.

'What do you see, Catherine?'

This certainly isn't turning out as I'd planned. But one thing I've learnt in this investigating lark is, if you let people have their head, let them talk, then you'll eventually learn what you need to know. Even if it's not what you expected.

'I see a family of three people, two adults, who I presume are the parents of the small child. I see a cottage, not much more than a shack, dirty and not very well maintained. I see...'

'Yes, yes. Those are just the cold facts. Try harder. What do you feel?'

I want to retort it's a photo, how on earth am I meant to feel anything? But then my stomach clenches so I try to unhitch my brain and tune in to my gut.

When I sneak a quiet look at my companion, she's still staring at the picture, so I do the same.

Moments pass into minutes. My brain reminds me we're now missing the Episcopal lunch and I tell it to be quiet – that's a first when it's food. Concentrate. My brain tells me I need a pee. I clench my legs and tell it to shut up. There's something in that wretched photo, I know there is. My brain tells me this is ridiculous, how on earth can I expect a thirty-year-old piece of photographic paper to speak to me?

More to silence my thoughts than anything else, I say, 'They look like a happy family. But there's no colour in the parents, only in the child.'

Anna nods. 'Go on. What makes you feel that?'

'The little girl, Pixie. She's twirling that stick like a cheerleader, like she hasn't a care in the world, she's happy. She's beautifully dressed, her dress looks vibrant. Even her underskirts look unusually bright for such grubby surroundings. I can feel the warmth in her half-look at her mother.'

I concentrate harder. When I look more closely at her mother, I shudder. It's very odd, it's as if she's looking in two different directions at the same time, but the facts tell me that's impossible because she's not cross-eyed and also because, in the photo, she's looking straight ahead. Yet I still feel she's looking in two directions: at her child and at her husband.

Then I feel a jolt, because I can see that the looks are completely different. Her look at Pixie is exactly what you'd expect from a loving mother towards a lively, excited precious daughter. But her look at her husband is altogether more complex and difficult. It takes some moments of stillness before I sense that this is because her feelings are multi-layered. I can sense love and familiarity but also something altogether darker. But try as I might, I can't get any further and it occurs to me then, that maybe that's because the woman herself has buried her feelings.

I realise I'm sweating. This is so much harder than I'd thought it would be. And much more enlightening.

When I turn my attention to Roby, there's even less. I move my head from side to side and up and down, wondering if changing the angle might loosen some inspiration. It doesn't. It's just black. It had never occurred to me that colours might trigger feelings or, rather, that feelings might evoke a colour. But *he* does, the darkness of the night, thick, inky blackness.

'Anna, Roby, I can't...' My voice trails off, I have no words to explain.

She smiles weakly, unsurprised. 'From the photo, Cat, what do you see about Roby?'

'Factually, a worn man, probably not that old but stooped over. He's not looking at either his wife or his daughter. He's not even looking at the camera. He's looking off into the distance, maybe at something only he can see. That's the easy part. When it comes to feelings, he just feels very black.' I slump into the chair opposite.

Anna leans across and squeezes my arm. 'I'm impressed, Ms de Barnes. I can see why Chief Inspector Parva rates your insights so highly.'

Wow. High praise indeed. Or sarcasm?

'Let me fill you in on some facts, then.' She smiles slightly. 'I'll put you out of your misery. And, as you listen, see what you feel.'

She stretches her legs out in front of her and puts her hands behind her head, looking intently into the middle distance somewhere beyond my left shoulder. I can almost hear her brain ticking over. Or, in view of the last few minutes, maybe it's her gut.

'You already know Roby lost both his jobs, here and in St Cyril's, because he was a drunk. What you probably don't know is that his wife bore the brunt of his anger and drunkenness. For decades, far longer than anyone outside the family even suspected. She was an absolutely saintly woman. And his daughter, well she found her own way of dealing with it all, went into her own world, cut everyone else out - and who can blame her? We keep the photo up to honour the two women's work, despite Roby's unhappy history.'

'How does Pixie feel about that, though?'

'We did ask her. She just shrugged and said, *it's a different life*.' Plus, she was such a cute girl. An absolute angel. She got no end of stick at school and in the village, she did, because of her dad's reputation. And all he'd ever say was, "it'll toughen her up." And it did.'

Before I can ask the unusually eloquent and indiscreet major anything more, there's a gentle knock and Bishop Norton pokes his head around the vestry door. Anna's face sets and the whole scene disintegrates in an instant. 'Major, Ms de Barnes, lunch is served.' He grins broadly, and with me on one arm and Anna on the other, he marches us down the main aisle of the church, down the path and into a large, detached cottage two doors away.

However, I'm absolutely certain there's something important Anna still isn't telling me and I need to find out what.

***

Swimming straight after a meal is never recommended, especially in cold open water, so after gorging myself on St Iggy's sumptuous banquet, with its silently trumpeted challenge to St Cyril's to match it after Evensong, I'm free to enjoy a leisurely stroll with Linton, both of us unusually free from the pressure of time.

The sun is still pleasantly warm as we amble through the meadows towards the lake while Daggers gambols ahead of us like a new-born lamb. The doctor has discarded his linen suit in favour of calf-length linen shorts and the same still-crisp shirt, now unbuttoned and flapping invitingly in the slight breeze. Crikey, I mean, I know the man's hot – but even o, shorts in March? I've discarded my outfit for a dark blue cotton sarong over a long-sleeved tee-shirt anf my thickest swimming costume. Sensibly, but inelegantly, we both wear boots and calf-length thick socks to thwart any risk of bites or Lyme disease or whatever. I've also brought a walking stick, not the kind you use for support but the type you take with you in order to thrash your way through undergrowth: brambles, nettles and thistles. And to keep inquisitive cattle at bay. Linton, on the other hand, assures me he needs no stick: one medical stare is sufficient to see off all bovine threats.

With perfect timing, we arrive at the lakeside just as the sun starts to slip behind the encircling trees. It's still warm enough to ensure that when I unwrap my sarong I don't break out into goosebumps the size of Symonds Yat rocks. Dagenham gives me a brief, pitying look before setting off to sniff the latest scents and explore.

After my previous swims, undertaken in temperatures that made me fearful I'd encounter as much danger from icebergs as weeds, and after careful online research, I've finally been authorised to increase my water time to up to fifteen minutes. And, joy of joys, to be the only one swimming, providing there's at least one person on the bank to summon help should I get into difficulties. Mind you, I nearly failed to get authorisation when I suggested they'd be more use leaping in to drag me out, rather than running halfway back to the village before they got a phone signal. Skye had dropped in to instructor mode and told me in no uncertain terms that the last thing a rescuer should do is to enter the water and risk their own life, given that a drowning person might latch on like superglue to the nearest available object and hold on for dear life irrespective of doubling the risk. Use a lifebelt first, I was lectured. Suitably chastened, I sensibly opted *not* to point out that these are noticeably absent in unauthorised spots like this. The second option is a rope (also not provided) or a long branch – a little more hopeful, especially since Linton has already selected one to perch on. And then, I suppose he's probably done emergency training as part of his medical studies.

Discarding boots and socks, I finally throw myself into the blissful beckoning water. Not that this makes the cold any the less shocking nor my squeals any the less high-pitched, nor Linton's peals of laughter any the less gleeful. All it does is set a few crows flapping and complaining as they fly out from the trees.

Throwing myself in is, of course, a euphemism for letting the water lap gently around my feet and ankles, then creep painfully slowly up my calves and even more slowly up to my thighs. A little higher, at the point delicacy forbids me to name it, is the point of no return. Stay at this depth for more than a few seconds and you'll never venture deeper. This is where the brave ones take a deep breath, bend their knees and strike out, and the more sane amongst us take a few more seconds to splash around and rub handfuls of water over our shoulders, chest and face before also sliding under the surface. It's amazing how much faster one's strokes are in cold open water compared with in a warm swimming pool.

Once the initial shock is over and my shoulders have been underwater, I turn onto my back and float, looking up at the darkening sky. This is the sweet spot, that fleeting, transitory time where the initial chill has been banished and before the deeper more dangerous chill sets in.

It's perfectly, blissfully quiet. Even the crows have settled and shut up. I could be alone in the universe – apart from my gallant lifeguard, of course, bless him. All of life's pressures float away and I'm free. Just me.

Gosh, I'm on my own.

Slowly, so slowly, that there are no ripples on the still water, I slide my hands under the straps of my costume and peel it down to my waist as I tread water. It's far less cold on my newly exposed skin than I'd imagined so with only a few extra wriggles I peel it all the way down and loop my feet out.

On the shore, both dog and human seem unaware so I tread water for some time, letting the water lap around my body and luxuriating in the novel sensations of skinny-dipping. Yes, I know, I led a sheltered life at uni, in that respect at least, if not in others.

Finally, I let out a loud whoop and wave my costume above my head. Daggers takes one look and carries on where he left off; water is never his favourite thing and cold water is very definitely off his menu. Linton's response is more gratifying. His eyes pop out on stalks so far they almost reach me and for a moment I think he's about to strip off and join me. But he soon thinks better of it, or possibly remembers he's on safety duty and just wanders down to the water's edge, tapping his wrist to remind me of the time, and shouts, 'It's a lovely view from here. You must try it more often,' while grinning like a randy schoolboy.

With a strong leg kick, I rise out the water to my waist and shout, 'Just another few minutes, doctor, and then I'll be out.'

I'm sure he makes some wisecrack but I've already sunk back in. I turn onto my stomach, my bottom exposed to the air as I do breaststroke, parallel to the shoreline. Normally this is my best thinking time. And today, feeling particularly unencumbered, it takes only moments before a revelation strikes me, my body goes rigid and I strike out for the shore. Why on earth hadn't I thought of it before?

There's someone I really need to track down.

Chapter 23

My determination to spend the day doing some online and phone tracking and checking up evaporates as soon as I draw back my heavy sitting room curtains to reveal a perfect blue sky. 'A British Bank Holiday and it's not raining. We need to get out into the fresh air.' Dagenham barks a cursory agreement before pointedly sniffing at the kitchen door and breakfast.

I quickly take the hint, not least because appearing in your cottage window dressed only in your sleeping attire of a thin vest and loose shorts meets with high disapproval in village circles. Plus, it's still only early April and until the sun reaches here later in the day this is the coldest room in my cottage.

Daggers shows his approval by winding himself around my legs, his furry tail lashing my bum like some over-enthusiastic masseuse, making sure he keeps his pleading eyes laser focused on me until his filled bowl is safely deposited on the floor. Then, for the next thirty seconds his entire world is contained in one red plastic bowl and the particularly nutritious and expensive dog food recommended by Martin, our vet, to avoid 'puppy fat' – which he'd said looking so pointedly at me that, at first, I didn't realise he meant Daggers.

I've just filled my own bowl with muesli, a chopped banana and natural yoghurt (*see, Martin*) when my phone bleeps with a text from Linton.

On call but fancy a picnic lunch?

This lovely thought is only mildly diluted by a row of *ccccccc*, which I immediately translate into eight kisses. The healthy doctor suffers from a severe case of fat-finger syndrome, which, along with an over-enthusiastic autocorrect, has produced some interesting moments. I remember when I popped into our local WOMAD music festival for the day, last year. The heavens had opened in a way not seen since the days of Noah, so I'd sent Linton a rather pathetic text lamenting that I was drenched to the skin. By return, I got, *There's nothing like a wet Woman*. Rapidly followed by, *I meant Womad Woman*. Well, no-one's perfect. Especially in the age of autocorrect.

With that and autocorrect in mind, I merely reply with a thumbs-up emoji. Linton's response is equally brief: *Pick you up at 12.*

I have a huge smile and a warm glow as I grab my breakfast and wander into my back garden. I sink into my canvas director's chair on my small but perfectly formed patio just as a robin flits down onto the far edge of the paving stones, his red chest iridescent for the mating season. He cocks his head to one side to watch me – or more likely, to check for Daggers – and hops back onto the fence as Daggers lumbers out and plonks himself across my feet. I let out a long sigh, I feel so content and lucky. I have an amazing dog, the perfect cottage, a heart-throbbing boyfriend – and my health. Plus, the sun's shining and it's a Bank Holiday, so I don't need an excuse not to think about business plans, kitchen equipment or even murder-theft. I stretch out my legs in the warm sunshine and rest my eyes for a few moments.

The next thing I know, my neck feels as if someone's twisting every single muscle and my back jerks like elastic as my phone bleeps, waking me up from my snooze. A glance at the screen shoots me to my feet: it's ten-thirty and I've a picnic to get ready for.

Luckily, the text is Linton informing me he's got the picnic basket in hand so all I need to bring is my 'beautiful self'. That man is a marvel. Sadly, my beautiful self doesn't emerge like a butterfly from a chrysalis, so I've barely had time to stuff my breakfast pots into the dishwasher, shower, wash and dry my hair, apply the lightest of lip, eye and face make-up, climb into my sixth clothing combination, push Daggers into the garden to do his business, then settle him into his bed, before my beau knocks on the door.

Mind you, although I say it myself, the result is worth every bit of my effort. Over my best green satin underwear, I've chosen a cream cotton dress with delicate mint green thin vertical stripes, and backless sandals.

And my reward for all this due diligence, apart from feeling like a million dollars, is watching his hungry eyes rove over every inch of me before he lets out a low whistle and mutters, 'You look amazing.'

I smooth my dress down slowly, turning my head to one side coquettishly. 'Well, kind sir, you don't look so bad yourself.'

Linton is dressed in a flamboyant Hawaiian shirt in bright greens and blues that goes perfectly with his olive skin. His baggy khaki shorts have the same effect on his brown legs and my heart doesn't just flutter, it threatens an explosion of nuclear proportions. The whole outfit is matched perfectly with rich brown leather deck shoes (I hate it when men take inordinate care over everything else and then clump around in a pair of scratched dirty shoes that would be offensive even for gardening). It's all set off with a large-brimmed Panama hat and large dark sunglasses that reflect like polished steel.

He finally drags his eyes away from my get up and waves his hand towards his vintage Jaguar sports car parked at the end of my front garden. I especially love it when, like today, it's top down. And I especially admire a man who can not only buy a car that's bright pink but also get away with driving it with such panache. But that sums up Dr Heath – panache.

He makes a grand show of taking my arm and leading me down the path as if we're heading into some formal banquet in a sumptuous manor house. He even opens my door for me, gently guiding me into the low-swung seat, before hopping over to his own closed door to slide behind the wheel. Pretentious, but I still giggle as the engine roars into life and we speed away in a pleasing flurry of gravel chipping.

Linton's chosen site turns out to be a forty-minute drive away, forty glorious minutes of wind blowing through my hair as we race through Cotswolds country lanes, tiny Bath stone villages and onto the Lambourn Downs. The combination of the vintage Jag and its eye-catching colour guarantees people turn to stare and, quite often, to wave. At least, it's mainly the men who wave and as I wave back I feel like an old-fashioned film star, Greta Garbo or Marilyn Monroe. I could *so* get used to this.

Linton spends the entire journey silent and tight-lipped. Apparently, it's much harder to drive a vintage sports car than it might seem from the comfort of the deep leather passenger seat. Who knew? Who cares – it's glorious to bask in the warmth, wave at the admiring crowds and just be. My heart feels so full.

Finally, with a flick of his wrists, my chauffeur, sorry, my lovely boyfriend, swings the car between two wrought iron gateposts and onto a long, paved driveway. A small track leads off to the left and at the last moment he swings onto it, a huge grin spreading across his handsome brown face. I so want to kiss him. (Apparently leaning over to kiss the driver of a vintage sports car while it's in motion is not allowed. I tried once and was firmly put in my place.)

On either side the track, fields of what I now recognise as wheat are just starting to make themselves known. This is perfect and I snuggle down deeper into the contoured seats.

A few hundred yards further on, Linton swings the car off to the left again and pulls up at the gate of the most perfect meadow I have ever seen in my life, especially since it's mercifully free of sheep or cattle. The grass looks every bit as green as grass should, neatly manicured to lawn standard, even the tramlines. And since the engine roar has stopped and my ears no longer throb, the silence is magical. It's as if I've been transported to another world. There's even a green swinging double seat swaying gently in the breeze about fifty yards into the meadow. Hang on, there's what? Even I know you don't usually find garden furniture in the middle of an isolated field.

'Linton, are we in someone's back garden? Should we even be here?'

He looks around solemnly and furtively for a moment, then opens my car door, slips off my sandals and tosses them into the passenger well.

'Relax. The owner's one of my patients. He's always said that I could use his land anytime I wanted. And today – I wanted.'

I grin as he takes my hand to help me out and leads me through the gate towards the seat, the grass tickling my toes and still slightly damp and glorious under my bare feet.

Suddenly, I freeze. 'What about ticks? I need to...'

'Relax, darling. He rents this out for events several times a year, so, believe me, he takes every precaution known to man to keep it safe.'

Reassured (mostly), I settle into the remarkably comfy seat and swing gently back and forth while my gallant man scoots back to the car and returns with a green bag and a huge tartan woollen rug which, with the merest flick of his wrist, he settles flat on the grass. From the bag he pulls out four metal pegs and pushes them through eyelets in each corner to anchor it down. This man thinks of everything. He settles down next to me on the swing and I rest my hand on his warm knee.

We both stare across the meadow, as I feel the sun warming my body through my loose cotton dress. Linton lifts my fingers from his leg to his lips and kisses them softly causing my temperature to rocket.

'Hungry, Cat?'

More than you'll ever know. 'Always am,' I say.

He starts to climb off the swinging bench, then stops suddenly, causing it to swing back so violently I'm almost pitched out forwards onto my nose. 'Oh no!' He looks mortified as he strikes his forehead with the flat of his hand.

'What is it, my love?' I spring off the seat towards him, getting catapulted into him as the bench swings back and hits me squarely on the back of my legs.

'Cat, I'm so sorry. I've forgotten the food. I'm *so* stupid.'

I reach up to kiss the tip of his nose. 'It's fine, you're more than enough,' I say, a sentiment immediately contradicted by the loudest stomach rumble ever, as I fold my arms around his back and hug the dear man close to my chest (while wondering if my phone has enough signal to find the nearest McDonalds).

It takes a few more moments of being bathed in his scent and the warmth of his body before I realise he's shaking and I pull back, worried he's having a stroke.

It's no stroke – he's laughing like a drain.

'You monster!' I splutter.

'Sorry, I couldn't help it, sweetheart.' There are actual tears running down his face –which are likely to become tears of real pain if I have my way.

Luckily I don't, because he ducks out of my reach and scuttles away. As I watch him trot back, I make a conscious effort to manage my expectations. If this was a classic movie, an immaculate butler in full tails would gallop over the horizon and I'd whisper, *Saved by the cavalry* as he unloaded several Harrods-style hampers, and surrounded me with caviar, a huge richly crusted game pie, pickles and crusty bread still hot from the oven, along with strawberries, and enough chocolates to sink a battleship. The reality is that our mobile catering truck is a vintage sports car not known for its storage space. And Linton's Jag doesn't even boast the ubiquitous wire hamper rack at the back.

He returns laden with – what's this? A speaker? Beethoven's *Pastoral* fills the air and I sigh. Not in a good way. If music be the food of love – I'm going to be mighty hungry.

Gone again, Linton leans into the car, his bottom stuck in the air as his shoulders burrow into the interior. And what a lovely bottom it is. I admire it, just as my stomach rumbles again. At least there's one thing I can feast on.

All too soon Linton unfurls himself. He marches towards me, a look of absolute pride on his face, a mildly bulging bag in his hand. He looks like a small boy with his Christmas presents. More importantly, he's wielding a bottle of white wine and two glasses in his other hand.

The bag is dumped in the shade behind the seat and Linton flops down beside me holding a corkscrew. Before I can say, 'You're a genius,' I'm holding a large glass of cold white wine and looking more than a little surprised.

'Yes, Cat, they're glass. None of your common or garden earth-ruining plastic for my special one.' We clink glasses.

Wow, that tastes good – the wine that is, not the words. (Although the words tasted pretty good as well). It has a cool, rich flavour, slightly lemony but not acidic with clear overtones of *drink more*.

Only with my second sip – my glass is already half empty – do I remember that Linton is the driver and I look across with some concern. 'Are you... I mean, are we staying long enough?' I have a momentary nightmare flash of him suddenly producing a tent from the car and announcing we're here for the night.

He raises his glass, downs the remainder in one gulp and, to my look of deepening horror, replies, 'Zero alcohol,' as he replenishes both our glasses.

'I never knew zero alcohol wine could taste as good as this.'

He stares at me for a few moments. 'And just how much zero alcohol wine have you consumed, Ms de Barnes?'

I pause. 'Now you come to mention it…'

'Ye-es?'

'Not a drop! This is the first. It always seemed to be a waste of a perfectly good drink.'

He looks hurt.

'No, don't get me wrong, Linton, this is lovely. How did you track it down?'

'Wine Club.'

Of course he did. Shouldn't have needed to ask.

'Though it did take a few appallingly bad attempts before I came across this one. I nearly didn't try it. It's called Tetbury Tipple, which doesn't exactly sound promising.'

'It's worth every sacrificial sip, my man. I raise my glass to you.'

His gallantry is rewarded with a very loud growl from my stomach.

'Ah, Madame would like to be fed.'

'Madame always likes to be fed,' I murmur, picturing him as a Greek god dropping tasty morsels of grapes into my mouth as I recline on the swinging bench.

Linton twists round and reaches into the bag, which I have a feeling is going to turn out as capacious as Mary Poppins' carpet bag. It doesn't produce any grapes, but neither does it disappoint and, within a couple of minutes, Linton has covered most of the rug with smart plastic plates, proper cutlery, fresh bread and pate as well as several cheeses I don't even recognise, a huge bowl of mixed salad and coleslaw.

Finally, he stands to one side, waves his arm over the mouth-watering display and announces in his best servant voice, 'Madame, luncheon is served.' He reaches out, takes my hand and settles me in the small remaining space.

'Do join me, Heath,' I say, in my best cultured tone, before ruining any delusions of grandeur by loading my plate to the height of a small Cotswold hill.

Linton hands me a white linen napkin (of course it's linen) and for a few moments watches the food tottering precariously on my plate before cutting himself a small piece of cheese, little more than a crumb of bread and two slices of cucumber, all of which look positively lost on his plate.

'Oh come on, Heath,' I mutter, 'you're really not trying.'

He grins and finally starts to do some justice to the spread before us.

This carries on through seconds (him) and thirds (me), through a bowl of perfect strawberries and cream with an amazing chocolate and caramel sauce, and finally, enough petits fours to satisfy a small army (i.e. me).

I could honestly believe I've died and gone to heaven, especially when Linton pushes aside the debris and invites me to loll beside him on the rug. I stretch out, my head on his chest, my hand running through his thick hair, all's right with the world.

The next thing I'm aware of is a cool drop on my chest. In the warmth of the day and the replete-ness of the lunch, it's rather refreshing.

When it's followed by a second, I decide it must be Linton playing tricks, probably with the cold condensation from another bottle of wine.

But when that's followed in rapid succession by a third, fourth and fifth, I force my heavy eyelids open just as Linton begins to stir.

Seconds later, he leaps to his feet, rolling me to one side as he sprints towards his car, yelling 'Get that stuff into the box, pronto.'

The gentle drops of cooling water have now turned into a full-blown April shower complete with black clouds and a damp breeze. As I bundle everything together in the blanket and drag it across to the box, I wonder why it is that life's black clouds always gather behind you and catch you totally unprepared?

Linton is busy fumbling with something in his car, oblivious to me shovelling bits away as carefully as I dare while getting drenched to the skin, my dress sticking damply to my legs and displaying my green underwear as clearly as if I was wearing it on the outside.

So I'm not exactly a happy bunny when I slide beneath the now-hooded car and onto the towel Linton has managed to conjure up from goodness knows where and spread across his precious upholstery. Especially when I see he's grinning like the Cheshire Cat, his hair plastered flat on his head and also very visible through his damp shirt. Poldark in a sports car. I'm only slightly appeased.

'Sorry, my love.' He leans over to kiss me and I can feel his warm skin underneath that damp shirt. 'I had to get the hood up. The last time this beauty got caught in a torrential downpour it caused a couple of grand's worth of damage.'

'And the last time *this* beauty got caught in a downpour she was not amused.' I glare at him. 'And you might find you got off lightly with a couple of grand.'

He places his poker-hot hands on my cheeks, wipes strands of damp hair back behind my ears and instantly warms me up as his lips land on mine. Well, what can I say? He's gone to so much effort to put all this together.

'Just remember, my man, classic glamour girls don't like being soaked any more than classic cars.'

He pouts in mock guilt for a few moments before another long, luxurious kiss.

'Now, let's get you back and out of those wet clothes before you catch your death of cold.' Sounds good to me. 'Your place or mine?'

Since the now-pardoned doctor has the most amazing Amazon rainforest shower, it's no contest. 'Yours. Just need to provide for Daggers.'

He grins. 'And I'm sure I can find you an old rugby shirt while your clothes are drying.'

Chapter 24

As payback for allowing us two and a half days of warm sunshine and having the hope that spring's here, Tuesday is cold, windy and wet, the epitome of winter once more. Or, as the BBC *Points West* forecaster solemnly announces, 'a cool front has rolled in from the north, bringing with it....'

Dagenham's morning walk consists of a quick dash round The Green, followed by at least an hour hosing him down and brushing the mud and knots out of his bedraggled light golden fur, after which he slinks away in front of the fire, steam rising like a sauna, the odour far from as pleasant. Beyond that, if I can get him to do anything, it's thirty seconds in the garden to do the minimum and a light growl of refusal if I try him for anything else.

It's also an excellent opportunity to try out some new chocolate lines, with a range of samples lined up on my (still not marble) worktop along with the more regular Crimson Courgette orders. Bad weather tends to drive more people into the coffee shop which in turn ups my sales – the silver lining to some literally very heavy clouds.

In between, I've been dropping some data into a business plan template that Skye mailed me. I say data: to be honest it's more like: *think of a number then double it (if it's sales) or halve it (if it's profits)*. I'm in the middle of an internet trawl of 'The World's 100 Best Mission Statements', my eyes drooping from boredom and the stuffy kitchen when, in the midst of a particular dense section on marketing, two words leap out and sear into my brain: *think film.*

I'm jolted wide awake, but not by the thought of filming myself hard at work in my lovely little kitchen surrounded by my kit as I pull out the most perfectly formed Irish cream-filled dark chocolate bonbons and lay them to cool on my immaculately clean worktop. No, what actually has jolted me awake is the lively but nervy leather-clad film runner, the one who looked shifty when she was speaking of her forthcoming nuptials. No disrespect, but she isn't a woman I can imagine in traditional white wedding dress, embracing a traditional wedding service, in a traditional Anglican Church. I know – don't judge a book by its cover or a film runner by her gear. But, really? And if she *was* checking locations for her wedding, wouldn't she have looked excited rather than secretive? It's not as if we were going to blab the secret to her betrothed, is it? Like the major, there's something she's not letting on. I can feel it. Plus, I still have some tracking down to do. My gut agrees.

Right, time for some action.

Which is easier said than done. The film shebang had upped sticks and left literally at dawn several days ago, leaving behind some angry woken-up-early villagers and some deep tyre ruts across the surface of The Green. Word had it, they'd paid a large sum for permission to film but half the village had sworn tyres would burst if they ever returned. The other half couldn't wait to see if they'd made it onto the screen.

It turns out you can't just ring a TV channel and ask how to contact a crew member. The sniffy production office receptionist informed me coldly that it wasn't their policy to give out such information and, in any case, they'd commissioned a specialist outside broadcast production company, and no, she couldn't give me their details. Or even their name.

Four hours later, I make a phone call. After having tracked down an old episode of *One Dog and his Sheep* on YouTube and learnt the name the production company, delved into their website to glean as many names as possible (thankfully I only needed the female ones), compiled a shortlist of twenty people and, finally, by way of Facebook, LinkedIn, IMDb and a hard-earned favour from my old social media guru which will cost me a very expensive meal next time I'm in London, and with a fair bit of guesswork, I got lucky.

'Yes?' The voice is surly, cautious and barely the right side of being downright rude. 'If you're selling, I've got no money. If you're lending, get lost.'

Clearly she's not expecting this to be an offer of work, then.

'Hello. This is Catherine de Barnes. We met when you were filming recently in Much Slaughter. I was working alongside Chief Inspector Parva.' I didn't say *with*.

'Oh, yes. The posh bint.'

Let it pass, Cat. You need her onside.

Okay, this isn't going to be one of those Jessica Fletcher conversations in *Murder She Wrote*, where we start with the pleasantries and gently build up to me asking the killer question. And, yes, the pun was intended.

Speaking of which, if Jessica Fletcher was to write the definitive Amateur Sleuth's Handbook, what would be her top tip? I reckon it'd be: *When in doubt, say nowt* (I paraphrase).

The silence lengthens.

Finally she cracks. 'I told you and that bloke all I know.'

I wait a few moments, then jump in with the sting. 'Except we both know that's not true, don't we?' I can almost see the diminutive figure shrinking on the other and of the phone.

Again, silence. How about Jessica's top tip number two: *The guilty party will feel far more pressure to break the silence than will you, the investigator.* I can imagine her voice saying it. And – it works.

A loud sigh rumbles down the phone and echoes in my ear. 'Alright, I suppose I can tell you now. You're right. It was just a cover story. There's no-one wants to marry me.'

Rule three (see above) would probably state: *Once they've started, don't stop them. Your burning question might be the most important thing in the world to you, but if you interrupt, your rapier question will become the bung that stops the flow.* Not the most eloquent of points, but a good sentiment.

And silent I stay, although common humanity means I want to reassure her I'm sure that's not the case, and plenty of young men – and young women for that matter – would be happy to… you get the gist.

It works again. Eventually, she can resist no longer. 'I was actually scouting locations, for a brilliant new TV drama. Top secret. If the plot, or the list of the talent attached, gets out, everyone would jump on the bandwagon, the production company would be bankrupt and I'd be out of a job. Worse than that, if they thought it was me who blabbed, I'd be finished in this industry. And before you ask – yes, it is that cut-throat.'

An interesting turn of phrase.

'Anyway, I was sworn to secrecy. And since I knew I'd got nothing to do with the murder, I knew I could just keep quiet. Truth will out and all that.'

Except that it sounds a little too glib, a little hollow, like stage lines practised too many times.

I'm sure that's as much as she's planned to say, so it's time to break rule three. 'If that's the case, why are you telling me now? And why haven't you told the inspector?'

There's another long pause and I can't tell if she's rehearsing her lines or just surprised by the question and not sure of the answer.

When she speaks, there's a new excitement in her voice. 'Because last week we signed the contracts. Read-throughs start in a month. Now, if anyone else nicks the idea, we can sue. It could be the biggest break of my career.'

My heart wants to believe her. Even I know how hard it is to get a big break in that industry and she sounds so excited. But my brain has other ideas: it still sounds too pat, too convenient: the top-secret mission, the career opportunity. Almost as if she's presenting a plot.

She senses my scepticism. Perhaps she's used to it. Maybe crew are no different to actors, always clutching at the straw of the next big thing, even though ninety-nine times out of a hundred it comes to nothing. 'I'll text you the producer's details, you'll recognise her. Just make sure you tell her it's a murder enquiry and not just me blabbing my mouth off in the pub.'

There's a note of bitterness there. Personal experience, perhaps?

A loud click announces she's ended the call, and seconds later a buzz announces the arrival of the contact details.

I dial another number. 'Glen, I've been speaking to that runner.'

The ensuing splutter is so loud I hold my phone away from my ear. So, before he has chance to say anything, I end the call.

At this time on a Tuesday afternoon, the Crimson Courgette Coffee Emporium is blissfully quiet and I'm able to slip straight into my favourite corner, laptop already primed to go. Skye always tells customers, quite correctly, that there's no Wi-Fi in the café because of the thick stone walls, so they might as well enjoy some downtime along with their coffee and cakes. One of the advantages of being both a regular and a good friend of the proprietor, however, is being given the (secret) code to the business Wi-Fi. Hence, in less time than it takes to consume my hot buttered teacake, I've Googled the producer, the production company and an industry website that also came through on her text.

It's all going so well until Chief Inspector Glen Parva ambles in and automatically gravitates to my corner, although he still looks surprised to see me there. Skye has now accepted him as a regular and his strong black coffee arrives only moments after he does. Unbelievably, he treats me to a warm smile, followed by words I never thought I'd hear him say: 'Cat, I'm glad to see you here.'

He notes my surprise (he's not one of Gloucestershire's finest detectives for nothing) and his grin widens. 'It's a bit tense in the office. The boss is unhappy so he's on my back, which means I'm on their backs. Which means nobody's happy. I'm glad of the excuse to get out, to be honest.'

I gaze at the officer for a few moments. His broad-shouldered good looks and rich baritone voice, along with his expensively cut grey hair and his tasteful choice of work clothing make him seem calm, almost fatherly. Except when he's dealing with – what did he call me? Ah yes – the Slaughter Sleuth. I certainly ruffle his carefully coiffured feathers.

In a well-practised move, he slides his trendy sunglasses up and onto the top of his head and I smile as the action dislodges raindrops he then has to wipe from his forehead. Vanity comes with a price tag.

Now I can see his grey eyes clearly and they're flitting restlessly around the room, almost as if he's expecting someone to jump out and attack him. Oh, hang on, he's a detective, I guess that's simply par for the course. For the first time I realise the glasses aren't vanity, they're professionalism, so he can watch unnoticed.

Despite the office tension, or perhaps as a conscious response to it, Glen seems unusually relaxed. He sips his coffee and stretches his legs out, almost causing Skye, who's carrying a full tray of goodies, to trip up. He seems genuinely apologetic.

'I tried to bring the missus here once.'

Wonders will never cease. This is the first time I've heard Glen mention a wife. I pay more attention.

'The trouble is, she's heard so much about the shenanigans in this village, she reckons it would be about as romantic as a trip to the London Dungeon.' He stares out of the window as a couple of villagers amble past and I wonder if he's beginning to recognise people.

Without turning back, he murmurs, almost to himself, 'It's a difficult life, being married to a copper. She once compared it with being locked in a police cell when they've thrown away the key.'

Ever so gently, I reach across, put my hand lightly over his and squeeze. Glen jumps. He suddenly seems to remember where he is and who with.

'Now, tell me, Catherine, how the hell did you get hold of the runner's details?'

'Don't worry, Inspector, nothing illegal and only vaguely immoral.' Another gigantic splutter. 'Glen, relax. Have you never heard of social media? Facebook? Insta? Friends in high places? It honestly isn't that hard with a bit of... ingenuity.'

Rule four in Fletcher's handbook could be: *Quit while you're ahead or it won't end well*.

Part of me is glad to b e back on safer, familiar investigative ground. But another part of me recognises that as deflecting from what's obviously a personal sore point, with more to add. That's what I'd want, the chance to share with someone else, to talk it over. But Glen seems to be what my ex would call, rather admiringly, a 'man's man' and not a 'touchy-feely girlie', as he'd once called me. Didn't stop him running off with a girlie, though,

Glen glances down at the table and seems surprised to see my hand is still covering his. He pulls it away to extract his official notebook and begins to suck the end of his official pencil. Well, his choice. But I've made a mental note to offer him another chance at a more appropriate time.

'As you know, Glen, rather like with the major, I felt the runner had been holding something back. I mean, if I'd been scouting for my wedding venue, I'd be bouncing up and down like the spring bunny and be as happy as Larry.'

Despite the mixed metaphor, I'm picturing myself in a huge white gown, gliding slowly down the aisle at St Cyril's, with Linton resplendent and glowingly handsome at the front, in complete awe and gazing at me with love. Scott, fully robed and equally joyful, is also there, service book in hand. Glen coughs.

'Glad as I am to get out of the office, please don't tell me you called me all the way here're just to tell me you doubt her story. Which, as you know, we've checked out.'

Snatched back from my somewhat premature daydream, I gather my thoughts.

'Yes, that's true. She did get a phone call at the right time calling her back on set. It was the other bit that wasn't accurate, the wedding venue.'

'Ah, yes, the costume drama.' He turns bright red in embarrassment. 'I took a lot of gip for that. The team reckoned my research was all an excuse to ogle bosoms, as they so delightfully put it.'

I raise an eyebrow.

'Well, okay, they didn't put it anywhere near as politely.'

What a shame!

'Anyway, Cat, it did all seem to be legit.' He sighs. 'Another one bites the dust.'

I sigh. 'Even I have to admit it, it does all seem above board. I followed all the links I could find, and there were plenty. I even managed to see the news featured on *Ariel*, the BBC's own internal comms journal. There's quite a media sensation in certain circles. So I guess I can understand the need for secrecy. And, if it wasn't just my job but my whole career which depended on me keeping shtum, I'd keep quiet.'

Glen grins in disbelief.

'Yes, Chief Inspector, even Catherine de Barnes can keep a secret, *occasionally*.' I grin back, just as my phone vibrates with *Ride of the Valkyries*. The carefully personalised ringtone means only one person, and guilt kicks in as I remember I owe her a call.

'Hello, Mum. What is it?'

The voice on the other end of the phone sounds unusually croaky and uncertain.

Moments later, I feel the colour drain from my face, my legs feel wobbly and I think I'm about to be sick.

Chapter 25

It's a bad sign when ninety percent of what you know about a member of your family is gleaned from their eulogy. I thought I'd been close to my gran. As I sit, damp-eyed and with a numb-bum on the hard polished wooden seats of Birmingham Crematorium it seems I was wrong. Either that or the older woman in clerical robes and a long blue preaching scarf has mixed up her notes. Which, given the way she greeted me by name as I shot into the crematorium chapel with barely two minutes to go, doesn't seem likely. But at least I'll be spared conversation time with my parents, especially about the absentee Linton, who's excused himself via an urgent medical training update. His reluctance to attend has left me feeling confused, upset and horribly unsupported. It also resulted in us both stomping off in different directions.

My parents and I are sitting at the front, in a RESERVED pew. I'm not quite sure why that was thought necessary since there are only a handful of others here, none of whom I recognise. Neither do my parents, it seems, as they stare, steely-eyed, towards the front, jaws set.

Even so, the three of us *are* squashed together in one pew, the closest I've been to my father and mother in years. Normally we're perched on deep upholstered armchairs (my parents) and a hard, lumpy sofa (me). Today, my dad is on the end, as if he's blocking any escape. Next to him is my mother, her elbow digging painfully into my side. Then there's me. On my other side is an elderly woman in a high-necked old-fashioned black lace mourning dress. I suppose she must be a distant relative. Possibly a friend. Or, given how uncertain she seems, maybe even in the wrong funeral. Although Gran's name has been mentioned enough times and she's shown no sign of leaving.

'Midge Hall was born in 1926, a true Lancashire lass,' the celebrant announces in a firm, clear voice, looking around as if daring anyone to disagree.

I tune out, taking the opportunity to fan the flames of resentment against Mum. It turns out that Gran had died a whole week before my dear mother had decided to pick up the phone and impart that piece of life-shaking news. Clearly only birthdays warrant an immediate phone call, not a relative's death.

Shock does strange things and her phone call had unleashed years of anger and resentment towards her, only made worse by her defence, 'I thought it better to wait until we knew the funeral details'. I mean, who on earth believes you only know those three days before the event? For the first time, ever, I put the phone down on her and she didn't call me back, just sent me a text with date, time and location.

'Midge, it seems, was always a feisty lass,' says the celebrant. I feel my mother tense, her elbow digging even more painfully into my ribs. My father looks as stony-faced as a gargoyle.

The gran I'd known, tiny and round like a bouncing ball, had the loudest, dirtiest laugh I'd ever heard. She took no nonsense from anyone, and a single look or a few carefully chosen words could reduce a grown man to a gibbering wreck – and had done, more than once. The celebrant continues.

'In 1942, shortly before her sixteenth birthday, she lied about her age so she could enlist and soon found herself delivering trucks and land rovers from her home in Birmingham to far-flung parts of the country. Which, considering her height, was no small achievement!'

The woman to my left chortles loudly. My father mutters something under his breath and from his tone it doesn't sound approving. I however am all ears. Trailblazers are right up my street. I swallow hard and rather noisily, realising she's gone. At this rate the minister will think all the family is capable of doing is to emit strange noises.

I glance up apologetically at the minister, who seems a little embarrassed. There's a long pause and some scanning of notes before she clears her throat to continue. 'After a rather eventful war, Midge finally settled in Birmingham, in the house that would become her home for almost eighty years. And where Peter was born and raised.' It feels odd hearing my father mentioned like that, although I'm not sure why it should. The woman looks uncomfortable and I get the impression she knows there's far more not being said.

It seems my mother has also picked up on this as she turns and whispers in my ear, 'We'll talk later.' Wonders will never cease.

I don't take in much of the rest of the service. I stand when everyone else stands – my mother's elbow ensures that – I sing when they sing and I probably mutter the appropriate amens in the prayers. The occasional phrase such as 'long battle with cancer' and 'very private person' filter through to me. But overall, I'm numb. It's unreal, as if it's me in the wrong funeral not the woman next to me. This isn't the gran I knew. Or, perhaps didn't know. I mean, I knew nothing about the cancer.

She was ninety-seven for goodness' sake, so I'd known this would happen sooner or later– as she'd often remind me, it got ever more sooner and less later. You know it's bound to happen. But that's an abstract concept. It's a 'someday', not a 'today'. So when 'today' actually happens it's no less of a shock. Gran dying leaves an empty space.

Later, at the wake, which is at Gran's house, Mum flutters round like a butterfly, always busy but never settling for more than a moment, impossible to tie down. Dad plants himself in the kitchen boiling the kettle and washing dishes. A few neighbours pop in, anxious to pay their last respects, having been unable to make the service, but mostly they stay in their own clique, more interested in reminiscing on past funerals and wakes than in sharing stories of my gran. Of the elderly person from my pew there's no trace.

The talk with my mother never happens, of course. The most I get is a large wooden box thrust into my arms and a muttered, 'That'll tell you all you need to know,' before I'm almost pushed outside and the door closed behind me. Of my father, there is no sign. *Families.*

My journey home, through Friday evening traffic, is horrendous. The slow crawl of the M42 traffic would put a snail to shame and, expecting the M5 to be just as bad, I turn off to travel down close to Stratford upon Avon and then head south to join the A429, the old Roman Fosse Way.

Big mistake.

It takes me five miles before I can overtake the small car attempting to pull a caravan twice its length, and another five to overtake a huge refrigerated lorry, only to be forced to stop at a mini roundabout in picturesque Stow-on-the-Wold for a car joining from the right. This car then edges through the rest of the town at an ultra-cautious five miles an hour and the remaining miles to the outskirts of Cirencester at a speed not once exceeding 32 miles an hour – or just over half my desired (legal) speed, the driver even planting themselves in the middle of two lanes on the only stretch dedicated to overtaking. I have no regrets for doubting the driver's ability and their parentage.

Tired and hungry, the approach to Much Slaughter has never seemed more welcoming. Just like the light in my neighbour's doorway as Wickham calls out, 'Supper's ready, put your feet up and I'll bring it across.' I swear the man's a living saint.

As I unlock my front door, Daggers bounds up to welcome me home, his tail wagging nineteen to the dozen and with only a slight disapproving look at being left for so long with only Carlton to release him briefly. But then he seems to take an inordinate amount of time to do his duty, as if he's making a point.

'Come on, Daggers, Wickham will be here in a moment.'

At the sound of the name, Daggers bounds up the garden and hurtles back inside, while I grab a bottle of wine and pour two glasses, then scuttle into my sitting room to set the fire going. A couple of puffs from the leather bellows and a handful of small branches later, it's a roaring inferno. It took me weeks to perfect the art of the log fire but maybe there's hope yet for me to win country girl status.

By the time I've positioned two side tables, Wickham taps lightly at the door and lets himself in. 'Just need to put the final touches on supper, dear lady.' Daggers loops around his legs as the dear man makes his way into the kitchen. There's only one thing that persuades my pooch to forego an open fire and that's food. Not for the first time I suspect that my strictures about not feeding a dog during food prep or consumption are not shared by my neighbour.

Wickham returns bearing a huge rectangular wooden tray. Daggers follows at his heels licking his lips and glancing guiltily in my direction before dropping in front of the log fire with a long, contented sigh.

Saint Wickham lowers the tray onto my lap as the heavenly aroma of hot food fills my nostrils. 'Boeuf Bourguignon,' he announces. 'I didn't know what time you'd be back so it's been gently bubbling away. I'm afraid I ate earlier; at my age it doesn't do to eat a big meal too close to bedtime.'

'Oh my goodness, Wickham, I'm so sorry. I didn't mean to keep you up.'

He snorts. 'I don't go to bed at six o'clock you know, this isn't a rest home for the elderly.' He sinks into the armchair across from me, stretches his legs and smiles. 'Now, enjoy your food.'

For the next few minutes the only sound is the clatter of my cutlery on the very large dinner plate, the occasional splutter from the fire and the almost continuous snores from my pooch. Wickham's eyes are closed, his fingers laced across his stomach.

With each mouthful of food and each sip of the excellent wine, a little more of today's anger ebbs away, replaced by feelings of loss, emptiness and sadness.

By some miracle of intuition or, knowing my neighbour, through watching me through almost closed eyes, the moment my plate is empty and I settle back replete, Wickham springs up and removes the tray. 'No dessert, I'm afraid, Catherine. Although I could rustle up some fruit?'

'I honestly couldn't manage another mouthful.' I intended a sigh of contentment. Unfortunately, it comes out as a very long burp and I go as red as the fire's flames. 'I'm so sorry.'

Wickham grins. 'In some countries, that would be considered a great compliment after a meal,' then he powers off to the kitchen. He's one of the fastidious ones who insist on instantaneous washing up.

I take the opportunity to delve into the heavy box I'd been given so unceremoniously.

When my host returns, I'm on the floor on my hands and knees, surrounded by half a dozen photo albums. It's immediately apparent my gran wasn't the most meticulous archivist: none of the albums are labelled with years and even the photos inside are labelled only randomly, sometimes with a location or name and sometimes with a whole sentence.

Placing a mug of hot cocoa by my elbow and a small cup of hot water next to his chair, Wickham watches me in silence until I sit back on my haunches and wipe a tear on my sleeve.

'Was it as bad as you'd feared, Catherine?'

I nod, and wipe another tear away, gazing at the only snap I've been able to find of me and Gran together, taken just a few years ago by the council house statue known locally as the *Floozie in the Jacuzzi.* Gran is wearing the most outrageously colourful woollen coat, all reds, greens and blues, and goodness knows what else, as we both mime surprised faces looking for water in the fountain. I remember taking it as a selfie, conscious how dowdy I looked in my sensible grey coat, and in no doubt as to who looked more in keeping with the statue. I can still hear her laughter as she recounted tales of all she'd got up to in her dating days around Victoria Square and the surrounding streets. 'It was much darker in those days, dearie. Much more fun, if you catch my drift.' *Go, girl.* I always loved her independent spirit.

In the middle of one album one particular snap catches my eye. I hold it up to show Wickham, forgetting that he's beaten a tactful retreat, content to leave me with my souvenirs. The photo is of an older couple, the beaming woman clearly Gran, with a young boy of six or seven, obviously my father, surrounded by a veritable ocean of toys and staring morosely at the camera. They're in a neatly manicured garden that's nothing like Gran's. But I suppose decades of growth, planting, pruning and replanting would account for that. The photo's black and white but, judging by the flowers, it's summer. Something of the pose stirs a memory of Pixie's photo on the vestry wall. Goodness knows what brought that to mind because the three people in her photo, the location and the look couldn't be more different. Nevertheless, my gut rumbles, and since, courtesy of Wickham, it can't be from hunger, I guess I'd better pay attention. Then I realise, it's not the photo itself but Anna's challenge that matters: look behind the facts and feel the emotions.

In the vestry, the key had been the young child, so I start at the same point, with my father, and wonder how much can be hidden behind the eyes of a child. His face shows the classic resentment of a small child told to sit still and behave when all he wants to do is be free and play. But staring at his eyes, the thin line of his mouth, the tightness of his skin, that's not what I feel. There's something deeper.

Try as I might, I can't get any further, anymore more than I can with his father, Gran's husband and my grandfather. He feels like a cardboard cut-out, one of those pop singer images you can have your picture taken with, almost real, yet totally false. Which ties in with how little I know about him. I guess every family has a person like that: someone about whom all questions are deflected, buried or ignored. My father took exactly that approach with his father, at any mention of him he'd stand up, leave the room and slam the door. My grandfather died years before I was born and this is one of the few images I've ever seen. And it's giving no feelings away. Just a sense that there's some connection between the boy in the album in front of me and the girl, Pixie, in the vestry frame.

Frustrated, I turn back to the box. In the bottom is a Christmas-themed plastic bag. I'm expecting it to hold more albums but as I empty the contents out, it turns out to be bundles of letters. My heart races. How romantic. I've seen this on countless TV drama and films. The young woman, the handsome young man. Convention or mismatched parents attempting to thwart young love. The illicit correspondence. And finally, the magic moment when they walk up the aisle, united in Holy Matrimony.

But the story these letters have to tell is far darker and unpleasant.

Chapter 26

The next morning finds four of us sitting on uncomfortable wooden folding chairs in the vestry of St Cyril's church.

Wickham, Boothby, Glen and I (Scott had inexplicably declined) had initially assembled, at Glen's request, at the Crimson Courgette hoping our combined brainpower might generate a breakthrough in the investigation. But we'd soon been driven out by the mass of noisy and inquisitive Saturday brunchers. I'd volunteered my cottage but the chief inspector had pulled himself up to his full six feet and announced, rather officiously, that he didn't conduct formal police business in the comfort of people's homes.

'Goodness, Inspector,' I retort, as we arrive in the vestry, 'anyone would think you were about to arrest me.'

'Don't tempt me, Ms de Barnes.'

Thankfully, just as my blood runs cold, there's the hint of a raised eyebrow. I punch him lightly on his arm.

'Ah, assaulting a police officer. Definitely an arrestable offence.'

'Inspector Parva.' Boothby's voice echoes around the room. 'I'm sure you didn't convene this conference simply to find out how many charges you can lay on our beloved chocolatier. Although, to be honest, Catherine does look as if she's just spent the night in a police cell.'

'Enough, Wing Commander.' Wickham intervenes to protect me, waving his hand in Boothby's face. 'Ms de Barnes attended a family funeral yesterday and it wasn't an easy time.'

Boothby splutters. 'Absolutely. Got it, Church Warden. Mouth buttoned.'

'To be fair, guys,' I interrupt, 'my appearance probably owes more to me delving into family secrets well into the small hours.'

'That's interesting. Would you like to tell us about it?' Wickham's question sounds like something out of a coaching manual but I know he means well. And, in view of what I learnt *and* in the ongoing absence of my boyfriend, I feel the need to bare my soul.

I nod. 'Just give me a moment. It's like something out of that TV programme, *Who Do You Think You Are*?'

We've only been here five minutes and already my neck and shoulders are aching from the uncomfortable chairs so I gain time by rolling my shoulders and then my head.

'Did you get any sleep at all, Cat?' Wickham looks worried.

I shrug. I'm not about to admit it, but I didn't, as I could tell from my mirror, before I left the house. I've enough bags under my eyes to carry a family's weekly shop. And as for my hair, don't get me started...

'Strangely enough, guys, it turned into something like a police investigation.'

Glen grunts. 'Well I hope you had more success with that than you've had with our current investigation.'

I take a deep breath, hoping I can get through the next few minutes without becoming an emotional wreck. *These are your friends, Cat. It doesn't matter.*

Okay, here we go. 'There are two things you need to know. First, I'm not close to my parents. And second, my gran, who's just died, was the most wonderful woman I've ever known.' My throat constricts and I swallow hard at the memories flooding in.

'Nobody in my family would ever talk much about her, my father's mother. At least, not in any detail. And the slightest mention of Grandad, who died before I was born, would be met with a silent shrug from my mother and my father storming out of the room. And being in a huff for days. It was the same yesterday at the wake. And the neighbours spent so much time conducting a review of past funerals that it was like an episode of *Wish You Were Here...?* No chance to pump them for any information about her. I learnt more from the minister's eulogy than I did from the wake and four decades with my family.'

Wickham comes over and gives me the biggest hug.

Boothby mutters, 'Families, not easy, what?'

And Glen nods, thoughtfully but I think sympathetically.

'But then, just as I'm leaving, my mother rushes up and thrusts a large box at me. Which was the cause of my sleepless night – and might just be the start of a breakthrough in our cases.'

I feel the atmosphere change, and I can see from their faces that they're puzzled and curious. 'Bear with me, you'll see the link. Now, my parents would never say anything openly, but there have always been hints about some alleged disgrace in the family, something to do with Gran and the war. There were a few interesting photos in the album that looked as if they might be clues, but as Gran rarely labelled anything properly, things only began to make sense when I discovered the bag of letters in the bottom of the box.'

I glance at my friends. Boothby's so caught up in the story that he's twiddling his moustache so hard I fear he'll pull out every single hair. Wickham is perched close to the edge of his seat, so close that he looks as if he'll topple over. And even Glen has forgotten to play with his sunglasses or his pencil.

'It took me all night and goodness knows how many false starts, to piece the story together into something that makes sense. It may not be the right story, or totally right, but it's close. And it does have relevance for us.

'The story starts with a man, a good-looking military type a bit older than Gran and one who crops up in a few of the photos, often in front of a racing car, but none of them are ever labelled. Not once. Which made me wonder if it was deliberate.'

Boothby mutters, 'It's not what you see, it's what you don't see, eh?'

I nod. 'Exactly. That's where the letters come in. It seems he was an army captain Gran met when she was delivering trucks during the war. He was a former racing driver and one day he made the mistake of letting Gran sit in one of them. Gran, being Gran, started it up and before the man could stop her, she'd raced round the track at such a speed that two things happened: one, the captain nearly fainted with fear, and two, when he recovered he was madly in love.

'There are no photos for the next bit but it seems they got together, she got pregnant and in less than a year, it was all over. Her family forced her to give up the baby for adoption and she never forgave them. The *Great Family Shame* had been buried. Then later, she met and married my grandfather. But even when my father came along, she never wanted to talk about any of it. She reluctantly shared a little bit with me over the last few years but it was never more than a couple of sentences. It's probably not surprising that my father left home as soon as he could and had virtually no contact with them.'

Wickham squeezes my hand and his warmth brings a lump to my throat as he murmurs, 'It's never easy being brought up in a place full of secrets.'

I swallow. 'The stupid thing is, it never occurred to me to wonder why he had a different surname to my gran. I mean, I just grew up with it. It was only last night looking through the photos that I realised that he took my mum's surname when they got married. So instead of becoming Hall, they became Peter and Mary Tavy.

'Anyway, when I was growing up, I did ask my parents why I never saw those grandparents, but they just got cross and shut me up. I don't remember my father hugging me much or showing much emotion and maybe that's why – he was just used to closing down anything unpleasant. When I got into my teens, they relented, I met my gran and finally started getting close to her.'

Wickham sighs. 'All that, just from a few photos and letters.'

'That's where it helps us. It's all about the stories behind the stories, what we're told and what we're not told. We need to start looking at the stories behind the stories our suspects have told us.'

Glen drums his fingers on the chair. 'Which means what, exactly?'

I remind myself that, as a police officer, he's a facts man and all this 'stories behind stories' stuff must be leaving him uneasy. 'The point is, Glen, we have to look deeper, behind what our suspects have told us. Suppose we start with the stories around the theft. Dale would be the most obvious suspect because he'd know the value of the pyx and probably have the contacts to sell it on. But his story stacks up – even the customer whose unexpected call made him late checks out.'

Glen nods. 'We've also done a background check on the customer in case they were in it together. We found nothing untoward and there were no obvious influences. Everything is as it seems.'

'So who else had knowledge and access?' I take a deep breath and look at each of them, suddenly apprehensive.

Glen shakes his head. 'You're going to point the finger at the major, I suppose.'

'I simply go where the evidence points, Chief Inspector.'

He glowers.

'I remember her saying that the diocese has been trying to get rid of her for years. But she didn't want to say why. It seems a lot of effort for them to go through if it's just that her face doesn't fit, or that she's offended some bigwig, so I reckon there must be more to it. Sadly, she wouldn't be the first church warden to help themselves from the till.'

This time it's Wickham who interrupts. 'She's honest as the day is long, that one, I'm certain of it. Anna comes down like a ton of bricks if there's even the merest hint of impropriety.'

I value his character judgement highly, even if it's pretty much, word for word, what Boothby said.

'But there's another story somewhere, something that not quite right. It's all a little too smooth, too practised. So, for example, all this about tending her horses the day of the murder. And yet she was jolted almost out of her skin when she met a horse on our walk. Hardly what you'd expect from someone who's used to being close to them.'

Boothby shakes his head. 'I still don't see it. She walks a straight line, that one.'

'Anyone else?' Glen extracts his notebook. 'The administrator? My specialist boys have been looking at her, but apart from a few minor skirmishes when she was a teenager, she's another one who seems off the hook. And the major seems sure the vicar would never let her near the safe or any sets of keys.'

'Besides, what motive would she have had, Inspector?' Boothby seems rather troubled at the idea she might be involved.

'Apart from money, you mean?' Glen snorts.

'She's never struck me as being in particular financial need.'

I nod. 'Her husband has a pretty good job at that place over in Swindon. Anna speaks very highly of how well she's done after a rough start. Would she really want to jeopardise all that? I don't think this story is about the need for money.'

Boothby strokes his whiskers. 'Surely there are more people with access to the safe?'

'Probably not. Anna says Reverend Cross was an absolute stickler for security, so very few people had access. Mind you, Scott's the same at St Cyril's.'

Glen jumps to his feet. 'Of course. It has to be Cross. Unlimited access. No wonder he was so cagey about security if he'd already stolen the goods and put in a replica. The fewer people who had access, the better his chances of concealing the switch. If he did swap them, though, the original will be long gone by now.' He slumps back down, dejected.

'Which leads us neatly onto his murder and the events in Much Slaughter.' Now it's my turn to feel discouraged. 'I still think they're connected. But for the moment, there's a missing link.'

Glen makes a big show of flicking through his notes. 'The only people we've been able to place anywhere near the murder scene have cast-iron alibis. Dale's the only link between the two, but he's already been eliminated.' He winces. 'Sorry. The mysterious runner and her TV drama stack up. So too does that suspicious Culkerton bloke, although I'll nick him one of these days for something.'

I immediately feel sorry for Ashley, so to divert Glen, I add, 'Even the boy's story about finding the stolen items by the roadside is backed up by CCTV.'

'Photographic evidence, what?' adds the Wing Commander, helpfully.

'Which is my point. Every picture tells a story. Like in this one.'

I dig around in my handbag and with a theatrical flourish produce Gran's snap of the trio. 'Remind you of anything?'

'It's as if they've been posed in the same position as the one in St Ignatius,' Glen mutters.

Boothby peers long and hard at it. 'By jove, you think it's the same photographer, don't you?'

'Not quite. But hang in there, Wing Commander, while I explain. As I said earlier, every picture tells a story and this one's no exception. But the story captured in the moment the picture was taken, the story you put together when you look at the picture and the story lying behind the picture aren't necessarily all the same. And to be fair, mostly it doesn't matter too much.'

I pause to check they're following my drift. Wickham nods encouragingly, Boothby harrumphs 'exactly', and Glen looks like all three of us are the wise monkeys.

'Sometimes the message you get from the picture is simply the message you need to hear at that moment because the picture mirrors something in you.'

My gut rumbles and my throat constricts, so I take a gulp of water. 'To be honest, I would have seen this photo of Gran and her family as nothing more than a sad reminder of her lovely lively self, her completely forgotten husband and my cold father if Anna Valley hadn't challenged me to look at the photo in their vestry and work out not so much what I saw but what I felt.' I gulp and Boothby pats me warmly on the shoulder.

'When I did the same with a load of my gran's photos, I found I could string some sort of narrative together. And however I played that narrative, this photo...' I wave it in the air like a trophy, 'demanded to be the centrepiece. If I left it out or put it to one side, the other pieces wouldn't hold together.' I blow my nose.

Now they're all looking blank. Sympathetic, but blank.

'When I turned that idea on the vestry photo, things got really interesting. If that photo demanded to be the centre of the narrative, where was the story similar? Was it about an illegitimate child? Was it about a woman with a secret past? Or a man with history? What was the unseen story between the two adults while the child played innocently in front of them? And finally, the penny dropped. It was none of those. It was about something I already knew but didn't realise I knew.'

I fold my hands across my lap as if I'm Miss Marple about to take up her knitting at the end of another success. 'I just need to check a couple of loose ends and then I believe you'll have your man, as the saying goes. At least for the theft. But we need the element of surprise, so if you'd care to walk me home, Inspector, I'll tell you my plan. Assuming you agree.'

Chapter 27

If Anna Valley is surprised to see Glen and myself march into St Iggy's shortly before the start of Sunday's Matins service, she doesn't show it. Indeed, we're barely through the door before she shoots across to shake hands with Glen, kiss me on both cheeks, grab service and hymn books from a startled usher and show us into a pew just a few rows from the front. Then she continues across the front of the church, her shoes rattling on the stone flagstones, and disappears into the vestry. I imagine her issuing last minute detailed instructions to whoever's down to lead today's service, which brings a smile to my face, and I imagine, for a stranger, she'd be just what the doctor ordered. Which brings a scowl to my face. There's been neither sight nor sound of Linton since he let me down so badly, not the slightest hint of an apology, and I'm *not* making the first move. I'm so over him, I decide, while at the same time wiping a tear from my eye. I blow my nose and force myself back in to the here and now.

I hate being too close to the front in an unfamiliar church: there's no chance to watch and copy the regulars, and while anyone I've ever asked always answers, 'we do it the normal way here', I can guarantee *their* normal is bound to be different. At least I'll have one person to follow: a tall, slim woman, her short hair swallowed up in an enormous straw hat.

I swivel in the pew, pretending to be listening to Glen wittering on about something or other, but actually so I can check out our fellow worshippers. Or rather, worshipper. The only person behind us is an elderly man in a loud check jacket who, I just know, when he stands up, will be wearing bright red trousers. He's parked himself in the middle of the middle pew and as I turn, he drops to his knees, resting his prayer book on the top of the pew in front of him. Maybe my move hasn't been as subtle as I'd hoped.

The door opens to admit a couple who must be in their mid-eighties. He leans heavily on a walking frame and she leans heavily on his arm so I can't work out who's supporting who. They wave away the proffered books and slowly progress to the pew opposite the elderly man with whom they exchange a brief nod.

All three stand as the vestry door opens so Glen and I scramble to our feet. 'Oh good grief,' he mutters as the minister walking out in cassock, surplice and blue preaching scarf turns out to be none other than Anna Valley. His shock is nothing compared to mine: the blue scarf has instantly taken me back to Gran's funeral and I search fruitlessly in my handbag for a tissue. Glen, bless him, offers me a pristine ironed white handkerchief (yep, definitely married) and I snuffle as quietly as possible while Anna walks across to the small litany desk and rearranges her books. I don't remember Gran ever going to church or talking about having any kind of faith, but in a strange way, I feel she's here with me.

'Welcome to this service of Matins.' Anna's voice is strong and clear, and her eyes range across the pews to look each of us in the eye. 'And a special welcome to our visitors this morning.' She stares right at us, possibly for a few moments too long, then without even glancing at her service book she starts, 'Beloved, we are come together in the presence of Almighty God...'

Forty minutes later, Anna proceeds past us on her way to the church door. By the time Glen and I have sat down for the customary few moments of prayer and then prepare to leave, the rest of the congregation (such as it is) has vanished and Anna is on her way back towards us.

'I'm assuming this isn't a social or a religious visit?' Her eyebrows arch and I can feel an edgier tone to her voice and the tension in her body.'

'No, Major, it isn't.' Glen's voice is calm and low.

She pauses for a moment and nods. 'You'd better join me in the vestry then, while I tidy up.'

Glen follows her, while I pop to the back of the church to replace the service and hymn books in their correct places. I know from past misdemeanours how important this can be in some places.

By the time I reach the vestry, Anna is hanging her robes on two stout wooden hangers.

'Anna, I didn't realise you were...'

'A minister? Yes, a rare CofE courtesy, on account of my previous role in the Sally.'

Glen looks confused.

'The Salvation Army, Chief Inspector. As an officer, I was accorded certain training and given the status of leading services. When I transferred my allegiance to the Church of England, a kind bishop, Bishop Norton actually, bent the rules slightly and licensed me as a reader. Of course, it helps the diocese and the parish as well. It means we don't have to have a vicar for non-Eucharistic services. That is, services which don't have Holy Communion and therefore don't require a vicar, Inspector.' She smiles and he nods his understanding, scribbling some notes in his book. When he starts to suck his pen, I realise he's omitted his customary sunglasses for the occasion. We are honoured indeed.

Glen skims through his notes and looks thoughtful while Anna's gaze moves from one of us to the other, her eyebrows raised in enquiry. My attention is drawn once more to the photo. The silence lengthens.

With a deep breath, I look her straight in the eye. 'Anna, I need to be honest with you.' Her questioning look becomes even more pronounced. 'I have the distinct impression there's something you're not...'

I get no further as the vestry door is flung open, causing all three of us to jump in surprise.

Pixie pops her head around the door, oblivious to the fact that she's almost caused three heart attacks, including even the customarily placid chief inspector. 'Anna, don't forget you've got a meeting at twelve.' She smiles at each of us briefly, her necklace flashing as it catches the light, and as she closes the door with a loud crash that shakes the vestry panels, I stare at the photo again. I wonder...

Running to the vestry door, I call her back.

'Pixie, is that the same necklace as in the photo over there?'

She pales as she stares at it, transfixed. Given my recent experience of feelings from photos, I can only imagine what she must be experiencing as she whispers, 'Yes'.

Anna crosses the room and puts her arms around her. 'It was an anonymous gift one Christmas when things with the family were at their worst. No-one ever knew who it came from, although the official story was that it came from her mother.'

Pixie sniffs. 'It was you, though, wasn't it, Anna?'

The major stiffens and turns bright red before mumbling simply, 'Yes.'

Pixie smiles weakly, let's out a sob and darts out, the three of us staring after her in stunned silence.

Anna swallows hard and turns to Glen. 'Chief Inspector, I wonder if we might continue this at my cottage? I'm feeling rather – uncomfortable, here.'

'I thought that woman said you needed to be here for a meeting, Major?'

Anna swallows heavily. 'The PCC meets at my house, Chief Inspector.'

'Of course we can, Anna.' I jump in before Glen has a chance to say anything else. He can be very officious when he's on duty and, in my gut, I know we'll get more from her if she feels like she's on secure territory. He nods.

***

The short walk, conducted in silence, gives me and, I suspect, the other two the opportunity to think. Although, so far, the encounter has left me completely befuddled. I only hope Glen has more ideas. All I've got is an even greater sense of something being held back, and the feeling that the fog is even denser.

Anna directs us into her sitting room before suddenly bolting out and returning only moments later. Odd. Too short to be a loo break, and definitely not long enough to put the kettle on, even if she'd asked us what we'd like to drink.

She then crosses to a glass-fronted low cabinet, drops the top and extracts three small glasses. 'Sherry?'

I nod agreement while Glen shakes his head and mutters, 'On duty.'

Anna winces as she pours two small portions and hands me one, waving us towards the sofa. I gratefully sink into the comfortable cushions but the police officer remains on his feet.

'Major, I think you owe us an explanation about what we just saw.'

I'm not sure she owes us any such thing but thankfully Anna doesn't seem to mind.

'It was one of the unspoken truths of the village, Chief Inspector. Everyone knew what she and her mother were put through. And everyone sympathised. These days of course, that horrible man wouldn't get away with it, the police and social services would make sure of that. But back then, well, we weren't so – enlightened. So we did little things behind the scenes to support them. My gift was just one of many.'

'But hang on, Anna.' Maths has never been my strong point but she's mid-forties and Pixie is thirty-five…

It seems she's been following my line of thought. 'Right. I was fourteen. But sometimes kids just sense what another kid's going through. Name-calling. Tripping up. Jeering. And in my case, as a teenager, hormones bubbling. A burning sense of righteous indignation. I wasn't the sort of person to beat up the thugs. So I gave her one of my necklaces.'

She wanders across the window and stares out, her back to us, while I'm trying to process this, the generous warm-hearted teenager and the suspected killer. Why is she suddenly so clipped? Was there more to the relationship back then than she's letting on? Or even now? Yet again, what's she holding back?

Sensing we need a change of direction, I put my glass carefully down on a coaster and walk across to join her at the window.

'Anna, can I ask you about you and horses?'

She half turns, stiffening, so I wonder if I've just blown any chance. She swallows the remains of her sherry in one gulp, clears her throat and crosses to the chairs. 'Let's sit down, Cat.'

I follow her and sink back down, sipping my own drink very slowly so as to keep a clear head. My gut rumbles.

Anna glances at Glen then back to me. 'Go on.'

'Well, it's just, erm, when we asked you for your whereabouts, you said you were tending horses, which you did every day.'

She stares at me for a few moments. 'So?'

'So, your behaviour seemed rather odd when we were out on our walk and we came across that rider. The horse really seemed to spook you. Yet you claim to be with horses every day.'

She stares hard as the seconds tick by, as if hoping I'm going to let her off the hook. Having got this far, no way am I about to do that. I stare her out, acutely aware of Glen, pen poised, and pray he won't give in to impatience.

He doesn't, and finally, she sighs. 'I could say the horse and rider caught me unawares and made me jump. But you're right. What I told you wasn't quite accurate – although not untrue.'

She pauses. Glen and I exchange confused looks and wait. She needs to find her own words in her own time.

As she turns away to stare out of the window or, more likely, to avoid looking at us, I notice her neck has turned red and blotchy. She's clearly embarrassed.

'I *was* with a filly,' she sighs. 'It's just she had, has, two legs rather than four.'

She lets the implications of this sink in, before turning to face us square on, hands on her hips, defiance radiating from every pore.

'I'm gay. That's why I'm no longer in the Salvation Army.'

I'm shocked. Not by Anna being gay, but because she felt she had to leave a Christian body because of it. 'Is that really still an issue? Surely, these days...?'

Anna suddenly starts to cry, plunging her hand into her pocket and extracting a handful of tissues, all of which are soon soggy as she mops eyes and nose. Finally, she sags into a chair.

'If you're an officer, yes, it is. Especially in some of the more traditional rural enclaves. And if you're a major, well, as they so delicately put it, "we expected better of you." I sometimes felt there would have been more support and understanding if I'd assassinated the Archbishop of Canterbury.' She puts her head in her hands and her elbows sink onto her knees. 'After all those years struggling to come to terms with who I really was, their reaction felt like a kick in the teeth.'

'Anna, I'm so sorry.' I spring onto her chair arm and put my arms around her. 'I had no idea. I just felt you were hiding something. Sorry.'

She looks up, her eyes red. 'I understand, Cat. And it's not just a theft, it's also a murder investigation. I should have told you both earlier.'

'Yes, you should.' Glen sounds more hurt than angry.

'I know I should've trusted you. But you learn to be careful, to protect yourself.' She calls out, 'Honey, it's safe.'

The tall woman from church pops her head around the door, smiles and announces, 'I'm Glendalough, coffee coming up,' almost as if it's all one word, and in a broad southern Irish lilt, before darting back into the kitchen so fast I'm surprised she doesn't meet herself coming out.

'Anna, forgive me for asking.' I loosen my hug slightly. 'Is that why the diocese wants to get rid of you?'

She gives a weak smile, her lips barely moving. 'I think so. Of course, no-one is actually saying so, they're too afraid of legal action. But I was only able to transfer across because Bishop Norton was so kind.'

Another horrible thought pops into my head, one I really don't want to ask at this moment but know I must. 'Where did Mark Cross stand on this?'

She shakes her head. 'That's a very good question, Catherine. To my face, he was always coolly polite and proper. I got the distinct impression that as long as I was of use to him in the parish and providing we were discrete, he wouldn't actively rock the boat. But I was left in no doubt that should I feel it was "time I moved on" as he put It, more than once, that far from standing in my way, he'd be very relieved.'

Glen shakes his head while writing copious notes in his little book. I really feel for the two women, caught in an impossible situation.

Anna's partner returns and places a tray of steaming coffee, milk, sugar and biscuits by my side. I smile at her warmly. 'Thanks, Glendalough.' She halts mid-stride before bursting into laughter. Anna's laughing too.

'What?' I'm confused. Especially since the inspector also seems to be struggling to keep a professional straight face.

The two women are in such hysterics they can't speak, they just reach out and link hands.

The chief inspector, however, seems only too happy to enlighten me. 'Her name is Glenda, Catherine. It's Glenda Lough. Two words.'

Anna's partner smiles at me. 'Don't worry, it's a common mistake. I do speak rather fast.' She lifts Anna's hands, and lovingly, gently, kisses them. I look away, to give them their moment of intimacy.

As I do so, my mind floats back to the intimacy in the vestry photo and I jolt. What an idiot. I've been reading quite the wrong story. 'Anna, I know you've got a meeting shortly, but can you text me when you finish? I think I know who stole the pyx.'

The atmosphere immediately chills and both she and the inspector look totally taken aback. But before anyone can say anything else, her doorbell rings and moments later, the first two attendees wander in, oblivious.

'Chief Inspector, we have another invite to issue.'

Chapter 28

An hour and a half later Glen and I return to St Iggy's vestry. Anna is setting up an electric three-bar fire which is dutifully setting about removing the worst of the chill. It also adds an eerie scarlet glow to the immediate surroundings, including giving the major's eyes a fiery almost-devilish red glow.

Anna stares at us, her face an interesting mix of worry and wariness, a few wrinkles showing around the edge of her eyes and the corners of her mouth. I'm not sure she's going to find what I've got to say any easier than it must have been for her to share about her partner and my hackles rise at all she's been put through by those in authority.

The chief inspector sets four chairs in a square, like the corners of a Rubik's cube. Which, come to think of it, is quite appropriate for the puzzle I'm about to lay out, which has taken me as long to solve as the original puzzle did.

Anna throws herself onto one of the chairs, which creaks ominously. Glen hesitates for a moment before sinking into the chair opposite, slowly and methodically taking out his notebook, skimming through a few pages and extracting his pen which he proceeds to suck while his gaze wanders around the room. He is patently avoiding looking directly at Anna.

I circle the chairs a couple of times before, with growing apprehension, announcing 'We're just waiting for one more person to join us...'

Right on cue, the vestry door opens and relief floods my body, along with a fresh blast of cold air. The new entrant peers uncertainly around the door before creeping in and hovering by the doorway.

'Come in, Pixie. Do join us.'

She stares at the two vacant chairs as if trying to work out which would be safer, although the only difference is whether Glen or Anna is on her left.

I solve her dilemma by perching carefully on one of them and waving her to the other. Pixie looks relieved as she sits and adjusts the hem of her blue cotton dress to cover her knees, before places her hands decorously in her lap.

I smile gently at the two women, going over in my mind all they've had to put up with in their different lives, until finally their uncomfortable shuffling prompts me to begin.

'Thank you both for joining us.'

They grunt in oddly similar tones before Pixie mutters, 'There's not exactly much choice when it's a murder enquiry and a police inspector "requests your presence".' She adds air punctuation to the last bit, causing the merest hint of a smirk to flit across Anna's face.

I nod, as my gut rumbles, then take a deep breath, ready to plunge in head-first. 'In this case, there have been two completely different puzzles. In that respect, Chief Inspector, you were absolutely right.'

Glen gently inclines his head and nods, without gloating too obviously. He knows what's coming, because I've spent our waiting time filling him in on what I'm about to reveal, inviting his scepticism and finally gaining his agreement.

'I admit,' I say, 'for much of the past few weeks, I've been looking in totally the wrong direction.'

'Too right,' the church warden mutters.

'I was so busy looking at the common links: Mark Cross, Dale Hill and the theft as a motive for murder, that I missed a far simpler explanation. There are indeed two totally different stories, each with their own cast of villains and heroes. Each with their own motives and secrets. Even with different locations.'

I sigh. It's no good, I can't do the Great Reveal sitting on this dreadful folding chair, so I move behind it, putting my hands firmly on the wooden back so I can look from Anna to Pixie.

'It was in this very room that our first story begins.' *Careful, Cat, this sounds less Great Reveal and more like Great British Bake Off.* 'Our first perpetrator had a long association with the church. Then something happened, and I'll come back to what that was, something which prompted them to creep into this room, cross to this safe…' I give a dramatic sweep of my arm, pointing to the far corner and gratifyingly see all three of them twist to follow my direction 'and remove the gloriously decorated and much reviled sixteenth century pyx. I'm guessing the person had no idea of its actual history and hence it's true value, just that it seemed valuable. And now we have more of a timeframe, the Chief Inspector is confident his specialist officers will be able to corroborate this. It was only when the person tried to get it valued that they had the dilemma of whether to put it back. Putting it back would've spoilt the whole point, so wasn't an option, because this wasn't supposed to be about the money – although that plays a part later. No, the only real option was to put in a replica. You see, because of the person's long association with the church, they were perfectly happy to play the long game. I think that maybe they even hoped that when the replica was discovered, the finger of blame would be pointed at Mark Cross.'

'Oh really, Ms de Barnes, this is starting to sound like some second-rate movie.'

Good heavens, she speaks! I cross to stand behind Glen's chair, so I can stare at both the tetchy major and the timid Pixie. 'Yes, it does, doesn't it? But nothing about this crime is sophisticated or well-thought-out.'

'Surely if it was done on the spur of the moment, then it was about the money?' Anna looks very confused and I can't blame her. I'd felt the same until very recently.

'Except that you mustn't confuse not well-thought-out with unplanned. Stealing the pyx was definitely planned. It wasn't about money, it was about revenge. And revenge is an emotion that tends to cloud judgement and get in the way of clear planning, wouldn't you say?'

Both women nod, as does Glen. Although he adds a knowing smile.

'So, who could have been so keen for vengeance?'

I walk two complete circuits before halting and putting my hands on the back of Pixie's chair. She stiffens. But my gaze is elsewhere.

'As you know, Church Warden, I've long suspected you were holding something back. And after what you told us this lunchtime, it turns out, I was right.'

Pixie leans forward, her necklace-comforter grasped tightly in her hand. 'Anna, what have they made you say? Tell them it isn't true.'

Anna shakes her head as she leans forward and grabs Pixie's hands. 'It's okay, love. I just didn't tell them about Glenda quite as soon as I should have.'

'Which is hardly surprising, since the authorities haven't exactly always treated you well. Especially your vicar. I can understand why you'd want revenge. And stealing a valuable item from under his nose would've been doubly sweet because it would incriminate him and make the diocese look foolish.'

'Now, wait a minute.' Anna's nostrils flare and she leaps up, but the Inspector lightly taps her arm and motions her back into her seat, where she continues to huff and puff. The words 'preposterous' and 'slander' feature several times.

'As it turns out, Major, you're absolutely right. That explanation would be possible but preposterous. No, I think your revenge for how you've been treated has been to make sure you did outstanding work, both as a warden and as a minister. And indeed, as a partner.'

Anna nods vigorously and a large tear rolls down her face. She hastens to the vestry table to retrieve a box of tissues.

'Unfortunately, that means my attention turns to you, Pixie.'

Pixie jolts and turns deathly pale.

I cross to behind her chair and put my hands on her shoulders. 'Don't worry, I'm not suggesting you stole the pyx. I really don't think that's your style. Although I'm sure you had plenty of opportunities.'

Glen stares at her for a few moments before announcing, almost reluctantly, 'We know you didn't have anything to do with it, Mrs Combe.'

She gives him the sweetest smile. Which makes what I'm about to say even harder. I start to feel queasy.

'Although we know *you* weren't responsible, I'm afraid the culprit is near to home. It was your father, Roby.'

She starts, but less than I would have expected and makes no move to disagree. I'm left with the impression that even if she didn't know for certain, she'd had her suspicions.

'When I began to suspect Roby, I asked the Inspector to do some discrete and off-the-record enquiries. It was reasonably easy to deduce roughly when the theft had occurred, because the most likely time for him to have done it would have been very soon after he'd been sacked. And guess what? The team had no trouble finding a fence who remembered the object. It seems your father made quite the impression, although I'm sorry to say, Pixie, not in a good way. "A sodden old drunk with a foul temper and a piece so valuable and distinctive that they wouldn't touch it with a bargepole." The fence apparently told your father that the best thing he could do would be to put it back.'

Anna pats Pixie's arm. 'I'm so sorry, sweetie.'

Glen, however, glances up from his note-taking. 'I wouldn't waste too much sympathy, Major. You knew, didn't you, Mrs Combe?'

I watch Pixie's face race through a range of emotions from defiance through fear to resignation.

'Until recently, I had no idea. Mum and I never saw a penny extra and he never dropped so much as a hint.'

'It must have taken a lot of the tarnish off his wish for revenge if he couldn't tell anyone, though.' Anna looks grim.

'Actually, Dad never cared what other people thought. The older he got, and the more sodden with the booze, the more he went into himself. So it doesn't really surprise me. Although, come to think of it, when he got particularly hammered, he'd mutter something about, "They messed with the wrong man when they did me over".'

Anna still looks as if she needs to find some solid ground. 'All those gifts we left. And he had a fortune all along. You really had no idea?'

Pixie looks pleadingly at her, then at Glen then me. When she speaks, there's desperation in her voice. 'You've got to believe me. It was only after the switch was discovered that I had my suspicions. But I had no proof. If he did manage to sell it, he certainly didn't stash the proceeds under his bed – there were plenty of empty booze bottles, yes. But no money and no pyx.'

My gut reckons she's telling the truth. So does my brain. And from what I've heard, the family never seemed to have even the smallest of luxuries. An idea strikes me. 'Could he have had a secret bank account?'

She snorts contemptuously. 'I'm the first person in my family to even have a bank account. And I won't begin to tell you dad's opinion of banks, so you can be sure my mum wouldn't have had one, either.'

'That's exactly why I don't think this had anything to do with money. My hunch is that he took it in lieu of the severance pay he reckoned he was owed. And because of the chance to get one over the authorities. Then, when he found out how much it was worth, he certainly wasn't going to hand it back, that would've seemed like yet another humiliation. That's probably when he got the idea of a cheap copy. To his mind, making a switch for something worthless would be yet another little victory, making his revenge even sweeter.'

Anna looks at Glen and me. 'So, what you're saying is, we've got some cheap seaside knock-off pyx. We've no idea where the proceeds of the crime are, or even if there are any proceeds because we've no idea what happened to the original?' She lets out a hollow laugh. 'Bloody typical.'

I shake my head. 'I fear you're right, Anna.'

Glen signs off his notes with a flourish. 'Of course, there's always the off chance it might turn up, one day. Out of the blue. You never know.'

Anna turns on him. 'You don't believe that for a moment, Chief Inspector.'

He shrugs. 'It's probably been melted down, I reckon.'

'And, Catherine, do you really believe that this has nothing to do with Mark's murder?'

I shrug. 'That, I'm afraid, I've yet to work out. At least fully, anyway.' My gut rumbles so loudly that everyone stares, which usually means that I'm on the right lines and, more urgently, that I need some food. 'Chief Inspector, shall we...?'

Chapter 29

Monday morning dawns bright and, for spring, relatively mild. The perfect opportunity to do some catching up with my lovely vicar friend, the Reverend Scott Willoughby. Dagenham's tail wags faster the closer we get to our destination.

My route doesn't take me past Bedside Manor so there's less chance of meeting Linton and delivering the speech I've practised a hundred times in my head and delivered full blast to both my bathroom mirror and my poor pooch. Which might be a good thing since, even though I'm so over him, we're bound to come across each other in a small village. Not that being over him has stopped me feeling unsupported at Gran's funeral or any the less puzzled as to what has happened. There have still been no texts or calls. Well, maybe now I'll get round to planning my business venture properly – there'll be no time for romance with all that. Men!

By the time Cherry conducts us through the vicarage garden, Daggers is so excited that anyone whose legs came into contact with his tail would be at severe risk of a broken limb. And once Daggers and Scott's dog, Barking, catch sight of each other, well, all hell's let loose in a flurry of tails, yapping and rolling in the grass. Within moments, Dagenham's fur, which I'd foolishly spent nearly two hours grooming before we left, is a matted tangle of leaves, mud and twigs. The two dogs bound around, making full use of the large garden.

I, however, am altogether more apprehensive.

Today is Scott's day off and he's dressed in a thick blue woollen turtle-neck and battered but expensive-looking sandy coloured chinos, probably going back to his days in the City years ago. He's lounging on a double swing seat and makes no effort to make room, although before I left the village a few months back, that's exactly what he'd have done, and we'd have spent a contented hour or so putting the world to rights.

Cherry produces a fold-up picnic chair and places it near to her partner. 'I'll leave you to it, then.'

As I watch her scurry back into the kitchen, I sense a deep sadness, so I fear Scott's re-entry into village life isn't improving. He merely nods as I sit in the creaking chair and we both stare ahead in silence. This is so far from the Scott I used to know, I have no idea how to start.

Mind you, there's no denying it is very pleasant just sitting in the early sunshine watching the two dogs rollicking around. Barking seems to be taking Daggers into every nook and cranny, reintroducing him to the smells after a break. And I suppose thirty-odd days in doggie-time is quite a break.

An early bee buzzes in a rather premature search for nectar. Several pigeons hoot amorously in the churchyard trees. Somewhere behind us a ewe bleats to her lamb. A tractor trundles past the bottom of the driveway on its way through the village and I smile as I picture the long queue of frustrated fuming motorists trapped behind it. Most of our local farmers are considerate and will pull into a gap if the line gets too long. A horn is honked out, so I'm guessing this isn't one of them. Welcome to the Cotswolds countryside.

I glance at Scott but he's still detached so I think I'll stretch my legs and do a little wander before I try to enlist his thoughts.

Everywhere there is new blossom and buds, although we're not yet at the bright colours and rich scents stage. If a fabulous aromatic, rainbow-coloured garden is God's gift, then weeds must be the grit in the oyster. And Scott's garden is both gem and grit: the weeds are giving the plants a good run for their money and at this stage I'm not sure which will prevail. I think back to last summer and I can hardly recall seeing a single weed. Even the grass beneath my feet seems uncharacteristically long. What on earth happened to Scott during his retreat to make it so hard for him to be here? One thing I do know is that there's no point in asking him outright: he'll tell us in his own good time.

As I amble, I wonder how Pixie and Anna are feeling today. Neither has been in touch, not that I expected they would be. And it will probably be a while before I can comfortably show my face in St Iggy's. Although all I've done is solve a theft from long ago. I take a vicious kick at the head of a dandelion and then wince as a shower of seeds scatters across even more of Scott's ill-kempt lawn.

My circle of the garden complete, I once more crouch on the picnic chair. 'Scott, I know you probably don't feel like this, but I need your advice.'

He grunts.

'Or at least the opportunity to put things into words.'

No response.

'I don't know if you read my email about yesterday's events up at St Iggy's?'

He doesn't respond, so I plough on and hope that I'm making some sort of sense.

'I'm grateful that the theft of the pyx has been resolved. But it's raised another dilemma. Solving the murder is as far off as ever. We're back where we started. Roby stole the pyx, we can be certain about that. But he can hardly have murdered Mark Cross.'

I pause for a few moments, but there's no response either from Scott or from my own thoughts.

'Let's assume for a moment that the murderer has some association with either St Iggy's or St Cyril's, given that Reverend Cross was associated with both. And, since Pixie doesn't seem to have known anything about her father's theft, I can't see why she'd want to get rid of the reverend, can you, Scott?'

If I'd hoped this might draw him out, I'm disappointed. He merely shrugs. But at least I know he's listening. And, unless I'm very much mistaken, a slight flicker of interest skims his eyes.

'Well, let's leave her for the moment. I still wonder about the major. We know Mark made life difficult for her, and her relationship with him was hardly what you'd expect between vicar and warden, even less vicar and a fellow minister of the gospel. But does his opposition to her lifestyle really give her a motive for murder? It's pretty drastic. And it's been going on for so long, so why would she disturb status quo now? Nothing seems to have changed. And even if it had, murder hardly seems likely. Is she really the type to fly off the handle so uncontrollably she'd kill him in a fit of anger? And if she'd planned it, I'm sure she'd have been more subtle about it. Unless, I suppose, he'd finally decided to take a stand? Even so, I can't imagine they had anything left to disagree about that hadn't already been said. It doesn't seem likely, does it?'

'No,' Scott mutters, almost under his breath. Which is progress, I suppose. He shifts slightly towards me.

'Of course it could be her partner, Glenda Lough. Perhaps in Anna's defence? But why now? And again, why rock the boat? Anyway, the chief inspector's done background checks and they're all clear. Do you know, I thought she was called Glendalough because she talked so fast.'

Scott smiles.

'You heard?'

'Of course. Ministers do talk to people. We're not hermits.'

'I'm perfectly aware of that, Scott. I remember meeting a whole clan of them last year. And if they were anything to go by, I can understand why becoming a hermit might have its attractions. Anyway, what do you think? Could Anna or Glenda be in the frame?'

He thinks long and hard, but just as I fear he's slipped back into his own world, he shakes his head. 'From what I've seen during the time I've been at St Cyril's, I'd have to say no. I just can't see it. With either of them.'

'I agree. And why in St Cyril's? If they'd been having an argument, it would hardly have been in our vestry, it would've been up in St Iggy's. And if it had been an argument that had got out of control, they wouldn't be thinking of stealing the 'silver'. This smacks of premeditation.'

Which brings no response from my friend, so I watch our two pets for a while as they curl up together on Barking's mat, Daggers with his head on his pal's haunches. From the outset they've been at ease with each other, Barking, marginally older, taking great delight in showing his younger protégée his own territory and the best smells. A role he picked up when Scott and I walked the countryside together before winter intervened.

'Maybe it was opportunistic.' Scott's first major contribution calls me back from my musing. 'What if Chief Inspector Parva was right all along and it was a theft gone wrong?'

I sigh. It would pain me to admit it, but it is a consideration. And at least I've finally piqued Scott's interest. 'Go on.'

'Well, if so, there would be two possibilities. Firstly, it was planned. By someone who'd need to be sufficiently familiar with our routines to know when the safe was likely to be open. Then they'd slip in and grab whatever they could lay their hands on, like the collections from the previous services.'

'Good thought, Scott.' Highly unlikely, in my opinion, but I don't want to discourage him now. 'Go on.'

'The second possibility is that someone just took a chance. Then they couldn't believe their luck when they noticed the safe was open with no sign of the vicar, so they simply helped themselves. In either case, when Mark came back and disturbed them, they just hit out indiscriminately and bolted with the first things they could lay their hands on.'

I sigh. 'And that's where I struggle with Glen's idea. If Mark had been pushed and struck his head on the edge of the vestry table, yes. But for some petty thief or chancer to grab a heavy candlestick and swing it with that force – it just doesn't feel right. Sorry.'

Scott gives the slightest smile. 'As it happens, I agree with you. So…'

'The trouble is, killing someone is a whole different ball game to theft. I mean, a lot of us might steal something if the motive and the conditions were right. But murder? Not many of us could commit a murder, not a cold, calculating, bloody one like Mark's, especially given that he was a relatively old man. And a vicar.'

'So, if we rule out theft as being the trigger, what are you left with?'

'Absolutely no idea, Scott. You?
'Nope.'

Oh dear, one step forward, two steps back.

With impeccable timing, Cherry arrives with two cups of coffee and (bringing a huge smile to my face), a plate of my very own chocolate macaroons. She grins as she places them between Scott and me. 'Bought, with my own fair hand, Ms de Barnes'.

She nods towards her partner and raises an enquiring eyebrow. I shrug and mouth, 'So-so'.

She nods, pensively, as she goes back to the house. I really feel for her, her shoulders droop and she seems so lost.

Scott's eyes are closed so I stretch out my legs and let the sun do it's relaxing, warming job while I try to empty my mind of murders and thefts and wardens and police officers, filling it instead with the soothing sounds of birds, bees, snoring pooches and a snoring vicar: what a wonderful countryside orchestra.

This seems like a good moment to practise what I've learnt about photos and their stories with Mark in our vestry. I've no photo, of course, just the fuzzy detail of my mind's picture, so I follow it from the bloody body of Reverend Cross splayed out on the floor in a seemingly posed cross shape. *That's an interesting thought: is there a link between his last name and the way he was posed?* It's a bit of a cliché, but you never know.

What about the rest of the vestry? My memory scans the closed safe, the messy desk, the closed drawers – I feel absolutely nothing from any of it. I can't picture anyone else in the room and get no sense of whether there'd been an argument or a deliberate confrontation.

I visualise the route the killer would have taken after the event: Glen hasn't said anything about bloody fingerprints on the vestry door so it's safe to assume it was open. There is an outside door from the vestry but I've never known anyone to use it and, judging by the huge ancient lock, it would have needed an equally huge key. So, the person will have left via the church. Then presumably they'd skirted round to get some protection from the trees and shadows, which is where some movement was seen. Again, I try to allow my feelings free rein but it's no more successful than it was indoors, except having a vague sense of a shadowy figure.

I sigh and grab another macaroon. Apart from my abortive investigations, this is such a lovely time. The sun's starting to warm my skin and I wonder if I can get the first tones of my summer tan. A slight breeze catches the hanging CDs Scott suspended causing them to tinkle.

As I turn towards the sound, a flash of bright sunlight catches them, causing me to screw up my eyes at the reflection, it's as bright as a torch. Which is what our witness said about the mysterious figure: that there was a glint, like a flash, from a phone or a torch. My mind whirs: what if what they saw was a reflection rather than a torch or a phone? After all, there would have been more than enough daylight to see where they were, they wouldn't need a torch. My gut rumbles as I try to recall where I've seen a similar effect recently.

Oh my goodness. I grab my phone. That might just be the key to unlock the *who*, if not the *why*. But in my experience – a sum total of two cases – if you know who the murderer is, you're very close to knowing *why* they did it because it lowers the number of options.

There's a click as my call is answered. 'Chief Inspector, I think I know who murdered Reverend Cross. No, I really don't want to tell you over the phone, it would be like announcing it to the entire village. How soon can you meet me in the vestry at St Cyril's? Excellent'

Scott turns his head towards me, his eyes still half-closed.

'Sorry, Vicar, did my excitement disturb you? Well, I can promise you, you ain't seen nothin' yet!'

He grunts.

'Having difficulty containing your own excitement, then, Scott? Look, can you let me check something in the vestry safe, please?'

He looks blank but thankfully agrees and, getting up, leads the way. I really don't want to voice my suspicions at the moment, not even to him.

Chapter 30

The next day, feeling every bit the TV detective gathering the crowds for the spectacular denouement, I corral Chief Inspector Glen Parva, church wardens Wickham and Anna Valley and Pixie, St Iggy's administrator, into the vestry at St Cyril's. After a sleepless night going over every single detail multiple times, taking the pieces and shuffling them in any number of permutations, I'm absolutely certain I finally have the story. Well, maybe ninety percent certain. Okay – pretty confident.

I stand up, survey the group and in best detective fashion, wander around behind each chair, doing a complete circuit before launching my over-rehearsed opening line.

'If Roby Mill stole the pyx, and I'm certain he did, what did he do with it? That's the key to unravelling this whole thing. You see, Roby couldn't peddle it straight away – he'd already tried and failed – and now knew that if he wasn't extremely careful, it would soon be traced back to him. It was about as hot a stolen property as you can get.'

There are gratifying nods of agreement.

'At first, I wondered if, when he stole it, he hoped the loss would be discovered so it would discredit his former employer, Mark Cross. But it wasn't discovered. So, given that he could easily have dropped a hint, plus the fact that we have a replica, I had to conclude that revenge for his sacking wasn't his motive. Or at least, not his main one.'

I pause for another circuit behind the chairs.

'Things only began to make sense when I realised that there was another person at the heart of all this, not just Roby. The shadowy figure spotted by two of our suspects. We identified the film runner, but she in turn saw someone, although she couldn't make out much.' I time my circuit perfectly to drop my hands on the person in front of me.

'It was you the runner saw in the churchyard, wasn't it, Pixie? The flash she saw was something glinting on the necklace Anna gave you.'

Anna looks shocked. 'Pixie, tell me it wasn't...'

'What of it? Aren't I allowed a few minutes to talk to my dad on the first anniversary of his passing?'

'Of course you are.' Beneath my hands, I feel her shoulders tense and as she moves slightly forward, I ease her back into the chair, just a gentle hint.

'But if that was the case, why didn't you just come forward and say it was you? Nobody would have thought any more about it.'

'That's not the way it works when it's my family, though, is it?' Goodness, I can feel a lifetime of resentment in those few words. She twists round to face me. 'Dad always told me, never say more than you have to. They'll only use it against you.'

This time, she glares at Glen. Goodness, this is a completely different side to the quiet administrator. Her eyes flit round the group, daring them to disagree. I've never seen anyone look more defiant. But as those eyes turn back on me, I sense something else. Fear, maybe? Or something darker?

'What did you so desperately want to talk to your father about at his grave?' Anna looks puzzled. 'As far as I could see, you two were barely on speaking terms.'

Something flickers in Pixie as I watch. That hit a nerve. If my theory is right, now's the moment to prod.

'There's something you're not telling us, isn't there, Pixie? Something you've just discovered.' Okay, that last part was a bit of a shot in the dark. My TV hero Jessica Fletcher would be proud.

'How did you...?'

I smile, while my heart pounds in my ears and I have to lean against the vestry wall, hoping I look nonchalant, fearing I look anything but. 'It's time to tell us what you found.'

For a split second, I think I've mistimed things, but then she deflates, her shoulders sag and she looks a lot older than her thirty-five years.

'Alright.'

Wickham produces a glass of water and as she drinks it, I get the impression Pixie wishes it was poisoned.

'When my father died last year, the only thing he left me, apart from a load of debts, was a grubby envelope. I was so fed up and angry at all he'd put us through, I stuffed it away in a drawer in our spare room so Milton wouldn't see it and I could forget about it. Her neck reddens and a vein pulses. Her voice is strained and a part of me feels sorry for her, or at least for the pain she's suffered and shouldn't have. 'When I was little, he'd always be setting me secret trails, treasure hunts. There was never any treasure at the end of them, of course. At the time I thought it was fun. It was only later that I realised he just enjoyed the power of secrets.' She sobs.

'That's right. And that's what this whole thing is about, isn't it, Pixie? Secret trails.'

She nods and my gut churns. 'When I realised it was you in the churchyard, I couldn't help wondering why you'd be there, especially since, when

I checked, it wasn't anywhere near your father's plot.'

She looks up ad I can see defeat in her eyes. Yesterday's record inspections with Scott weren't in vain. 'You see...' I look around the group who are hanging on my every word. 'I was right all along. The two cases are interlinked, as in a chain.'

I nod at Scott who wordlessly crosses to the safe, unlocks it and extracts a black leather record book.

'Follow me.' Feeling like a tour guide, I lead them out of the vestry, though the church and to the graves. 'Scott?'

The vicar traces a careful route through the burial plots, checking the register in his hand. Suddenly, he halts and looks puzzled. 'That's odd, there's an extra headstone between these two entries, with no record in the register.'

The chief inspector snorts. 'Couldn't that be someone else taking a burial and just not making a note?'

I feel Wickham stiffen, as if his church warden responsibilities have been called into doubt. 'Hardly, Inspector. As I'm sure is the case with your important documents, there are all sorts of cross checks. We're very mindful our legal requirements, you know. Plus, we now have a very keen archdeacon snapping at our heels.' He grins at me and I roll my eyes in sympathy, as does Scott, the first positive reaction I've seen from him since his return.

The major is nodding her agreement vigorously at the mention of the ecclesiastical Rottweiler. 'You'll back us up, won't you, Pixie?'

Unfortunately, her administrator is staring vacantly into the middle distance, her hand at her throat, so it's Scott who provides the affirmation. 'None of our local clergy would do that. Neither would any of the funeral directors. It makes no sense.'

I let them ponder for a while, my heart still pounding. What if I've got this all wrong? *Trust your gut, Cat.*

I look from one to the other, then realise I look even more like a tour guide and take a deep breath. 'You're right, it makes no sense. Until you consider two things. Firstly, what do you notice about this grave?'

They look blank. Finally, Wickham says in an uncertain voice, 'It looks as if the soil on the top's been disturbed recently. Maybe a predator's been foraging?'

I smile, encouragingly, although I'm so nervous I worry I might look more like a deranged old woman. 'Truer than you realise, Church Warden. Predator and forager.'

I wait a few more seconds to let that sink in. Now for the second thing. 'What do you notice about the headstone?'

If anything, they look even more puzzled. 'Oh come on, guys, look closely.'

Glen actually produces a magnifying glass. I mean, has any police officer ever carried one of those since Sherlock Holmes or Poirot? He examines the surface but shakes his head. 'You can hardly see any inscription. It's been weathered off.'

'Exactly, Chief Inspector.' I could start enjoying this. 'And if I asked you to do the same with the headstones on either side?'

Anna reels off both sets of details, top to bottom, as if she's running down an eye test chart.

Beside me, a knowing smile emerges from the bristles of Wickham as I rub the stone, covering my fingers with powder.

He turns to address the group. 'Any self-respecting stone mason would use granite or marble because they last longer. This is cheap sandstone.'

I nod. 'But then, this one wasn't meant to last, not even the decade it's been here.' I turn to each of the group in turn, watching their faces, enjoying my moment in the spotlight. 'Was it, Pixie?'

The administrator jolts as if she's received an electric shock. Her hands are welded to her necklace like a baby to a dummy.

'I think you'll find the inscription on the headstone, the entry missing from the register, is invented. But it's also very revealing. Inspector, I think you've finished deciphering?' He nods agreement. 'In fact, as I'm sure Glen will confirm in a moment, it's the key to unlocking this whole case. Inspector?'

The policeman tucks his magnifier away and reads: '*After years of suffering, a brighter tomorrow*. I don't understand.'

I turn to Pixie, whose face now looks granite-hard, unlike the headstone. 'But it does make sense, doesn't it? Why don't you explain? After all, it's your family.'

The young woman looks totally defeated. When she speaks, we all have to lean in to hear her words before they're carried off into the air, thin as a spider's web.

She shivers but no one seems inclined to offer her anything warm. 'The nearer we got to the anniversary of his death, the more that wretched envelope seemed to call to me. So finally, when I knew Milton would be out of the way, I took it out the drawer. That's when I noticed it was addressed to MY LITTLE PYXIE. I thought it was an odd spelling but then Dad was never going to win Mastermind.' She reaches into a pocket and tosses a grubby envelope at the Inspector, who lets it fall to his feet. Then he produces a fresh set of blue evidence gloves and picks it up by one corner as if t it might explode. As he turns it over, we can see the jagged edge where it's been opened and simultaneously our eyes swivel back to the woman, while Glen carefully removes its contents.

He waves a single scruffy piece of paper in the air and we crane our necks to read, 'MY BELOVED PYXIE – GRAVE TODAY FOR A BRIGHTER TOMORROW.'

She shakes her head. 'My first thought was, *how stupid*. I thought it was just some drunken joke. Until one day, when I was down here weeding his plot in preparation for his anniversary and I noticed the headstone next to his was crumbling. I could only just make out the name, SUNNY DAY, but there were no dates, which seemed really weird, quite unnerving. In the middle of the night, the penny dropped: Brighter Tomorrow and Sunny Day, it was almost as if I could hear Dad laughing. His last message to me had nothing to do with bad spelling. He'd deliberately spelt my name like that to make me think of that hideous thing in the safe. It was another secret trail. What he didn't account for, though, is that with the shock of his death, it took me so long to work it out.'

She stares ahead, lost in things I can't reach or understand. But I know she needs to be left to talk in her own way, not be prompted or led, and I can see Glen taking notes and, I suspect, probably also recoding this on his phone. He'd been crystal clear when I'd told him my suspicions. No witness-leading, at ANY point. His emphasis.

At last, Pixie clears her throat. 'Just before his anniversary, I woke up in the middle of the night. I'd been dreaming I was at work, he'd not long finished and I'd just started. It was the first time I'd ever known him show the slightest interest in any of my jobs. He just marched into my office and demanded to be left alone so he could make his final peace with the place. Everything was locked up so I couldn't see any harm in it. He only wanted five minutes. That was all I gave him. The thing is, I know dreams can feel as real as real life, but it did happen, exactly like that. And when I woke up, my first thought was that it would've been more than enough time to open the safe and swap the pyxes.

The thought that he might have had something to do with the pyx made me get out of bed and fetch the letter. Luckily, Milton's such a deep sleeper, I knew he'd never stir. I spent ages staring at the note and then, just as it started to get light and I was thinking I ought to go back to bed, it made sense. You see, for all my father's faults, he loved his job and he was good at it. He'd make sure every service was set up perfectly, and everything had its correct place for safekeeping. He always said he didn't dig graves, he prepared final resting places. This had to do with a grave. So I told Reverend Cross that for the

Archdeacon's visit I needed to check the burial records at St Cyril's, when he was next down in Much Slaughter.

'The old fool had no idea. It was easy to get him to open the safe and get the records out. I only needed a quick check of the plots to confirm what I suspected, that it wasn't a proper grave. But he never trusted anyone. He crept up behind me, saw my dad's letter on the vestry table in St Cyril's and realised what I'd spotted. The stupid man said I should "surrender the pyx to the authorities" and turned his back on me. I ask you, after all he and "the authorities" put my family through. I was *so* angry. I just grabbed the nearest thing to hand, stretched up and belted him. I honestly only wanted to stun him so I could get away.'

She makes pleading eye contact with us all in turn, but from my perspective, I'm looking at a cold-blooded killer, given after she'd lashed out she made no attempt to call for help, just left.

My impression is justified as she shrugs and continues. 'I knew I'd done the right thing, though, when he fell with his arms out, as if he was one of the thieves on the cross. It was *so* fitting, like something in a film.'

I shudder. It's what I'd expected but hearing the words spoken out loud, and with such lack of emotion, makes me feel nauseous. Pixie goes on.

'All I had to do then was to pop outside and five minutes later, I'd dug up my reward.'

Glen snaps his notebook shut with such a clap Anna and Carlton jump in their seats. 'The missing pyx.'

She shrugs and we all shudder at her cold indifference.

'But what if you'd been seen?'

'What, little inconspicuous me, doing a little harmless weeding around my family plot?'

This seems a different person to the one I thought I knew. And judging from the look on the major's face, she's having the same struggle.

'Then I stuffed it in my bag and I was on my way back into the vestry to do some tidying up but I heard footsteps and someone's mobile ring, so I just scarpered.'

At this point, two uniformed police officers appear and stand either side of the defiant perpetrator, while Glen informs her, 'You're under arrest for the murder of Reverend Mark Cross.' One of the officers produces a pair of handcuffs and the rest, as they say, is a matter of public record.

Chapter 31

'I just don't get it. If she did do this, what's she done with the pyx? Or the proceeds?' Boothby scratches his wingspan moustache and glances from me to Chief Inspector Parva.

Glen looks rather pleased with himself. 'We traced the pyx through her browser history, they're not the easiest of things to get rid of, being so identifiable. Even the dodgy dealer didn't really know what he'd got his hands on, so he was only too keen to co-operate with us.'

Boothby nods his head. 'What'll happen to it? It wasn't exactly popular before, to say nothing of the extra connotations it now carries.'

Glen nods. 'Once the case has finished, it'll probably go to a museum, so at least it'll be on show...'

I'm sitting with Glen, Boothby and Wickham in our favourite corner of the Crimson Courgette Coffee Emporium. Skye drifts between us and a handful of customers while my pooch dozes, entirely unimpressed and oblivious, on his special blanket near a radiator, as I fill Boothby in on my finest hour. Finest, that is, since I helped solve the murder of a local police sergeant. Which itself had been my finest hour since I helped Glen solve the murder of a visiting celebrity chef.

Outside, another burst of rain batters the window of our wonderful homey cafe, the only place to be when the forecast is squally, with scattered April showers: i.e., rain, wind and more rain.

The whole village is still buzzing over the recent spectacle of no less than three police cars and a van with flashing blue lights tearing into the village on full blues-and-twos, the previous afternoon. Speculation was rife about who'd been taken into custody. Those who knew weren't saying. And those who didn't were sharing their opinion with absolute certainty. Their uninformed choices included the vicar, various newcomers, a passing stranger who looked shifty and an extra-terrestrial being.

So far, no-one seemed to have got the right person, which was a tribute to Glen's compassionate shrouding of Pixie with his jacket as she was led into the back of one of the police vehicles. Part of me was relieved and several times I have to remind myself that, as well as being the ill-treated child, timid adult, dedicated wife and efficient administrator, she's also, by her own admission, a killer.

So it's a rather subdued bunch of us that are sitting around the table in the half-empty coffee shop. Skye finally joins us and sits next to a rather gloomy Glen. To his left are our two church wardens, Wickham and Boothby, then there's an empty chair, then me.

Finally, Scott stumbles in, shaking the rain off his long coat and adjusting his clerical collar as he drops into the vacant seat. Barking waddles over to join Daggers, treating him to his own heavy shower as Barking shakes the rain out of his fur. And believe me, an Old English Sheepdog's fur can carry an awful lot of rain.

As if triggered into action, Boothby shakes his head sadly and announces in an usually quiet voice, 'I can hardly believe it! She seemed such a pleasant lass. Always willing to help with any enquiries I had. No doubt, I suppose?'

I shake my head. 'I'm sorry, Boothby, but no. She's confessed. Isn't that right, Glen?'

He nods agreement. 'Carry on, Cat, it's your show.'

Not quite the way I'd have put it but at least he's acknowledging my contribution.

'It seems Pixie blamed Reverend Cross for triggering her father's descent into alcoholism *and* his death because she reckoned Cross didn't pay him properly when he was employed and then didn't give him a penny when he sacked him. After years of service. But you're right, Wing Commander, she wasn't the sort to do anything about it, she just buried the resentment.'

'Poor girl.' Scott looks genuinely concerned so I guess he must be fully back into vicar mode after his super-spiritual other-worldly thirty-day retreat.

Wickham sighs. 'There's no way St Iggy's could have kept him on, though, he'd became so unreliable.'

'That's not the story she chose to tell herself, though.' I glance at each of my friends. 'It didn't fit with her story about her father. Although, oddly, she didn't seem to feel the same resentment towards St Cyril's.'

Wickham stares at his empty cup. 'Perhaps because he only worked for us as and when needed. And we did pay him a reasonable fee. Usually directly to his wife, so it didn't end up in the pub. I'm not sure even Pixie knew that.'

Glen gives a dry cough. 'It appears from our enquiries that everything changed when the perpetrator finally opened the envelope her father left for her at his death.'

There's a collective wince at his terminology so I soften the official line a little.

'Yes. Roby didn't really steal the pyx for the money. It was more about snatching something of value from under the noses of those who'd never really valued him.'

Skye shakes her head, her curls swishing across her face. I've rarely seen her look so sad. 'Why didn't Roby sell it – or just tell her straight away?'

I pat her arm. 'We'll never know. Maybe he thought he'd get a better offer. Maybe as an alcoholic deep down he knew what would happen to the proceeds if he suddenly had a stash of money in his pocket. Or maybe he had a rare moment of conscience and wanted to make it a legacy for his daughter, who knows? What we do know is that he buried it in a special plot in our churchyard and left a cryptic clue for Pixie. From what she said, she wanted to check that she was right about the plot: it seems that she had some scruples about rummaging around if someone was actually buried there along with the pyx. She told Reverend Cross it was all to do with the Archdeacon's visit but then he caught her out and said if she didn't report it to the police, he would.'

Glen chips in. 'We're working on the assumption that this triggered all the things she'd buried over the years and she just hit out.'

The full force of it all leaves us without words and we're left with our thoughts.

Moments later, in my mind, I can hear Gran's voice. 'You got there in the end then, Catherine. You finally realised what I'd been trying to tell you.' Her laugh tinkles in my brain. I can't help smiling.

'Thanks, Gran.'

'I'm proud of you, my girl. Now when are you going to get down off that high horse of yours and patch things up with the gorgeous doc? If I was fifty years younger...'

'Gran, I've got a business to run, to get off the ground. I don't have time for that arrogant Dr Linton Heath, not at the moment.'

There's a bellow of laughter from the group and everyone turns to look at me. *Oops*, I think. I probably said those words out loud.

Look out for their next adventure, *Who Killed The Dame*? The world of amateur dramatics becomes so much more dramatic when Much Slaughter's glamorous diva Dame Rosemary Lane is murdered and there seem to be more suspects than members of Much Slaughter's audiences.

Acknowledgements

Shannon Cave, via ALLi (the Alliance of Independent Authors), continues to do an amazing job as my Development Editor and leaves me in awe of her razor-sharp perception.

Ellie Stevenson, my copy editor, is masterful in herding my rampant punctuation and plot lapses, and also gives such generous advice and support.

Emma O'Brien has again drawn such wonderful artwork that really encapsulates the essence of Much Slaughter and its amazing characters.

I continue to learn so much through excellent articles provided by REEDSY (www.reedsy.com) and ALLi (www.allianceindependentauthors.org).

To everyone who's read, advised, encouraged and challenged – simply THANK YOU.

About the Author

Peter Hyson was born in the area of Nottingham that shares his name. Over the ensuing decades he's worked in a host of different areas, geographic and professional, as a teacher, professional swimming coach, radio reporter, video editor, business consultant and facilitator of leadership retreats – to name just a few. This means he's met a wide variety of people and backgrounds who've enriched his experiences and none of whom appear in any of his novels.

He's married to Hilary and between them they have four amazing children with two fantastic partners and two grandchildren all of whom bring such fun and joy.

Peter also helps run a Retreats business in the UK and around the world.

The Cotswold Capers series

If you've enjoyed this book, please leave a brief review.

For extra material and to be among the first to hear about Catney and Dagenham's future adventures, sign up for our quarterly newsletter, *Continuing Capers*, at www.peterhyson.com or via Substack at https://substack.com/@peterhysonauthor

The Taste of Murder is available as an e-book only.
ISBN: 978-1-7393489-0-8 https://amzn.to/43vcDbl

A Fair Cop is available as an e-book and paperback:

978-1-7393489-1-5 for e-book https://bit.ly/46U75ZH

978-1-7393489-2-2 paperback https://bit.ly/3sGKsrW

And now there's the chance to enjoy extracts from the first two earlier stories in this series…

Extract from The Taste of Murder

The Taste of Murder – a novella

Celebrity chef Lee Clump is cooking up big plans – and he's finally found the perfect village to serve up his latest trendy Restaurant. The trouble is, he has no premises, a number of established competitors & significant local opposition. He's convinced that his speciality sous vide wild boar and venison will establish MEAT & GREET on the culinary trail and finally provide him with all the trifles he's ever dreamt of. Others would say, gets his just desserts.

Until he's found dead at the Village Fete.

His death provides a spicey challenge to Catherine de Barnes and her trusty hound, Barking, in this tasty appetiser for The Cotswold Capers series set in the beautiful but deadly village of Much Slaughter...

'Oh, no, not again.' The loud click confirms my worst fear. I pound on the locked door even though there's only my pup inside and again regret the penalty for being the only person in the village of Much Slaughter to lock her door. I'm locked out. And I only popped out to collect my Monday morning milk order – yes, we do still have doorstep delivers, part of supporting local producers.

With a sigh, I pull my thick velvet dressing gown tighter around me, slip through the rickety wicker gate, my fluffy slippers squelching in the mud, and knock on my neighbour's door.

'Sorry, Wickham.' He's already dangling my spare keys and grinning from ear to ear behind his whiskers. This is not the reputation I'd hoped to create in the village. 'Glad I caught you before you left for work.'

'It's Monday, Catney. I don't open the bookshop till ten. I'd offer you coffee, but...' He averts his gaze, his blue eyes twinkling under bushy white eyebrows that must have taken all of his 68 years to nurture.

Face burning, I beat a hasty retreat. 'I'll call in later and grab a coffee with you. Thanks.'

Safely back inside, I glance in the hall mirror, grateful my dressing gown not only covers me neck to knees but also hides the absence of nightwear. Not bad for a 42 year-old, I reckon, as I toss my golden curls and sashay upstairs.

Showered and dressed, with minimal make-up applied, I'm almost ready to face the day.

But first, the call of homemade muesli, Greek yoghurt and local strawberries. Plus, my special treat, a steaming mug of freshly-ground black coffee. To my mind, a healthy start to the day gives you permission for a few little extravagances later. Especially if they're chocolate.

After breakfast and two mugs of coffee, it's time to pull on an apron and a pair of thin plastic catering gloves while humming the opening bars of *'Hey ho, hey ho, it's off to work we go'*. Well, we all have our own ways of preparing for our daily routines, don't we?

I snatch a tea towel off a tray of coconut pyramids and break a slab of dark chocolate into a freezer-bag before grabbing my wooden rolling pin and hammering the chocolate into smaller fragments. I heat some water in a saucepan, empty the chocolate fragments into a bowl and place it over the heat. This is one of my favourite parts, watching the dark blobs slowly melt into a wonderfully rich smelling sauce. My mouth's watering.

Once it's all fully melted, I swirl chocolate over each macaroon and carefully place it on a sheet of greaseproof paper. Next, the best part: running my finger around the bowl and blissfully sucking the remaining thick gooey chocolate.

A cold wet canine nose against my bare ankle makes me jump. 'Won't be long, Dag.' I toss a treat into my golden retriever's eager mouth and enjoy a few moments tickling his floppy ears, before I change my catering gloves and take another tray out of the fridge.

A few minutes later, thirty-six neatly wrapped cellophane packages are ready alongside my wicker basket. Just in time, I remember to add my latest touch: thin cardboard pennants in the shape of medieval knights' flags proclaiming CATNEY CHOCS.

'Right, Dagenham – time for your...' My gorgeous pup is already pawing the door, so I clip the leash onto his collar. Dag lollops down the paved path, tail spinning like a propellor, eager to greet all and sundry.

At my gate, we both pause to sniff the summer, the scent of new-mown grass and flower-strewn banks.

Near the main part of the village, the bank flattens into a wildlife strip planted with daisies, buttercups and cowslips, already alive with butterflies.

The *Bound to Please* bookshop has its own colourful display of window boxes and hanging baskets crammed with magenta petunias, white geraniums, bright red fuchsias and what look like daisies, but can't be. The smell is amazing and Dag sneezes loudly. I dodge half a dozen fat bees, their hairy legs already pollen-laden, and open the bright red wooden door, setting the brass bell tinkling.

The bookshop owner, my devoted neighbour Wickham Skeith, has already settled his waistcoated frame into an upholstered green armchair and waves me to its twin, across from a low wooden table set with two large mugs and a cafetiere of steaming coffee. Dag lollops off to nestle into a huge dog cushion underneath the window. By the time I'm settled, my damson and gold dress draped over my legs, my lovely pet is snoring loudly and twitching in time with his dreams.

Wickham pours the coffee, glances across at the dog and smiles, his rheumy blue eyes twinkling. 'Seems like he's been here forever. You too.'

'Yep – six months now. And I don't regret a day of it. Can't think how I lasted so long in London.' I lift the mug and take a moment to savour the rich tang of his coffee which he orders specially from the importer, while my body relaxes into the upholstery. 'Mind you, there are those round here who'll still see me as an outsider even after ten *years*, Wickham.'

'Catney de Barnes, don't you dare take any notice of them. The general opinion is, you've thrown yourself into village life good and proper. Much to everyone's surprise…' He glances over his half-moon spectacles. 'And pleasure, of course.'

'Oh dear, do they think I'm being too pushy? I've just been trying to meet people.'

'Well, perhaps at first. You can't blame them.' He wiggles his bushy eyebrows, then looks serious. 'Every village lives in fear of outsiders, hell-bent on the rural idyll and then complaining about noisy cockerels and church bells.'

'I know, Wickham. I've tried to be sensitive and low-key, but I need to keep myself occupied.'

'You have, Catney. After all, you've only joined, what, five committees?' He grins. 'Oh and become well-known for your chocolate goodies.'

I smile. 'Which reminds me.' I delve into my bag and remove five cellophane packages like a conjurer pulling rabbits out of a hat. 'A little thank you for rescuing me earlier. Don't eat 'em all at once.'

'You should lock yourself out more often, kid.'

'I'd never keep up with the baking. Now, I really need to go. Fête Committee in five minutes.'

'You lot still planning on having that ridiculous TV chef open it?'

'The committee's very excited. Well, most of us, anyway. Dag, come on, boy.' Dagenham raises a sleepy eye and promptly sinks back into the cushion, already snoring.

'Leave him be for now. And leave me in peace with…' Wickham flicks an invisible speck from his tweed waistcoat and reaches for one of the macaroons.

Moments later, I'm shouldering open the heavy oak door of the village hall, just as the church clock ends its eleven chimes.

'Morning, all. Perfect timing, eh?' I mop my forehead with the back of my hand and pause as the hall's smell of stale polish, musty air and stewed tea wafts over me.

The sole person in the room looks up from the wooden trestle table and runs his finger round the inside of his clerical collar. He's wearing a dark suit, well-fitted without looking overly expensive. He tugs down his jacket cuffs.

I speak. 'Scott, thanks for sending the agenda round last night. Didn't have time to read it, I'm afraid, but…'

'Clearly not, Catherine. Otherwise, you'd have seen the meeting started at ten o'clock. I'm afraid we've already finished.'

Oh dear, I think, *if it's Catherine I must be in trouble.* For the second time this morning, I blush. 'I am SO sorry. I didn't think anything in Much Slaughter got going before mid-morning.' This isn't helping, I can tell.

'Yes, we do realise that's the common perception of the outsider.' Scott glowers, pushes his spectacles back up to the bridge of his nose, then bursts out laughing, running his hand through thick black hair. 'Sorry, Catney, couldn't resist.'

'You absolute terror, you really had me going, there.' I slip into one of the empty chairs. 'So, where is everyone? We need to get going. Only a few days to go...'

The vicar clears his throat. 'Erm, the meeting did start at 10 and we actually have finished, I'm afraid. But don't worry. Trot back to the vicarage with me and I'll fill you in.'

With a couple of mighty strides, he's out the door. And I'm literally trotting behind.

The High Street is already busy with meandering tourists causing us to weave in and out as if we're following some complex pattern.

I smile as I watch him make a path for us through the throng like he's the rugby player of his youth. Friendship is a precious thing, especially when you're new to a place – although I never thought I'd number a vicar among my closest companions. But then Scott Willoughby is hardly your typical vicar: he's in his still in his forties so half the age of most other vicars I've known, he's still got his own hair (quite a lot of it actually) plus he's one of the kindest souls you'll ever meet, and his dog Barking is Dag's best mate. He's also got a live-in girlfriend, and a whiff of scandal from his previous post to boot. Definitely my kind of clergyman.

'Right, Scott, fill me in on the fête decisions.'

'Firstly, it's a *fair*, not a fête, or you'll offend an awful lot of people. Sorry.' He bumps into a young woman who has suddenly stopped dead in the middle of the pavement and is clicking off photos as if her life depends on it.

'The fet... the fair? What did I miss?'

'The main thing is this celebrity chef bloke has confirmed he'll open it. People seem to reckon he'll bring in the crowds. Apparently, he's well known in – certain circles.' He wrinkles his nose and I smother a giggle into a cough. 'Reckons he'll be around for a few hours as he's got some business or other in the area. The committee thought you might be the one to meet-and-greet, given you're in the same line of business.'

'Making a few novelty chocolates for special occasions hardly makes me a chef.'

'Yes, well, you weren't there so the committee decided.' He pushes his glasses up again and flexes his broad shoulders. 'Anyway, I reckon the word's already out. Saw a whole load of strange women nosing around Rose's Tea Shoppe yesterday. I reckon it's his fan club.'

As we draw near the bookshop, a crowd of brightly clad women ogle the window where Wickham's added a rolling video to his display of books, artfully scattered around a large cardboard cut-out of beaming CELEBRITY CHEF LEE CLUMP. The woman taking photos is now busily recording the shop front from every conceivable angle.

Scott turns as we pass. 'Well, at least Wickham will be happy. Unlike some others.'

'You mean, because of the rumour about Clump's business plans?' Several people swivel to stare.

Scott's reply however is lost in the general hubbub, by which time we've reached the vicarage driveway.

'Is there anything else I'm down for, apart from being the bit of fluff on the arm of our celebrity chef?'

I'm unable to stifle a laugh at his look of horror. 'Don't worry, just joking. I can't imagine me being just a bit of fluff on anyone's arm, can you? Not my style.'

Of course, if it was the *right* arm...

As a novella, The Taste of Murder is available as an e-book only. ISBN: 978-1-7393489-0-8

Extract from A Fair Cop

And from A Fair Cop...

When Catherine de Barnes – Catney - finds Much Slaughter's retired policeman draped over a motorbike, three knives in his back, she and her pooch Daggers face a frantic race to save an innocent villager from jail. But a grumpy police officer, a fledgling chocolate business and a romantic midnight dance threaten to distract her...

The familiar villagers from The Taste of Murder return in glorious technicolour, along with an eccentric retired RAF officer with a moustache the size of aeroplane wings, a vet who paints a road tunnel on his garage door and a coffee shop owner with a chequered reputation. Then there's the rather dishy doctor... and a whole host of others.

Will Catney be lured away by the many distractions as she seeks to track down the killer?......

Dagenham, my lovely golden retriever, gives me a long pitying stare when I grind to a halt, lungs heaving and face burning. I must have tackled this driveway ten or twenty times and it doesn't get the slightest bit easier, despite my twice daily dog walking. I wipe my forehead on the back of my hand, my blond, curly hair damp with sweat. Sorry, Mum, lady-glow. She regularly recycled that old saying, 'horses sweat, men perspire, ladies merely glow'. Dag, restless to meet his doggy pal Barking, scampers off again, towing me the final twenty metres up to the 1970s vicarage.

My friend Scott Willoughby stands at the open door, and I wonder if he's heard my approaching gasps but as we step into his cool hallway, I realise he can see the driveway from his study, and I laugh.

'Hours of endless entertainment, eh, Vicar?'

He follows my eyeline and smiles.

As we pass from the public arena into his domestic one, I'm greeted by the massive black and grey furball of Old English Sheepdog that is

Barking. Or rather Dag is, there's absolutely no interest in me or even Scott, and the two hounds tumble around, through the kitchen and out into the garden.

'Useless guard dog!' Scott gazes after his dog, looking like a proud father watching his child erupt into a playground. 'Good listener, though!'

'Aren't they just!' My six-month-old pup has seen me through many a lonely night since I moved into the village. It was Scott who suggested I needed a pet, though he was at pains to point out I shouldn't see it as filling the hole left in my life by my erstwhile straying husband. He'd even loaned me his own rescue pup Barking for a few days. When my own rescue hound arrived, it seemed only right to name him Dagenham after the London Borough, sure even then that they'd be the best of canine companions. And what a difference Dagenham has made, not only as the ever-willing listener and ever-keen sharer of affection, but also as the most effective finder of friends. Within a week I knew more people than in the previous two months in the village before I got him and there are few in Much Slaughter who don't know him by name. He's been the catalyst to a dozen supper invites. Sadly, no romantic interludes as yet. But hope springs eternal in the Catney breast.

I lower my rucksack carefully onto the floor, which leaves me with an unpleasant damp patch at the bottom of my back, so I'll need to make sure I keep facing Scott. And I'll definitely need to keep my arms plastered to my side. My calves are aching, but all the chairs are plastered with newspapers or worthy-looking books and the coffee table is submerged under the remains of breakfast and a whisky glass I hope was a nightcap, rather than a hair-of-the-dog from this morning.

'No Cherry this morning?' Cherry is Scott's... well, no-one seems quite sure what she is. Partner? Long-term girlfriend? A few other less savoury descriptions have also been suggested but she's actually well liked and arrived here with Scott and has been accepted along with him despite (or perhaps because of) the air of mystery.

'No – she's spending this week working on the renovation of her cottage back in Much Snoring. Unfortunately.' He gazes around the room with a bewildered lost-puppy look. 'Cat, I'm sorry but I can't stop. My clergy colleagues are due any minute and I've got masses to do – sorry, no pun intended.'

I smile. Yes, he does look rather haggard, so I suppose he must be missing Cherry's presence. In more ways than one. He's tall, broad-shouldered and has the classic sharp jawline but his eyes look puffy and dark and there's the start of crow's feet at their edges, even though I reckon he's probably only in his early forties. He's got a couple of days of beard stubble and being black-haired it looks as if it's been drawn with a felt-tip pen.

I take out a box of my favourite chocolate macaroons which I'd baked just a couple of hours earlier and hold them up proudly. 'Fifteen people, I think you said? I've done 25.' And though I say it myself, they're some of my best.

Scott seems pleased. 'Good move, Cat. I have to say that, judging by their waistlines, our local clergy are rather fond of their fodder. They seem to descend on food like locusts – very Biblical but not very edifying! Now, where on earth did I put my clerical collar?' He stands in the middle of the room and spins around, then just stands motionless.

It's disconcerting to see Scott so flustered. I've always thought of him as the archetypal cool, unflappable cleric, hovering saint-like above distractions. 'Look, I've nothing in the diary. Why don't you start in here while I set up the kitchen?' I'm not at all sure what I'll find if I tidy the sitting room, so I reckon I've got the better job.

Moments later, I'm not so sure. Dirty dishes and saucepans are piled in the sink and across the draining board and there are dirty plates, glasses and cutlery on the table, along with a half-empty bowl of shrivelled salad, probably older than last night. It all feels worryingly unlike Scott.

Ten minutes later, with a packed dishwasher churning away, the overflowing items have been washed and sit draining, and the emerging wooden work surfaces have been scrubbed clean. My search of the cupboards has located fifteen matching cups, saucers and side plates, admittedly in the typical shade of church green. Two huge metal kettles rumble away on the gas stove, while my macaroons stand like a valley of pyramids on a large stainless-steel platter.

Just as I drop the final teaspoon onto the final saucer, Scott returns. What a transformation. He already looks so much better. His dog collar has been found and inserted into his shirt, his still-damp black hair is brushed into place, he's clean-shaven, there's more than a hint of Old Spice in the air and he looks –and smells – like the vicar of old. I wonder if he misses Cherry's presence rather more than he'd prepared to let on.

'I hate these meetings, Cat. They can get so, well, argumentative. It's as if they bring all their frustrations from their parishes and vent them here.' He shudders. 'That's why I'm so tense.' The eye contact lasts a moment too long to be convincing and my heart lurches. He leans on the (now pristine) kitchen table. 'It's the only time I ever miss the City.'

'Gosh, yes, I'd forgotten that. Stock market, wasn't it?'

'Investment banking, actually. Twenty years. Sorry – I know, I know!' He holds up his hands in surrender.

'Scott, let's face it. I'm in no place to throw stones. Don't forget, I was ten years managing an advertising agency! Twenty staff and no holidays.'

'Don't you ever miss anything?'

'You mean the ridiculous deadlines, stroppy clients and colleagues and a mound of paperwork? Hardly!'

'Sounds to me like a vicar's job, Cat.' We both laugh, a little falsely.

'And, let's face it,' I turn to face him, 'it was my choice to up sticks and move here, so I can hardly complain, can I?'

He looks so desolate, my heart hurts and I add, quickly, 'I do know your story's very different.'

He stares. 'It felt as if my world was caving in. Getting made redundant and my wife running off. And that ridiculous business in my last parish.'

Now that last bit has intrigued me ever since I first heard there was something. But before I can say anything more, Scott glances at his watch as, bang on cue, the doorbell rings and in his eyes I see the shutters crash down. 'I'll be off and leave you to your vicaring,' I say. His face pales and a vein throbs in his neck, making him look like he's been condemned to a firing squad. 'But, Scott, you know where I am...'

I squeeze his arm and plant a quick kiss on his cheek.

I'm tempted to slip out the back way but even I realise that the sight of someone furtively slinking out by the tradesmen's entrance might not be a good look. Especially a blond babe. *Okay, Cat, in your dreams!*

'Dag – here boy.' Both pups look up and carry on racing around the garden. So much for obedience classes. Although, in fairness, my investigations into the horrible murder at the recent village fête – fair – meant we had missed a few classes. 'Dag – now.' He looks at Barking and I swear he rolls his eyes, before ambling across the lawn, tail drooping, while Barking remains glued to the spot as if he can't quite believe anyone would spoil their fun.

We pass quickly through the house. The open front door reveals three black-coated clergymen whose florid faces and rotund figures suggest they might be better served by a gym session than a meeting. Behind them are three battered old cars. The men push straight past me and don't even greet Scott: they clearly know where they're heading. Even Dag shows little interest in them which must be a first – but maybe he's sulking at being dragged away.

Behind them traipses a woman who seems to have tackled the driveway far more comfortably than her colleagues and looks remarkably cool despite sporting a rather resplendent flowing cardigan that flaps around her calves.

'The Area Dean. A good thing,' Scott whispers in my ear, as if I should know exactly what that means. All I do know is that she's a rather wrinkled woman, probably in her late fifties, with a taste for a long, knitted cardigan. She does at least nod at me as she passes and then greets Scott with a warm hug and, I swear, a flirtatious wink. She pauses and I wonder if she's also noticed something odd about him. But then she rushes inside, followed by Scott. The door closes.

Dag suddenly pulls on his leash, his tail wagging nineteen to the dozen, which is the way he greets long-time friends. All I can see is an elderly man in a purple shirt, his alpine sticks clicking to aid his ascent. His face lights up as he glimpses me, and his smile shows a full set of gleaming white teeth. 'Please tell me you're a lovely addition to our clergy team, my dear. I'm Bishop Norton...'

'Catherine de Barnes, Bishop. Usually known as Catney. And, no, I'm afraid I'm not.'

'Shame – could've done with someone to lighten the proceedings!' He grins, bends down to tickle Dag's ears, thereby wining a friend for life.

'Ah well, I'd better face my penance, I suppose.' He clicks across to the vicarage and disappears.

Good grief, what a motley crew! I'm not surprised Scott... I get no further as a young woman in a bright red MX5sports car roars up the driveway and screeches to a halt, almost mounting the doorstep in her enthusiasm. She hops out, showing rather more bare thigh than I'd have thought appropriate for a cleric, before following the tribe inside.

This morning's encounter with Scott and the foray back into both our pasts has left me feeling quite disorientated for some inexplicable reason, so I meander across the churchyard and push on the heavy oak door. Inside, it's refreshingly cool and I select a wooden pew about halfway down and sidle in by a pillar. The silence is immediately comforting, and in some weird way there's a sense of being surrounded by hundreds of years of prayers which have soaked into the limestone walls. Everything is plain and simple. Even the altar has only a single wooden cross and a rather battered candlestick on it; these days, the main silverware is securely locked away in a huge vestry safe. That's when I realise my hands are shaking. And it's not the cold.

I stare up ahead at the beautiful stained glass of the East Window and the colourful patterns it throws on the stone floor, my mind a jumble of thoughts and feelings. I have to admit, I wasn't being entirely honest with Scott. Or with myself. I find it quite hard to pretend when I'm in church. I know that might just be me. I'm not religious and I have no idea what I believe. And although I've probably sat in church more times in the ten months I've been in Much Slaughter than in my previous forty-two years, that's simply because it's much more prominent in a village. It's a very good way to meet people.

Anyway, Scott's words have made me realise something's missing. I'm sure it's not the gaudy, buzzy superficiality of the advertising world: that had lost its sheen long before I left. Although maybe I miss the cut-and-thrust of managing a business. I loved my tiny docker's cottage in a trendy part of East London. But the area was also noisy and dirty! So, not that either. And, while I certainly don't miss the philandering lump I called my husband, actually, I do miss male company.

Well, I guess a church is as a good place as any to count your blessings. I have a small cinema half an hour away and several theatres within an hour. And soon after I arrived in Much Slaughter, I realised that I didn't have friends in London, I had acquaintances. Whereas in the country, even if it's taken me a while, I've got my next-door neighbour, Wickham; Scott, of course, and Rose and her niece Skye at the *café*. Plus at least a dozen dinner guests. Now I've got twice the living space in my house, a huge garden and country walks from my doorstep. And my trusty pup Dagenham and my growing chocolate business. No mortgage and a small financial cushion in the bank. This was the independence I'd been craving. And I love it, I really do. Okay, so a nice hunk of man to cuddle up with would be the icing on the cake, but hey, you can't have it all, can you?

Mind you, a girl could do far worse than that nice Chief Inspector Parva: the man I helped a few months back. Together we solved the murder of a local celebrity chef. Although he did think me an interfering busybody... there have been worse starting points. And recently, one of the village worthies seems to have popped up significantly, more frequently than I'd have reason to expect...

Any further romantic conjectures are shattered as the church door is flung back, the crash echoing around the stones, and Scott's clergy colleagues tumble in. A couple of them seem to be continuing a dispute, something about who wrote some Bible book or other. Another is on the phone muttering about funeral arrangements. The Area Dean emerges from the vestry with all the communion paraphernalia (I never was very good at terminology) and as she arranges them on the altar, she starts a loud conversation with someone else whose church service it appears she's taking on Sunday. Bedlam! I know there's something wrong but all I can do is slip out for a much needed and very strong coffee. Scott has my sympathy...

978-1-7393489-1-5 for e-book
978-1-7393489-2-2 for paperback

Coming next...

Who Killed the Dame?

When Catherine de Barnes joined Much Slaughter's Thespian society, it was meant to be relaxing and fun. But when weeks of infighting lead to the murder of prima donna Dame Rosemary Lane during the Dress Rehearsal, Cat is sucked into a whole new plot. One where she really doesn't want to play the leading lady. Once again, Chief Inspector Glen Parva sets off on one track – and once again Cat is convinced he's wrong. But how to prove it when the cues – sorry, clues – seem lost in the mists of past histories, murky dealings in the wings and more pretending than at an Awards Gala.

Old friends Revd Scott Willoughby, Boothby Graffoe and Skye Green join Cat and her medic boyfriend Linton Heath, along with bickering twins Willow and Kitt Green, local Headteacher

Betwsy Coed as we draw back the curtain and shine the spotlight on the murky corners of Much Slaughter more than one person would prefer to keep in the dark – at any cost. While doggie palls Barking and Dagenham prove drama isn't the sole preserve of the humans...

Coming December 2024

www.ingramcontent.com/pod-product-compliance
Lightning Source LLC
Chambersburg PA
CBHW060547080526
44585CB00013B/470